UNBREAKABLE INVESTOR

Build the American Dream in Any Economic Cycle

by Charles Payne

Unbreakable Investor
Build the American Dream in Any Economic Cycle

Questions, simply reach out to my team.

Unbreakable Investor
351 W. Washington St.
Kearney, MO 64060
1-800-296-9890

support@PaynesEducation.com

Cover Design by Command G Design
Internal Design by Jeffective Design & Illustration
Published by Paradigm Direct, LLC
Printed in the United States of America

First Edition

Paperback ISBN: 979-8-9878784-1-5

*This book is dedicated to
my grandchildren and yours*

Cassidy

Jonathan

Samantha

Anthony

Michael

CONTENTS

Preface

Everyone wants to be financially secure. It's always been part of the American dream, but it's been my experience that everyone wants their families to be financially secure even more so than they are themselves. Parents take on dangerous jobs like law enforcement, firefighting, long haul truck driving, dangerous factory work, mining and exploration jobs, and so many others, so they can earn enough money to position their children for "a better life."

Some families have been at this for several generations, and despite debilitating tax policies, financial fortunes have been accumulated and will be passed on. However, words like "rich" and "fortune" have different meanings for different people. Essentially, you can be "rich" and have a good life with a satisfying job, a great family, and close friends. We are fortunate when we live long, healthy lives and get to share experiences and even adventures with the ones we love. When measuring life, there is no doubt there are so many aspects that matter beyond money.

With that in mind, however, we live in a nation that uses such sentiment to keep most of us trapped.

We sacrifice to save money and have a great credit score. We are told that a credit score is the key to "financial security," but for the most part it's a trap. A great credit score (FICO) allows us to engage in the Great Faustian Game of debt and interest payments. A high credit score only means a lower payment, but a payment nonetheless.

- College loans
- Home loans (several if we are lucky)
- Wedding loans
- Vacation loans
- Timeshares

These kinds of loans, and this arrangement, only ensure the status quo — the lender gets wealthier and the borrower might be able to pay everything off in time to pass something to the family, but it will only be a windfall, not life-changing fortunes. Not generational wealth.

You can have all of the things listed above for yourself and your family without entering into a deal with the devil. My goal and dream for everyone is to have those things that make life wonderful. I want everyone to have those moments and milestones. I want everyone to reach economic freedom, because all that other stuff tastes just a little sweeter when it's not followed by a lifelong trial of monthly bills.

Fortune is the goal, and, while it's up for interpretation, mine includes a financial component, not as a cherry on top of life, but as the crust holding it all together.

There are endless quotes about fortune. Here are a few that hit the nail on the head:

"Every man is the architect of his own fortune."

— Sallust

"Fortune always favors the brave, and never helps a man who does not help himself."

— P. T. Barnum

"Formal education will make you a living; self-education will make you a fortune."

— Jim Rohn

"You leave home to seek your fortune and, when you get it, you go home and share it with your family."

— Anita Baker

"Diligence is the mother of good fortune."

— Benjamin Disraeli

Seeking one's fortune is admirable, and if it includes trying to make a lot of money for yourself and your family — you have come to the right place.

The Great Wealth "Transfer"

America is the richest nation in the world at any given moment of time. Despite recessions, stock market crashes, and a once-in-a-lifetime pandemic, gobs of wealth have been accumulated and will be passed on over the next two decades.

As you can see from this chart below, more money is going to be passed on from one generation to the next over the next three decades than at any time in American history.

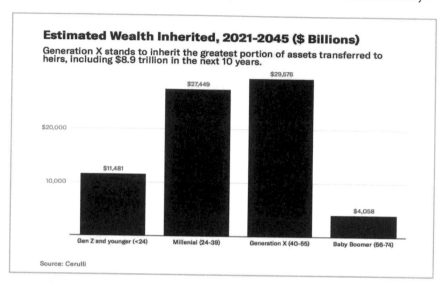

Estimated Wealth Inherited, 2021-2045 ($ Billions)

Generation X stands to inherit the greatest portion of assets transferred to heirs, including $8.9 trillion in the next 10 years.

Source: Cerulli

It is going to be a bonanza of cash that will invariably see the bulk of that cash mismanaged. Most of it will, unfortunately, be squandered. Depending on how much money is inherited, a goal of recipients should be to use this book to learn how to become good stewards of that money, and make sure there is something left to pass on to the next generation.

The goal of those not getting a piece of that action is to be invested in companies that will profit the most off the greatest transfer of wealth in human history. In fact, if human nature doesn't change, those who do not inherit the wealth could end up with most of it in the end.

Great Wealth "Creation"— It's Your Turn

Let's face it, most of us won't be the beneficiaries of an inheritance or the recipients of some significant windfall financially. Most of us must grind it out, which means making a living and, at the same time, trying to find ways to fund an enjoyable retirement and give future generations a leg up. It certainly seems daunting.

Many find it easier to succumb to the whims of life. People grudgingly ride out life by holding on as the winds of change blow them aimlessly through life. This book is designed to give you the knowledge, skills, and confidence needed to incorporate those same winds to steer the course toward your goals, even when those winds are coming at you with gale force.

The quest to change your life and build your own financial independence takes a number of steps. This book will guide you through the ones I have used, but you must make the decision to apply them for yourself.

Don't Let Perception Lead You Astray

How we see things is not always how they really are or have to be.

When European explorers found certain tribes deep in the African rain forest, they took some individuals back to their home countries. Once there, the explorers found there was an amazing adjustment period for those rain forest people, including adjusting to depth perception. Being born and raised in surroundings where the horizon was always immediately in front of their eyes, they had no conception of a three-dimensional perspective. The things that appeared small in the distance, like a building or an elephant, turned out to be much larger as they approached the object.

In so many ways, we have become dwellers in our own rain forest, with our views blocked by the non-stop bombardment of opinions and outrage, which fuels a combination of anger and fear. This has held back our personal journeys that, in the past, were so much a part of the human experience.

Moreover, because of it, we are not prepared for the inevitable challenges, of both the known and unknown, when we finally allow ourselves a chance to embark on such a journey.

This book will open your eyes to the reality of the opportunity in front on you.

Think for Yourself

There is an investing revolution happening, and traditional financial media is missing it, dismissing it, and, too often, actively trying to derail it. Like so many other things when it comes to the investing world, the financial media works for the masters of the universe. It is the platform the masters of the universe use to seduce ordinary folks to buy offerings that are criminally overpriced and to sow seeds of never-ending doubt.

Finally, the public is getting hip to the farce. This is happening, in part, because the public has gotten hip to the general farce of everyday living with institutions ostensibly designed to work for us but are instead working us. They are cramming agendas down our throats and working toward the goal of control.

Controlling the masses means keeping the masses dependent on that Faustian deal of debt and interest payments while creating the mirage of financial freedom.

It is in this regard that the New Investors Revolution is a larger revolution steeped in independent thought and with a goal of greater determination to control one's own destiny.

It's not just about taking back control for the sake of control, but the need for public rejection of large institutions and other reservoirs of power that have lorded over public opinion and decision-making for too long.

Don't get me wrong, those in power still control and manipulate the gargantuan media machine to generate opinions that create consensus (to their liking) and that create or inflame outrage. But more and more, people are either unplugging or offsetting those powerful tools of media, entertainment, and established public policy to find their own way.

There is another powerful factor at play, and that's a sense that there were better times in our past. As much as we celebrate the coming digital age as a way to communicate, learn, and do business, more and more Americans are choosing to devote parts of their lives to slowing down.

It is remarkable how many Americans believe life was better fifty years ago than it is now, and a much larger percentage believe the future will be even worse for people like themselves.

People are choosing to be more independent, to move away from blindly accepting the opinions of the media or others. They are actively trying to emulate and recreate the independent-minded generations that came before them.

They want to feel the dirt.

They want to smell fresh air.

They want to marvel at simplicity.

I guess it's like all those old sayings about slowing down and seeing what's around you and then being a part of that simple, yet marvelous, world. It's a world where identities are not boiled down to computer code or cataloged into cohorts.

The most compelling aspects to approaching life in this

manner can be very expensive when still holding onto day-to-day life and living.

However, technology and the tools of technology are making this embrace of yesteryear more possible to achieve and to share.

Last summer, my aunt in Alabama sent my wife and me a text saying hello and catching us up on the doings down her way. One remark that stood out was her complaint that there were no mason jars.

Mason jars? What could possibly cause a shortage of mason jars?

When I was growing up and would visit relatives in Alabama, every home had mason jars. All my kin used them as part of their survival. Yep, this wasn't a hobby but a way to sustain life. They were poor farmers who tended the soil with tools that were a generation out of date but with proven techniques that ensured they could feed themselves.

Each home had all these preserves in mason jars, and I always thought it was cool but quaint.

My Grandparents Were Super Heroes

It took me until my early thirties to truly understand and respect the ingenuity and determination of my grandparents. My grandfather never ate with utensils, and yet he ate his meals with a calm grace that I have never witnessed in the fanciest New York City restaurants.

I remember one summer sitting at the tiny table in the kitchen watching my grandmother work the cast iron stove, moving red hot embers around with her bare hands and then making my grandfather his plate. As he was eating, I looked down at the floor.

The Timing of This Book

Hundreds of thousands of folks have read my bestseller *Unstoppable Prosperity*, but maybe this is the book I should have written first...not knowing a pandemic was coming. Because of the lockdowns and influx of federal monies to families, many individuals decided to begin exploring the stock market to achieve the financial freedom we've been discussing. This is a great thing, a wonderful adventure. But without a proper understanding of how to survive and thrive in both bull and bear markets, it can become a fool's errand.

I've seen many boom-and-bust cycles and know that during boom times new investors don't take the time to learn or educate themselves. Instead, they assume that what is working when they made their first stock trade will work forever. And yet how long can a company with no earnings see their stock value continue to increase?

Another invariable part of boom-and-bust cycles is policy reactions from governments and central banks. The script never changes, except this time it was on steroids. A once-in-a-century pandemic rolled in, and record amounts of money from governments and central banks were deployed. The recipients used it as intended, which triggered the greatest inflation crisis in four decades (see chart on the next page). Then came the sobering part: Deliberate policy actions to slow the economy were ramped up, creating great economic uncertainty and fear for all, especially those who were not financially prepared.

This is the backdrop as I write this book.

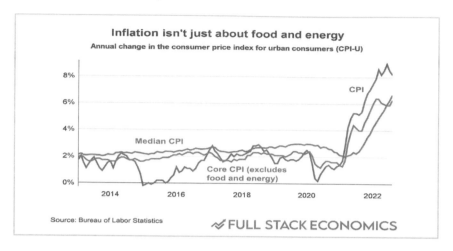

My goal is to help make sure you never get caught off guard or unprepared again.

This book will teach you how to identify changing market backdrops and investing conditions so you can both get ahead and stay ahead of them.

You'll learn ways to minimize losses during bear markets and maximize gains during bull markets just like I've done now for more than thirty-five years. This book is designed to transform the way you think about and invest in today's market so that you can continue to build the American dream throughout any economic cycle and truly become an Unbreakable Investor.

Introduction

Nobody said investing in the stock market would be easy. Although I will admit, there are times when it appears as easy as throwing darts at a board filled with bullseyes.

Nobody said investing in the stock market would be fair. I know it's advertised as such, but there are lots of powerful forces that have better information and execution that often comes at the detriment of the individual investor.

But then again, life isn't easy or fair. The same is true for our investing lives. But we must live both to the fullest and, along the way, make it our quest to make sure it's easier and fairer for those that come after us.

We must learn the most effective ways to invest in today's stock market.

We must become Unbreakable Investors.

The Secret to Investing Success

When I was in grade school, my teacher read us a poem that stuck with me my entire life. It's attributed to Aesop, but versions of it were authored throughout time around the world by wise observers of nature and humankind.

The Oak & the Reed
The Oak spoke one day to the Reed
"You have good reason to complain;
A Wren for you is a load indeed;
The smallest wind bends you in twain.
You are forced to bend your head;
While my crown faces the plains
And not content to block the sun
Braves the efforts of the rains.
What for you is a North Wind is for me but a zephyr.
Were you to grow within my shade
Which covers the whole neighborhood
You'd have no reason to be afraid
For I would keep you from the storm.
Instead, you usually grow
In places humid, where the winds doth blow.
Nature to thee hath been unkind."
"Your compassion", replied the Reed
"Shows a noble character indeed;
But do not worry: the winds for me
Are much less dangerous than for thee;
I bend, not break. You have 'til now
Resisted their great force unbowed,

But beware.
As he said these very words
A violent angry storm arose.
The tree held strong; the Reed he bent.
The wind redoubled and did not relent,
Until finally it uprooted the poor Oak
Whose head had been in the heavens
And roots among the dead folk.

There are several morals to this poem but the main point for me is the ability to shift positions to survive. To bend and not break. This means to constantly be learning, to grow stronger, and to never be so arrogant that you allow worst-case outcomes to dictate your future.

This is particularly critical for stock market investors.

As so many have learned the hard way, financial storms are going to happen, and there will be times when the ability to bend will make you and your investing goals unbreakable.

Ultimately, as an investor you want your portfolio to be as mighty as an oak, but as an investor you must also be flexible, like the reed. This means you must, from time to time, be able to adjust not just with the intent to survive, but with the mission to thrive during and after those inevitable storms.

Building Wealth

You must let your money work for you, or life means running in circles of despair that lead to dashed or delayed dreams.

Or, even worse, dreams and goals that are never reached.

Greater financial control of your life is freedom. The challenges to get to this place are worth the effort when we consider the rewards, and I'm honored you have chosen to get my book and allow me to be your guide.

Charles V. Payne
My Life as the Pied Piper

For years I have pleaded with people, from members of my family and close friends to complete strangers, to invest in the stock market. For as long as I can remember, I have been the Pied Piper of the stock market. Over time, I have become more successful in getting people to invest in it. But it's not enough to simply dabble or put some money in here and there.

The goal is to maximize the effort so you can maximize the return. That is why this book is critical to your long-term success as an investor.

I became an advocate when I was fourteen years old. I bought my first mutual fund when I was seventeen (my mother had to cosign the account form due to my age) and my first stock (MCIC) when I was nineteen. But investing in stocks was not something I grew up around.

In my Harlem neighborhood in the 1970s and '80s, most people were understandably concerned with short-term gains that came from hitting the winning number in the daily illegal lottery known as "The Numbers Game." So many people were behind on their rent, needed clothes for their children or just a few dollars extra to have a cushion, that playing the numbers seemed like a good idea.

If you could pick three numbers straight in succession, the payoff was huge. Nothing felt better than hitting the numbers back then.

The odds of picking the three numbers straight were

1:1,100, but the payoff of $700 for a one-dollar bet was enticing. I was considered lucky in my neighborhood, and I used to hit the single and two-digit numbers a lot. I spent an exorbitant amount of time in what we used to call the "Number Hole."

These were normally storefronts where you could walk in and place your bets (slips) with someone seated behind plexiglass like bank tellers. Inside these Number Holes were plenty of places to sit while filling out your slip.

It was there that I learned a lot about life in general from older folks, but one of my biggest takeaways was that these folks had been playing the numbers their entire lives, and despite hitting the jackpot from time to time, were not able to escape their overall circumstances.

I knew I was lucky at numbers. As I walked down the street adults would always shout out to me: "What number(s) do you like today, Charles?" I was quasi-famous LOL, but I came to understand my occasional luck would not be enough to change my financial situation in the longer term.

Moreover, I realized that while those short-term pops, like hitting the numbers, felt exciting, the great menace of time kept marching on. My epiphany came one day while chilling out in the Number Hole chatting with an older gentleman who I respected.

At one point he had been a big-time hustler and had all the vestiges of success, like big cars and nice clothes. His luck had changed, and he had fallen on hard times. He shared his lessons of life with me in our almost-daily conversations, which helped me navigate a tough environment but also encouraged me to look beyond the immediate walls that seemed like barriers (mental and physical).

He had been to prison and only survived by allowing his

brain to take him beyond those walls.

One day we were in the Number Hole chatting and I looked at his number slip. He had a dozen three-digit number bets for ten cents each.

I said, "You're not going to win any money with those tiny bets." He replied that he would be thrilled to hit any of them even though the payout would be paltry.

I began to think about all those dime bets. They came up to ten dollars a week. He made those bets day in and day out throughout his entire life. Even a low-yielding savings account would have, over time, seen better returns.

The operative word: returns.

When the odds are one thousand to one, the "house" always wins no matter what kind of lucky streak you might hit. That is the difference between investing with a gameplan or taking a shot, whether it's on numbers (lottery), horses, sporting events, or even the stock market. One is based on knowledge and careful research and planning while the other is wishful thinking and based on luck.

I signed up for the U.S. Air Force when I was seventeen years old and went in at eighteen. I sent half my check home to my mother and brothers and saved most of the rest. It wasn't a lot of money, but when I reached one thousand dollars, I went to the Dean Witter office in Minot, North Dakota, and opened an account.

I bought shares of an up-and-coming company called MCI that was competing with the world's largest business/ monopoly, AT&T. It was a real David versus Goliath story I couldn't resist.

The investment was an immediate grand slam, but I was in for the long haul, so I requested my certificate (lack of trust of large institutions came naturally to me) and put it in a strong box. I told all my friends about the success I was having, but nobody was interested.

Suddenly, I was in a position to begin lending money, because that stock was doing well, to the people around me. I could see that it was the same old story for them of focusing on the immediate while I was building for the inevitable.

Fast Forward

I became a stockbroker in my early twenties. By then the market was becoming more democratized. Discount brokers were popping up, and more and more regular folks began thinking they could dabble.

In my own personal circles, my pleas continued to fall on deaf ears until some saw my success and decided to give it a try.

Most times they would jump in the market looking for a quick buck.

They took stock touts from buddies at work or tips they read on numerous chat rooms that were popping up on the nascent Internet. Those who were more serious took stock touts from so-called Black Boxes that would magically spit out lots of trading ideas.

The plans I laid out to them seemed slow and plodding. Why settle for 20% a year when they had a buddy at work who knew about this hot technology stock that could do miraculous things?

Every stock was undiscovered by Wall Street (wink-wink), but soon everyone would know the company and the stock would pop 1000%, maybe 10,000%. Now those odds made the seven hundred bucks for a one-dollar bet seem like peanuts.

It's human nature to be drawn to get-rich-quick or even get-richer-quicker schemes. It's always amazed me how many well-off people lose huge sums in one scam after another, even though the victims who get sucked in are not trying to pay the rent or get money to buy the kids back-to-school clothes.

I have personally seen it too many times.

Twenty-five years ago, a sports agent reached out to me about joining forces with his firm. He was already representing a few young professionals and figured the ability to offer a long-term investment strategy would make his business even more attractive.

He fretted that his clients spent too much money too fast, and he really needed to impress upon them the need for fiscal responsibility and long-term thinking.

He shared the story of convincing one client at the start of his career that it didn't make sense to spend $150,000 on a car.

So, the client spent $150,000 on two cars. I guess it was a start in the right direction.

Heck, depending on the models and if he put one in a garage mostly untouched, it might have appreciated in value. But the pro athlete drove them a lot and enjoyed the attention. A star athlete is expected to sport the best whips, after all.

I got together with the agent and three athletes he represented for dinner one evening.

I thought I was laying it on thick, talking about potential returns of 20% or 30% or even more, in certain years, and beating the street in down markets by being down but less than everyone else.

Over the next two weeks, each came back to the agent to say someone else promised them 20% or 30% a month. They were flabbergasted and wondered why I was lowballing the potential they could earn in the stock market.

A few years later, the same agent got in legal trouble and many of his clients lost everything. When I came across the story in the newspaper all I could do was shake my head. My guess is he tried to accommodate these players and got into pie-in-the-sky stuff that was doomed.

So, it's easy to understand the allure of getting rich (or even richer) overnight, but the majority of wealth, like success in general, is the culmination of years of work, sacrifice, and smart investments.

And there is no such thing as going through a year without trials and tribulations. Being amenable is key. Even with a great game plan for life, we must all learn to bend so we don't break.

Getting Rich Is a Secondary Goal

As I write this book, runaway inflation has come back with a vengeance as the result of trillions of dollars pouring into society from central banks and eager governments looking to retain power (buy votes) even knowing those trillions would lead to a serious hangover.

But even in normal times, keeping up with day-to-day life has become a challenge, and far too many people are falling behind because prices never stop moving higher.

If you aren't earning high six-figure incomes, you are constantly chasing higher prices that negate wage gains while eroding purchasing power. It's almost a curse to reach that sweet spot of six figures a year when keeping up with those around you costs more than you earn and net. Try telling your children, relatives, and even friends you can't keep up.

Inflation makes that an even more daunting circumstance.

It's a constant reminder that we must put our money to work. If you are risk-averse, you can buy bonds, dividend paying stocks, and other alternatives, but cash sitting in a savings or checking account (as illustrated in the chart below) is dead money. I want to help you achieve financial security. That means putting your money to work. My purpose in this book is to provide the tools that will allow you to become an Unbreakable Investor.

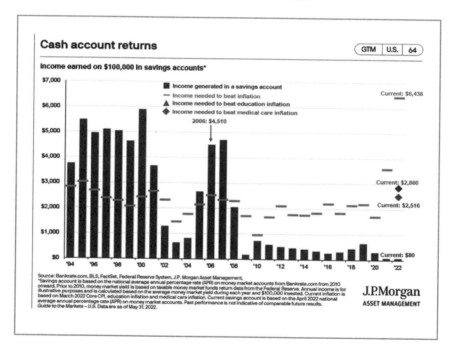

This book has dual goals. They are to provide you with:

In-depth strategies to supercharge your gains in good times as well as in the aftermath of market pull backs and crashes.

An investing approach that adjusts when markets turn south to mitigate losses and capitalize on opportunities.

The reality for 99.9% of people is that they get sucked into the hamster wheel of barely paying bills and trying to save money to pay for experiences, like short vacations (in lean times) or goods, like new cars (in flush times) and paying for these on credit, which becomes a lifelong shadow.

By spending on fewer experiences and cars and putting more into investing, you can own your life over time with money to spare to help others or leave to heirs rather than "renting" a good time or a temporary good look.

I've experienced both, and owning the future has a much sweeter taste and true sense of fulfillment.

Best Investing Weapons: Time, Patience, & Ability to Make Adjustments

Interestingly, in my own experience I have made big money in two ways.

Occasionally I have been successful with short-term "grand slams." These were high-risk ideas that often were withering on the vine until they finally lived up to the hype and then erupted "overnight." Of course, that overnight success might have been months in the making!

That waiting period, as you watch these investments lose value, can be excruciating. If it's the only funds you have in the market, and it's your gauge on whether to invest more, going for grand slams is a disservice to your own long-term wealth-creation goals.

It wasn't until I didn't need these funds, and didn't have to panic while these positions were dying on the vine, that I was able to hold them long enough to reap the rewards.

In fact, most moved to zero or languished so low that, eventually, I closed them for tax purposes.

I mention my experiences with these types of investments here because, all too often, investors who are new to the market see these rare events as the only way to make money investing. They often have a "friend" who knows of an investment that is about to explode. It's going to be the hottest stock out there. On rare occasions it just might be, but more often than not it underperforms at first, and the novice investor watches the value decline. I believe there is a smarter way.

To be sure, the ones that popped for me were nice, but I don't think this should be your primary approach to investing. I've had the luxury to take those kinds of moon shots because of the financial cushion I've made over a period of time using my 3 pillars approach:

Fundamental Changes

Technical Moves

Behavioral Reactions

I'll talk more about these 3 pillars later in the book.

Don't get me wrong, it feels great when something you had on the shelf and mostly had written off suddenly pops and you have a triple-digit gain.

But the better wins come with smarter risk management and far fewer sleepless nights. This is the essence of being an Unbreakable Investor. There are certain kinds of documented endorphins and emotions triggered when we get that big pop, but they pale in comparison to paying for your children's college education without taking out expensive loans or buying your vacation home with cash.

The kind of wins I'm talking about are based on the underlying story (potential) of an investment coming to fruition.

Theoretically, every publicly traded company has a chance to be something special. But it takes a combination of great products or services, foresight, and evolving thinking and management to get the brass ring.

And to hold onto that brass ring.

To be an Unbreakable Investor, you will have to be able to judge if these things are in place and will remain constant. The great news is this challenge is not as hard as you might imagine. The same tools I will teach you to use to identify potential buys are also the tools that will notify you when a particular investment is no longer viable for your portfolio.

Risk-reward Management Is the Key

All too often investors become enamored with the ideas used to hype a company and ignore the fact(s) about its product or service not living up to the hype. Or maybe so much success is already built into the share price (assumed and pumped by Wall Street) that the stock starts to move lower even as the company hits its goals. These are two situations the Unbreakable Investor must be aware of and know how to navigate.

This is the scenario that ensnares more newcomers to the market than anything. It's one thing when the pie-in-the-sky story starts to fade and the share price does as well. But it's another when management appears to be delivering but the stock goes down.

Hence one of the oldest axioms on Wall Street — buy the rumor (hype and tips), sell the news.

Investors become enamored with management and say things like "she is a brilliant visionary", which might be true. But checking boxes and making profits are two different things. For more than a decade the stock market has rewarded companies based on hype and prototypes but with nothing on the bottom line. That has changed, and those investors who haven't noticed or adjusted have been the mighty oaks trees — uprooted by the storm. I cannot wait to get deeper into the nitty gritty of this throughout the book.

Ultimately you want a stock portfolio of great businesses — some undiscovered by the masses and others that have been around — and understand how to remain relevant and to keep reinventing their own value proposition.

Great business always requires execution skills that a large portion of visionaries lack.

Great investors always need to be able to recognize the difference between these distinctly different skill sets. It's not always apparent, especially when there is a lot of noise (which is often a cover for those in the know on the inside to be selling while the rest of the world is buying). If you set aside your emotions, the signs will be there.

Again, I love it when lofty ideas live up to the hype because they not only line your pockets, but they make you feel smart. I won't dismiss the need for people to feel a pride of ownership. We do it with new products none of our friends know about or our favorite team that wins when we wear their jersey inside out. I understand this firsthand.

We are huge boxing fans in my family, and my brother feels special pride when he discovers an up-and-comer first. When that fighter wins, my brother enjoys a gratification that feels as good as making money.

It's what the folks on Wall Street don't understand when they chastise "retail investors" for swinging for the fence. People feel an emotional ownership of stocks, particularly when they initially buy stocks. It's how I felt with MCI. It was a personal litmus test for me and had nothing to do with fundamentals or technical or anything other than I was rooting for this business to win.

Do It Yourself

There is a phenomenon sweeping the nation — people are learning how to do everything for themselves. This sense of doing it yourself, from making a coffee table from driftwood to baking a cake from grandma's recipe, is even more important these days. Remember the shortage of mason jars my aunt mentioned? That was partially because so many people had gone back to "canning" and putting up their own fruits and vegetables. They were taking back a small part of their lives and gaining just a bit more control. So many folks want to get their hands dirty in a world that's rapidly drifting toward machines rubber stamping everything while humans do less.

Talk about a sense of pride and ownership. It is currently taking social media by storm and creating superstars of folks who can teach us by making complicated stuff look easy.

People are making things by hand and selling it to others who appreciate the time and craftsmanship.

The euphoric feeling of accomplishment can also be obtained in the stock market. It's fine to have the right financial advisor, but the person at the party who bought that super-hot stock with his or her own research gets the biggest applause and accolades.

The problem these days is that markets shift but many investors do not. The same people who got the round of applause in the last market phase are getting crushed right now, unless they made adjustments that included getting back to basics and listening to the market.

Those unable to bend, to learn to adjust, have been broken. My goal for you is for you to become unbreakable.

So, let's jump into Chapter 1!

The Challenges & Realities of Investing Today

I try not to ever get preachy — this is your journey. Moreover, there are many ways to make money in the stock market. By the same token, there are many ways to lose money as well.

In this book I share my approach based on personal knowledge and experience as well as the knowledge gained as someone being positioned to watch and study market trends and who has helped retail investors navigate the market for more than three decades.

In recent years, I have also been a professional television presenter and interacted with brilliant market experts, as well as those not-so-brilliant experts that mostly follow the herd.

I've learned there is little original thinking and lots of

hesitation as most experts wait for consensus, even when they are being contrarian.

Why Bother Investing?

I suspect the first question you are asking yourself is "Why bother?" Why invest during times when it feels like there is a market crash around each corner? Why invest if there isn't a level playing field? Why invest if there are so many outside influences that can make you quickly go from making money to losing money?

Why bother?

Because, with the right strategies and mindset, investing in the stock market is the best chance you have to change the direction of your life and the trajectory of your family's financial well-being. In a nutshell, it can change your life and help fulfill all your dreams and those of your family. The stock market delivered me from a life of poverty to the life I live today. Just imagine the future that awaits you!

High-probability, Life-changing Rewards

The S&P 500 is up every twelve months over the prior twelve months 74% of the time. It's an amazing statistic and one you should remember during those down periods that test your nerve or when you think it cannot move any higher. It has, and eventually it will. With that in mind, the longer you are in the market, the higher the probability you will make money. Take a minute and really look at the next couple of charts. This is why I keep saying that the market is the greatest money-making machine ever.

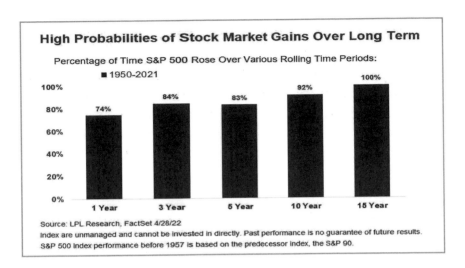

As you can see, there are enormous rewards for staying long — the longer you stay in, the less risk you incur.

S&P 500: 1926-2020		
Time Frame	Positive	Negative
Daily	56%	44%
1 Year	75%	25%
5 Years	88%	12%
10 Years	95%	5%
20 Years	100%	0%

Source: Dimensional Fund Advisors

S&P 500 Annual Returns: 1926-2020				
	5 Years	10 Years	20 Years	30 Years
Best	36.1%	21.4%	18.3%	14.8%
Worst	-17.4%	-4.9%	1.9%	7.8%
Average	10.1%	10.4%	10.9%	11.2%

Source: Dimensional Fund Advisors

In My Lifetime

How many times have you looked at a long-term chart and just said to yourself, "Why didn't I just put the money in the market and chill out?" Look at the chart below to see the gains in the stock market from the time I started to think it was a way out of poverty. It has been a juggernaut since I graduated high school in 1980.

Even if I could go back in a time machine and tell people about this, the growth has been so significant nobody would believe me.

But you have seen it firsthand. Now it's time for the next fifty years to be more than a curiosity. Let it be an integral part of the fabric in your journey to financial freedom.

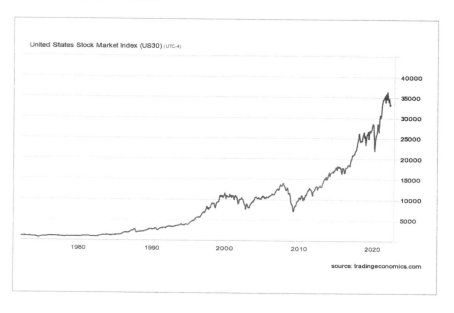

Not for Everyone? I Disagree!

Stock Picking Shouldn't Be Allowed for Everyone

Most people who own shares in individual companies don't really know what they're doing. Should the government set more guardrails?

– Bloomberg

The headline above threw me for a loop when I read it. But it echoes the elitist thinking on Wall Street. The idea that, maybe, regular folks should be barred from trading stocks could make its way to Capitol Hill one day.

I interviewed the author of this article on my "Making Money with Charles Payne" show where she was less vociferous about the topic than the headline suggested. But the idea is still out there and something Wall Street wouldn't mind seeing come to fruition.

Who decides how much risk another person should take? The day it's the government that makes those choices is the day the current economic and social standing becomes permanent. Not just for now, but for generations.

Your Right to Take Risks & Reap the Rewards

Part of the op-ed writer's position was that there is a good way to take risks and a not-so-good way. She then referred to advice an economist taught her about the disadvantage of owning individual stock — comparing it to owning a car muffler as a single part rather than owning all the parts and having a car to drive.

I think the goal was to underscore the advantages of diversification. But the way it's mentioned in the article underscores a beef I've had with investing "by the numbers" for years.

By focusing on the mitigation of downside risk, you can miss upside potential. I want you to think of the stocks in your portfolio as individual cars and not car parts. Would you like to own a Rolls Royce and an old station wagon just to tell your friends your garage is diversified?

Diversification and the Goal of Getting Rich

I agree folks should own more than one or two stocks, but the idea is to own the cream of the crop and not be overexposed to the stocks with deteriorating fundamentals. All of this really gets back to the establishment belief that most people are too dumb to figure out the direction of operating margins and market share gains, valuations metrics, etc.

There is a "knowledge" roadmap and an "emotional" roadmap. The latter can be more difficult to solve. The emotional side of investing is something we need to take a careful look at and completely understand. For a bit of context, take a look at this excerpt from a book about investing written almost 120 years ago.

The Pitfalls of Speculation written in 1906

X

What 500 Speculative Accounts Showed

A N examination of almost four thousand speculative accounts, extending over a period of ten years, developed results interesting and instructive in many ways. The examination was of an exhaustive character, and covered operations of every conceivable nature in both stocks and cereals.

In these accounts all the errors of speculation were distinctly illustrated.

The three principal points developed by the investigation were that 80% of the accounts showed a final loss; that the tendency to buy at the top and sell at the bottom was most prevalent; and that most of the operations appeared to be of a purely gambling character. The further fact was established that success almost invariably led to excesses.

The mass of figures derived from so exten-

101

Source: "The Pitfalls of Speculation" by Thomas Gibson

The book highlights mistakes made by investors over one hundred years ago and are the same mistakes made today. I believe they will be the same ones made one hundred years from now as well.

- 80% of speculators lose money
- Tendency to buy at the top and sell at the bottom
- Gambling characteristics

A very compelling point was the fact that folks who lived farthest away from brokerage offices had smaller losses and larger gains than local folks with access to those offices.

The author pointed to flurries and canards around brokerage offices that were available to those individuals living close to the brokerage houses and who could visit them on a regular basis. They were more susceptible to the rumors and whispers. The opportunity for those living farther away to make fools of themselves was much more restricted.

Being near the action back then might have been seen as an advantage, and that's when charlatans and rumor mongers take maximum advantage.

That reminds me of a story about the use of rumors in a famous gentlemen's club in the Wall Street area back in the day of the first stock market boom. An infamous trader was on the verge of losing everything on imminent news he had learned.

He hatched a plan to rush into a club of big hitters always

looking for an edge (anyway they could get it). Acting frantic to find a friend, the stock operator ripped off his coat and a note "fell" out of his pocket.

When he was told his friend wasn't there, he abruptly put his coat back on and left. Nobody told him he dropped the note, which was part of his plan. The "gentlemen" read the note and, thinking they had insider information, raced to the exchange to buy.

Of course, as they were buying, the stock operator was selling.

There is an intoxicating feeling in thinking we have the inside scoop or when we are riding a big-time winner. Some call this "irrational exuberance." My grandmother would have called it being just plain greedy.

Taking a Shot

I think swinging for the fences or taking a longshot from a successful plan is fine, as long as it's a small amount of money.

I take those occasional shots here and there to spice up my primary plan of wealth creation, more because it's fun and rewarding in a different way rather than trying to make a big score. This type of investing needs to be treated like going to the track and picking the 80-1 longshot. You root for that horse to win not only for money but because we all love an underdog. In the market, taking a shot on that "underdog," that stock nobody has heard of yet, is fine once in a while. You take a swing at the stock on the chance that it could pay off in the future. But it shouldn't be the focus of your investment strategy.

When Everyone Is Swinging for the Fences

There are also times when the market, in general, is

racing ahead with reckless abandon without underlying developments that would justify the gains.

Those periods can last anywhere from several weeks to several years. They are marked by an overwhelming sense of exuberance but always end in a river of tears. With that in mind, you can take an occasional shot as long as you understand the risk. When people say the stock market is a casino, I clarify: It's only a casino when you make it a casino, except there are no free drinks or great shows.

But it would be silly for me not to A) admit massive amounts of money can be made in a short period of time, B) acknowledge how powerfully enticing these periods can be, and C) recognize that no amount of intelligence or self-restraint is guaranteed to temper the allure of all that money everyone else seems to be making.

If you are going to occasionally treat the stock market like a casino, then at least know what makes a successful gambler.

Lessons to Be Learned from the Game of Poker

I like this list below a lot because most of it can be applied to being successful in the stock market or any investing endeavor. I've added my thoughts below the key points.

From Daniel Negreanu's Master Class

1. Study at least 20% of the time.

Studying the market means knowing what's going on in the present, how it relates to the past, and how it might inform future decision-making. I consider myself a constant student of the market.

2. Don't just play one type of poker.

Most investors, even professionals, learn one approach to the market. When it's not working, they always blame the market and market participants who simply don't get it and are ruining it. You need to be prepared to change your strategy as the market changes.

3. Treat it like a business.

This is your hard-earned money that you should treat most dearly, even the so-called "play money." You should treat your approach to investing like a business no matter how "small" the investment. All too often people tell me, "It's okay, it's not a lot of money, anyway." That approach is the first step in losing that money. The most successful businesses pay attention to details. So do the most successful investors. There is no such thing as "not a lot of money."

4. Use technology.

This seems self-explanatory but I would add that, while you want to use all the tools at your disposal, don't ever lose touch with both the computation process and thought process of investing. And be careful with so-called black box solutions that spit out ideas. Don't allow technology to become your only source of decision making.

5. Learn from other players.

There are so many books on investing success it's hard to believe any "maven" ever lost a penny. With that said, beware of any studies or investment guides that suggest retail investors are the only folks who ever lose money in the market. Institutions have massive losses. Even hedge funds, with unlimited resources and advantages over retail investors, haven't lived up to the hype for more than a decade. So, what I am advocating is that you can create your own success by listening and learning from others. Don't assume the market is too complex for you to successfully create that platform, which will assure your financial freedom and will be a stepping stone for your children and their children. Study other investors. Take their ideas and learn from them. You are capable of doing it for yourself.

6. Evaluate your bad beats objectively.

Study your stock market mistakes. Everybody makes them. I'll have more to say about that later in the book. Each scenario will come back around again at some point. There is no doubt 90% of the scenarios that you've lost money on will once again present themselves in the future. By studying your mistakes you'll be able to recognize the situations and not just avoid making the same mistakes but take advantage of them in the future.

7. Train your body as well as your mind.

There is a lot to be said about staying healthy. Investing involves mental challenges but you can't let yourself go, sitting in front of a screen all day. Get the blood flowing and do not allow emotions to make you psychically ill.

I've played poker at big casinos and it's boring as hell. I consider myself a good player but lack the patience to sit at a big table for hours. On the other hand, I could study the market for hours because I like reading the news, learning history, and trying to predict the future, all at the same time. So, the real difference for me between playing poker and investing in the market is that last statement. When playing poker, I am reacting to the cards being dealt. When I'm investing, I can do research and examine data. I can use that information to predict the future. I'm not passive at all. I get to dig out the facts and find the information. There is a wonderful sense of control in doing that research, learning all you can, and profiting from it.

In other words, investing is a lot of fun if you allow it to be a lot of fun.

But the one thing all professional card sharks (and smart investors) have in common is discipline. Knowing when to cut losses or knowing when to make the big bet is what separates the greats from the pretenders.

Pride and Ego?

There is a famous quote on Wall Street: "Beware of pride and ego." There are many other quotes that echo the same sentiment like the quote below from Charles Dow, the man who invented the Dow Jones Industrial Average.

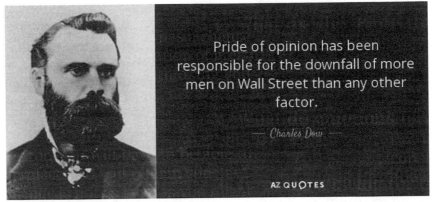

Pride of opinion has been responsible for the downfall of more men on Wall Street than any other factor.

— *Charles Dow* —

AZ QUOTES

Source: azquotes.com

This ancient quote proves that ego is a factor man has battled throughout time.

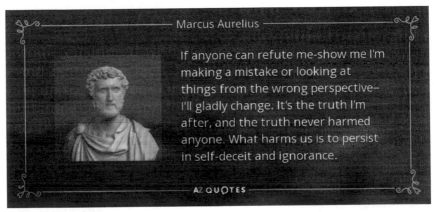

Marcus Aurelius

If anyone can refute me-show me I'm making a mistake or looking at things from the wrong perspective–I'll gladly change. It's the truth I'm after, and the truth never harmed anyone. What harms us is to persist in self-deceit and ignorance.

AZ QUOTES

Source: azquotes.com

Being wrong can be expensive but unwillingness to admit you're wrong can cost you everything. For most people, the embarrassment of getting something wrong is so powerful that it supersedes common sense and rationality. It's also a main cause of big mistakes in the stock market.

The quote by Marcus Aurelius can apply as a warning about getting too personal with losing positions and the realization that losses can have a major psychological blow greater than the loss of money. In so many endeavors in life when things go wrong, people shift from the economic loss to the mental or psychological loss. A fact of human nature is that you can always make money back, but those hits that live in your mind are a lot harder to shake.

I get that on so many levels, but it should NEVER happen from a bad investment or mistimed trade. It is true that certain things in the market, from companies lying in filings or large firms looking out for well-heeled investors over smaller investors, should stick in your craw, but they should not be confused with the actual investment(s).

Rule #1 for long-term success in the stock market is to identify your mistakes, bite the bullet, and leave it in the past. Otherwise, you will be victimized by it twice: first by the money lost by the original mistake and then by the opportunities missed as we dwell on those mistakes. Learn to live with, and learn from, your mistakes without letting them haunt you in the future.

While I agree with that Wall Street adage about being wary of ego, I think there is nothing wrong with having pride. I suspect that I would define pride differently than the adage might. I suspect the pride that is referred to in the saying is really arrogance. I believe that pride is not only good but necessary. In fact, I think there is too little of it in the world these days as people have been encouraged to be faceless parts of the crowd. We are being urged to have a sharing society and own nothing, but I believe you must own that pride that comes with personal effort.

Pride in individual accomplishment is the reward you get from hard work. It's the reward you will get at the end of your investing journey, if you stick with it through the ups and downs. This is especially true if you can improve the lives of your children and their children and help your local community.

What is Pride?

Pride is a feeling of satisfaction arising from what one has done or achieved. It is a sense of accomplishment that is healthy and good for a person and motivates him to be doing better all the time. A person who takes pride in the quality of his work is never satisfied with a below-par performance and strives to do well all the time.

Figure 02: Pride, unlike ego, is a feeling of pleasure and joy.

Pride, unlike ego, is a feeling of pleasure and joy. It is a sense of accomplishment that tends to bring humility in a person. You must have noticed how humble those who achieve everything in their field become. Pride gives a swollen heart, unlike ego, which gives a swollen head. A big heart gives nothing but humility. While ego is self-admiration, pride is self-satisfaction.

Source: differencebetween.com

There are other emotions you'll experience on the rollercoaster of stock market investing that you will need to avoid or mitigate. The best tool for navigating these inevitable emotions is knowledge.

Hanging Tough = Getting Paid

Warren Buffett famously said, "I will tell you how to become rich. Close the doors. Be fearful when others are greedy. Be greedy when others are fearful." Using the cycle of market emotions illustrated below, you certainly want to buy when everyone is despondent and depressed.

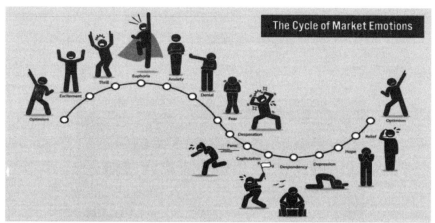

Source: stock.adobe.com

But beware, it's not your grandfather's Dow Jones Industrial Average.

The notion of owning the "stock market" is often based on the assumption that it's the same group of stocks that generally go up over a period of time as the indices do. The fallacy with that thinking is that there are changes being made to the stocks that make up those indices.

Dow Jones Industrial Average, S&P 500, Russell 2000, all see periodic changes where new names are added and old names are removed.

This gives the allure that the "stock market" always goes up. Hence, all you have to do is buy and hold.

This is why I want to get this point in early in the book. As an investor you will be told to "buy and hold" forever. The fact of the matter is nobody who's ultra-successful in the stock market simply buys and holds every position forever.

It's true there are amazing stocks that have returned enormous amounts of money via share applications, dividends, and spin-offs. Owning one of these and never thinking twice about closing your position would have made you fabulously wealthy. I read this (below) and thought to myself, "wow!"

> In 1902, the NYSE began trading stock in Philip Morris & Co. Ltd. This was the greatest investment opportunity in the history of the United States, with 247,500,000% returns to date.

That works out to 13% annualized, which is a strong gain. A cynic might say the only problem with these kinds of stories is you have to live 120 years to enjoy them. That misses the point, however. For me the real problem is the 99% of other names that also began trading in 1902 have long ago bitten the dust. If you had invested in those stocks and "held them forever" your return would be 0.0%.

The components of major indices have to change like players on professional sports teams. Nobody confuses the New York Knicks that won championships in the early 1970s with any Knicks teams since then. The major indices are like that. The stocks that make up an index are subject to change over time.

Dow Jones Industrial Average

The Dow is considered the granddaddy of all the indices.

The Dow Jones Industrial Average was created by Charles Dow, then editor of the *Wall Street Journal*, and statistician Edward Jones.

It's actually the second oldest stock market index, after the Dow Jones Transportation Index.

It was established on May 26, 1896, with twelve stocks. Of those twelve, you would only recognize one name: General Electric.

Some of the other names included:

- American Cotton — now a subsidiary of Unilever
- American Sugar — now a subsidiary of Domino Foods
- American Tobacco — was broken up due to antitrust laws the same day as Standard Oil and became four separate smaller companies
- Distillation and Cattle Feeding — was taken off during prohibition and put back in 1934
- Standard Rope and Twine — was added in 1896 and removed in 1899

If the Dow Jones Industrial Average were just those original stocks and they were never acquired or merged with others, it's safe to say that no one would invest in the Dow Jones Industrial Average.

The components of the Dow have been changed fifty-seven times. The components of the S&P 500 have been changed almost three hundred times. It's estimated that through 2030 there will be an average of thirty-five changes each year, with the average lifespan of an individual stock on the Index at just above fourteen years.

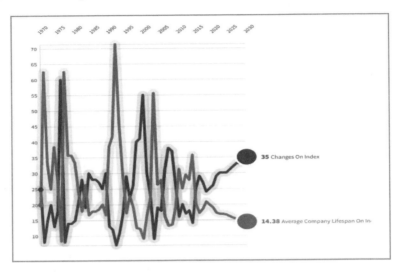

The bottom line is that you should treat your portfolio as your own personal investment index. It requires periodic changes. But you make the call on when those changes happen, which stocks are removed, and which are added. This is how you remain an Unbreakable Investor while those passively investing in the indices get broken by volatile market swings.

Passive Surrender

"The stock market is a giant distraction to the business of investing."
— Jack Bogle

Jack Bogle is considered the father of the mutual fund industry, a revolutionary investment vehicle that brought Main Street into the stock market.

As an introductory product or a part of a retirement portfolio, I think the mutual fund serves an important role. But the evolution of mutual funds and introduction of exchange traded funds (ETFs) have taken on a more sinister role.

Quite simply, they have become too large and powerful, and they skew market performance.

Risks Abound

A white paper from the Federal Reserve, last updated in 2020, laid out the pros and cons that hinted at some of the potential negative impacts. These risks included liquidity, redemption risks, and increased volatility of investing in mutual funds and ETF's.

The Board of Governers of the Federal Reserve also released this abstract statement below in a post entitled "The Shift from Active to Passive Investing: Potential Risks to Financial Stability."

Abstract:

The past couple of decades have seen a significant shift from active to passive investment strategies. We examine how this shift affects financial stability through its impacts on: (i) funds' liquidity and redemption risks, (ii) asset-market volatility, (iii) asset-management industry concentration, and (iv) comovement of asset returns and liquidity. Overall, the shift appears to be increasing some risks and reducing others. Some passive strategies amplify market volatility, and the shift has increased industry concentration, but it has diminished some liquidity and redemption risks. Finally, evidence is mixed on the links between indexing and comovement of asset returns and liquidity.

Source: Finance and Economics Discussion Series (FEDS)
https://www.federalreserve.gov/econres/feds/the-shift-from-active-to-passive-investing
-potential-risks-to-financial-stability.htm

Not-So-Passive Investing

In 1958 the sci-fi movie "The Blob" was released as a double feature with "I Married a Monster from Outer Space." The film launched the career of Steve McQueen, but it is better known for its plot. An amoeba-like creature crashes on Earth and begins to envelop everything in its path. The more it consumed, the larger and more menacing it became. The Blob was child's play compared to what passive investing is becoming today. As the chart below illustrates, over 50% of U.S. equities are now owned by passive funds.

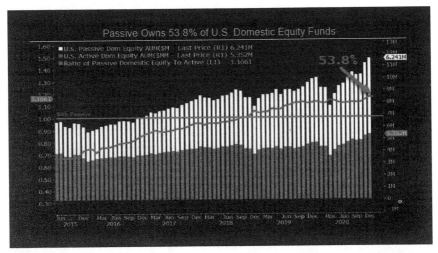

Source: Bloomberg Intelligence

The sheer amount of cash that has poured into these funds triggers buying that creates its own momentum. That momentum often attracts even more buying, which helps the market move higher, but what happens when that wave moves the wrong way?

In a Flash

I fear we are about to find out the answer to the question posed above. We've already gotten a glimpse of that outcome over the years with the emergence of the so-called "flash crashes."

For example, on May 6, 2010, ETFs lost 60% in twenty minutes. Another flash crash that occurred on August 24, 2015, served notice of risks from imbalances caused from excessive passive ETF investing. These are just two examples of what is now possible due to the ginormous "Blob-Like-Effects" that EFT's and passive investing have created.

Bears Take a Bite

Bear market's bites can leave deep scars. The rough outing for the stock market in 2022 (illustrated below) saw a sharp decline in ETF flows, but money was not redirected into active funds. Perhaps that means more investors are finally becoming wise to the dangers of this style of investing.

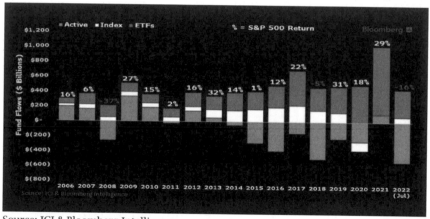

Source: ICI & Bloomberg Intelligence

Wave Machine

Have you ever seen one of those wave machines some people have as part of their décor at home or in the office? Most use either silicon oil or mineral oil, which is lighter than water, and thus, moves slower inside the case, giving it that feeling of a visible wave action. The more the oil moves to one side, the more rapid the pace and the higher the level of the wave crest gets until it peaks and the pattern reverses.

I think they are so cool and even meditative to watch, but imagine if you were in a tiny ship riding those waves back and forth. The ride up the wave would be exhilarating but the ride down the wave would be terrifying.

As a stock market investor, it's pure joy and excitement as the wave builds higher and higher, and, unlike those wave machines, there are times it feels like there will be no limits as to how high the wave can go. But there are limits, and a passive investor, just like a tiny ship, is stuck riding the wave back down.

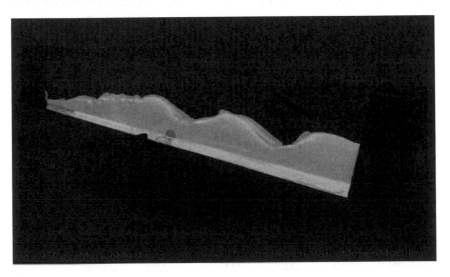

The Tide Turns

In 2021 and 2022, we saw the effects of reversing passive investing patterns as the most popular stocks in the market (mostly those hot mega-growth names in technology and communication services) started moving lower. The more they declined, the more passive funds were forced to sell. The more those funds sold, the faster the stocks declined.

When the market starts to turn lower, those passive funds move in reverse. Most passive ETFs allocate money based on market capitalization. This is one reason, in recent years, why the top ten market cap names have only gotten larger. It's a positive feedback loop when the market is going up, and it's a terrifying negative feedback loop when the market is going down.

Diversification?

Check out the top six holdings in some of the largest ETFs. It doesn't matter what the stated objective is, these giant ETFs all own the same stocks and are not as diversified as many investors think.

SPY	IVV	VTI	VOO	QQQ	IWF	VUG
U.S. large- and midcap stocks	U.S. large- and midcap stocks	entire mar-ket-cap spectrum	U.S. large- and mid-cap	Non-financial on NAS-DAQ	Russell 1000 Index	U.S. large-cap growth
AAPL	AAPL	AAPL	AAPL	AAPL	AAPL	AAPL
MSFT	MSFT	MSFT	MSFT	MSFT	MSFT	MSFT
AMZN	AMZN	AMZN	AMZN	AMZN	AMZN	AMZN
GOOGL	GOOGL	TSLA	TSLA	TSLA	TSLA	TSLA
GOOG	GOOG	GOOGL	GOOGL	GOOGL	GOOGL	GOOGL
TSLA	BRK.A	GOOG	GOOG	GOOG	FB	FB

I'm sure everyone has seen that funny GIF of how normal conversation in a crowded room morphs into a crescendo of fear and then greed.

Source: kaltoons.com
https://shop.kaltoons.com/collections/all

It's funny because we know it's true. But the story's moral is to not allow yourself to be sucked into these types of traps.

Market Efficiency

There are other elements to passive investing that might harm your long-term goals in the stock market that need a strategy. A strategy that, from time to time, ignores the herd in order to achieve outsized performance.

For example, too much money in passive funds makes the market less efficient. As defined by Investopedia, "market efficiency refers to the degree to which market prices reflect all available, relevant information. If markets are efficient, then all information is already incorporated into prices, and so there is no way to 'beat' the market because there are no undervalued or overvalued securities available."

This is a concept pushed by the mutual fund and ETF marketers to attract more funds, but it's far from reality. I want to help

41

you gain knowledge so that, as you become more sophisticated, you will be able to strategically take advantage of the effects passive investing has on the market or, at the very least, mitigate their negative impact on your own investing efforts.

Passive funds are big business and have made a few firms on Wall Street fabulously wealthy. There are five issuers with $100 billion or more in ETF assets under management:

- BlackRock: $2.117 trillion
- Vanguard Group: $1.619 trillion
- State Street Corp. $881 billion
- Invesco Ltd. $308 billion
- Charles Schwab: $262 billion

Marketing Bait

Wall Street is not unlike companies that need to come up with fresh products and marketing angles to keep consumers engaged and buying. Just think about your typical trip to the supermarket and a stroll through the cereal aisle. When I grew up there were only ten brands of cereal and only eight crayons came in a box. Now, the options seem endless, but they're still just cereal and crayons. Here's my point, don't let the fancy marketing bait of the endless array of funds and ETFs lure you in!

Source: blogspot.com
http://breakfastbowl.blogspot.com/2017/

Source: shop.crayola.com
https://shop.crayola.com/color-and-draw/crayons

Are Index Funds Capitalism?

One final thought to put an exclamation point on my concerns about index funds. I rarely agree with things written in *The Atlantic* but an article about index funds asking if they could be worse than Marxism has stayed with me. The publication's headline below says it all!

The Atlantic

IDEAS

Could Index Funds Be 'Worse Than Marxism'?

Economists and policy makers are worried that the Vanguard model of passive investment is hurting markets.

Now, let's review.

At the end of each chapter, I'll present you with a short quiz. Because I believe the material I'm presenting is essential to become an Unbreakable Investor, I want you to check and make sure you have mastered the key points along the way. If something isn't clear, or you forget an answer, take the time to go back into the chapter and make sure it is part of your working knowledge. These quizzes are for you. Take your time and make sure you "own" the material. I'll put the answers lower on the page so you can check. But test yourself first.

Quiz: Chapter 1

1. What is the Blob that impacts the market today?

2. What do emotions have to do with investing?

3. Is taking a swing for the fences on a long-shot stock a good or bad idea?

4. What do I believe is the greatest tool for achieving financial freedom?

Answers to Quiz - Chapter 1

1. The Blob is the huge amount of cash that has hit the market in the form of passive investing.

2. Emotions can have a huge impact on investing, and it is very important that the Unbreakable Investor be aware of his/her own emotions and be able to control them, especially when everyone else is in a panic.

3. Taking a chance on a long shot can be either good or bad. The important thing to remember here is that it **should not be** your primary investing strategy.

4. This should be an easy one! The Stock Market, of course!

2

Greatest Money-Making Machine in History

As many know, I am fond of calling the stock market the greatest money-making machine in history. There have been other ways to make a lot of money in a short period of time, and some have even been legal. These days a hot, online video could spring you into stardom overnight. And, of course, there are still folks tinkering with things in their garages that might change their fortunes. But none of these can touch the stock market for overall wealth creation.

The Wilshire 5000 was created in 1974 to track the entire stock market. The graph on the next page illustrates how it compares to the other indices. It was revamped in 1980, the year I graduated from high school, with a starting value of 1404.60 points, reflecting a total market capitalization of $1,404.596 billion. Back then each point on the index was equal to $1 billion.

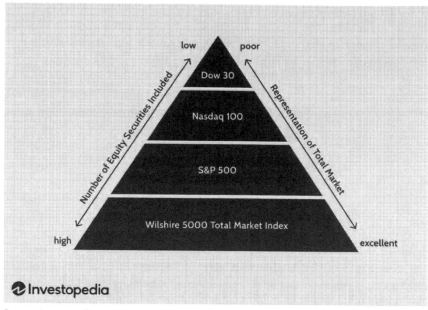

Source: investopedia.com
https://www.investopedia.com/terms/w/wilshire5000equityindex.asp

With adjustments (as shown below), the Wilshire has climbed from $2.0 trillion to a high of $233 trillion. You want a piece of that action. And that is not a question!

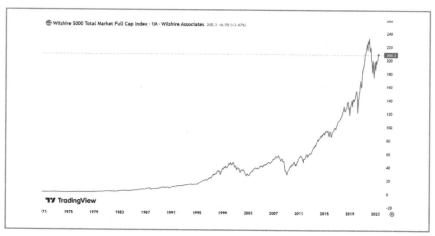

Source: investopedia.com
https://www.investopedia.com/terms/w/wilshire5000equityindex.asp

Everyone's Welcome

 The beauty of the stock market is how easy it is for anyone to participate. For the most part, this has always been the case but was made even easier in the 1970s when Charles Schwab introduced discount commissions.

This newfound ability for the actual individual investor to be in charge was novel at the time and only created a few ripples.

But the notion of being in charge of your destiny via the stock market should be appealing to everyone.

Since the advent of discount commissions, the self-directed movement has become a tidal wave and a serious dilemma for Wall Street. However, like so many things, the "street" has taken the issue of commissions and found ways to take advantage of investors.

Beware of Zero Commissions

Nobody is going to execute orders for you for free, unless they are monetizing your trade in a different way. Zero commissions are used to entice investors to trade too much and each of those trades is sold to the real client — hedge funds. This process is called Payment for Order Flow (PFOF). It's a form of compensation, usually in terms of fractions of a penny per share, that a brokerage firm gets for directing orders to a certain market maker or exchange. This can result in lower quality order execution, leading to slightly higher buy prices and marginally lower sell prices.

Annual Returns

Retail investors tend to assume that professional investors are always successful and will often take advice without doing any further research. Ironically, the pros tend to underperform the market.

But they have ways to mask that underperformance by selling the notion of "annual returns." Let me illustrate just how deceiving that can be.

In the four-year chart below, the average annual return is +10%. So, a typical investor might conclude that he would make 40% in four years plus all the benefits of the compounded returns. But in truth, the real return for an investor during that four-year period was –23%. BIG difference!

Annual vs. Real Rate of Return

		Initial Balance:	$100,000
Year	Annual Return	Annual Gain/Loss	End of Year Account Balance
1	-20%	-$20,000	$80,000
2	20%	$16,000	$96,000
3	-60%	-$57,600	$38,400
4	100%	$38,400	$76,800
Average Return:	10.00%	Real Return:	-23.20%

These return percentages below and not based on any security or investment product

Linear Performance Matters

Now you can see why I am staunchly against measuring your portfolio in annual terms. Investing is not like a sports season where it comes to a climactic finish with a single winner and then you start all over again. Nor is investing like playing a game of Monopoly, where you begin a new game with all the pieces standing on "Go."

Your portfolio is linear, and the gains and losses cross into the next year seamlessly. Don't be swayed by someone telling you the stock (or the professional investor) is having a great year and is making a great comeback. Look at the long-term picture. Investing isn't a snapshot but more like a whole photo album.

The notion of Wall Street firms or professional managers having a "great year" after a terrible year can mask the fact that stocks that lost value in the down year can still be underwater in the great year. And you can bet their marketing material will not mention this — not even with asterisks.

The point I'm stressing is that focusing on things like annual performance in your own portfolio can lead to big mistakes. There are tax advantages to making year-end decisions, but that should never supersede decisions based on strategy and fundamentals.

Don't get too caught up with trying to mimic metrics Wall Street uses to measure its own success, because there are often ulterior reasons for their decisions.

"Average Year" Myth

The "average year" performance is designed to contain investor optimism and erase the notion that anyone can beat the market. It wouldn't be beneficial to Wall Street for the average investor to assume he could beat the market.

I've read that the average return for the S&P 500 from 1957 to 2021 is 10.5%, and the average total return (dividends are added and reinvested) between 2001 and 2020 is 7.46%. Here's the rub — there is no such thing as an "average" return. The S&P, over the past forty years, has rarely had an "average year." In fact, it's been feast or famine — mostly feast.

Take a look at the averages chart below. Take a minute to focus on the period from 2001 to 2020. How often was the "average year" anywhere near the 7.46% Wall Street presents? There is nothing "average" in this period. There are several really rough years (we all remember 2008!) but mostly the market was up. In some years it was remarkably up! The idea of the "average year" has little value to the individual investor. What matters are your "real returns."

1980	32.42	1990	-3.10	2000	-9.50	2010	15.06
1981	-4.91	1991	30.47	2001	-11.89	2011	2.11
1982	21.55	1992	7.62	2002	-22.10	2012	16.00
1983	22.56	1993	10.08	2003	28.68	2013	32.39
1984	6.27	1994	1.32	2004	10.88	2014	13.69
1985	31.73	1995	37.58	2005	4.91	2015	1.38
1986	18.67	1996	22.96	2006	15.79	2016	11.96
1987	5.25	1997	33.36	2007	26.46	2017	21.83
1988	16.61	1998	28.58	2008	-37.00	2018	-4.38
1989	31.69	1999	21.04	2009	26.46	2019	31.49
						2020	18.40

Keeping Emotions at Bay

It's all about emotions, especially greed and fear. That's why you have to understand EQ.

Emotional Intelligence (otherwise known as Emotional Quotient or EQ) is the ability to understand, use, and manage your own emotions in positive ways to relieve stress, communicate effectively, empathize with others, overcome challenges, and defuse conflict. Emotional intelligence helps you build stronger relationships, succeed at school and work, and achieve your career and personal goals, like making a lot of money in the stock market.

Emotional intelligence is commonly defined by five attributes (as illustrated below):

Social Skills

Self-Awareness

Self-Regulation

Empathy

Motivation

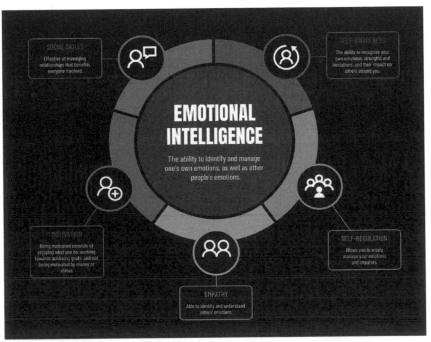

Why do I think having a high EQ is so important to investing and investors? Because I know being able to control your emotions at times of high stress can save you money and make you money. The stock market is reactive by nature. If you can stay calm when others are freaking out, you will find opportunities where others only see obstacles. The ability to be aware and manage your emotions is key to becoming an Unbreakable Investor.

You can make managing your emotions in times of high stress much easier by increasing your investing knowledge, which I am going to help you do.

You Are Already in the Market

By now anyone who knows me, and has seen me on television long enough, knows I'm the eternal advocate of everyone investing in the stock market and other smart assets. You must have your money working for you to change your financial life. That being said, I'm also fond of saying "everyone is in the stock market." I recognize that there are plenty of people who do not have a brokerage account or may have opened one in the past but it's not active.

But everyone is in the stock market — you cannot escape being in the stock market.

You might think, "Well, when I'm asleep I'm not in the stock market." Yes, you are. If you sleep on a bed with a mattress and sheets, you are in the market. If you sleep on the floor without a mattress or sheets, you are in the market.

Once you wake up in the morning and turn the handle on your sink, floss, brush your teeth, shower, towel off after the shower, shave, and use a cream (shaving, skin care, after shave, lotion, or beauty), you are knee-deep in the stock market because you are a consumer of products and services sold by publicly traded companies.

At this point you are a full-fledged member of the stock market — so why are you not an owner of stocks?

I bet you told your friends about the great products you used:

This is the best bed I ever had.

This is the firmest mattress I've ever had.

My bed sheets are divine.

Man, I love my new shaving kit — never have to change the blades.

I'm not big on aftershave creams but this stuff I'm using is amazing.

I only use two drops and my new beauty cream takes me back to my youth.

Not only do you take your hard-earned money to buy these products, but you then rave about them to your relatives, friends, and co-workers. This is where you should have your own epiphany – because not only are you paying for these things, but you have become an unpaid spokesperson. So why not become an owner?

I understand you cannot own every stock in the market but get this — you do not want to own every stock in the market. You don't need to own all the "hot" stocks right now. What you DO need to do is begin looking for opportunities.

The savvy investor recognizes that existing companies are always reinventing themselves and their products and services. Often, these are new opportunities.

Think about it — that great bed, bed sheets, slippers, razor blade, lotion, and beauty creams are often new versions of old products. The company that makes them spent a lot of time and money to revamp them and then lots more money to promote them. Or maybe there is a new company on the scene with a breakthrough product or service. But these products and services are not always quickly observed and many times it never occurs to folks that these are companies they can invest in — they can become part owners.

Buy What You Know but Know What You Buy

Most investors of a certain age know of the great Peter Lynch who ran the Fidelity Magellan Fund. From 1977 to 1990 he grew the fund's assets from $18 million to $14 billion. In the process he became a Wall Street superstar, and one willing to share his thoughts and experiences with the general public.

His most famous saying and mantra was: "Buy what you know."

Over the years this mantra became a commonplace saying for those looking to participate in the market. That is great advice for a starting point. Deal with products or services you know. But how can you tell if that company would be a good investment for you? That's where we have to turn the advice around. Now we want to "Know What We Buy." So, how do you do that?

Welcome to My 3 Pillars

Let's pause here for just a minute and let me introduce my 3 Pillars. These are the things I use to help make my decisions about both what to own and when to move into or out of a position. I'll talk more about them in the next chapter, but I want to introduce them here.

Pillar #1: Fundamental Changes

For me, this really consists of several parts. I look at the current financial facts about the company. I want to look at the current financial conditions and trends of any potential purchase. I also want to assess the company's ability to deliver against expectations. I look at the company's own valuations based on history and their peers in the marketplace. Finally, I need to look at the risks that might be known.

We need to recognize that all news is backward looking, telling only what has happened. However, using the news in those areas I just mentioned, we can get a better insight into what might happen in the near future.

I use the fundamentals to help me determine WHAT to buy.

Pillar #2: Technical Moves

Technical Moves has nothing to do with the fundamentals of the company. This is where I look to understand the buying and selling patterns of the current stockholders. The market is always in flux, and these constant changes are a test of the current shareholders. I look for the patterns of when shareholders choose to buy or sell these stocks. I am looking for *Resistance* on the upside of the stock's perceived highest value and *Support* on the downside of the stock's perceived lowest value. The analysis of these repeated *Support & Resistance* patterns tells me WHEN to either open or close a position for the highest probability results.

Pillar #3: Behavioral Reactions

Emotions can play a significant role in the short-term movement of stocks. Emotions can generate a buying or selling frenzy that may have nothing to do with the fundamentals or technical trends of the company. Fortunately, these emotional behaviors can be leveraged to extend gains or mitigate losses, especially when shares go parabolic.

This is when the price goes off the charts, in either direction, but is not something that can be sustained. When the movement is upward, it can seem like the ultimate party ride, but when it is downward, it feels like skydiving with no parachute!

By learning to use all three pillars together, you can more effectively manage your positions for bigger gains and smaller losses. You can confidently take advantage of upward trends and avoid selling on temporary downward swings that are triggered by unsubstantiated fear that doesn't match the fundamentals.

How heavily I rely on each pillar changes as the market shifts from a bear (downward) market to a bull (upward) market. You'll understand why when we dive deeper into the 3 Pillars in Chapter 3.

	Bear	Bull
Fundamental	80%	65%
Technical	5%	25%
Behavioral	15%	10%

Macroeconomic Factors

Learning to master the use of my 3 Pillars is the foundation for becoming an unbreakable investor. But, there are also macroeconomic factors that, from time to time, can have a big impact on stock prices and must be taken into consideration when they are in play.

Macroeconomics is a branch of economics that focuses on how the "overall economy" (the markets, businesses, consumers, and governments) behaves and influences everything else. Macroeconomics examines economy-wide phenomena such as inflation, price levels, rate of economic growth, income levels, gross domestic product (GDP), and changes in unemployment.

Today, the effects of macroeconomics go far beyond our national borders.

It's a Small World

The 1940 presidential candidate, Wendell Willkie, said it way back then...

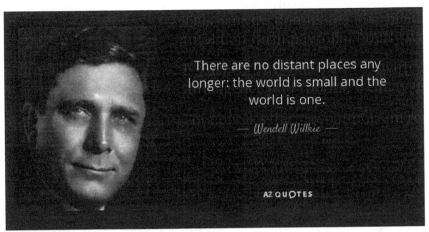

There are no distant places any longer: the world is small and the world is one.

— *Wendell Willkie* —

AZ QUOTES

Source: azquotes.com

The world has been shrinking for a long time, tied tighter by the advent of sailing ships, railroads, and airlines, which brought people and their goods and services to close proximity.

And recently, the COVID-19 pandemic made it abundantly clear that the idea of commerce being anything but global is a total fallacy. We are so interconnected today that successful investing needs to be done with an awareness of events and conditions around the world.

While recent events have demonstrated how interconnected we all are in a negative way, we can't ignore the power of the global economy for the individual investor.

As the chart below illustrates, the interconnectedness has seen the value of exported goods climb to 25% of global GDP since the end of the Great Depression. This has provided (and still provides) companies and investors with remarkable opportunities.

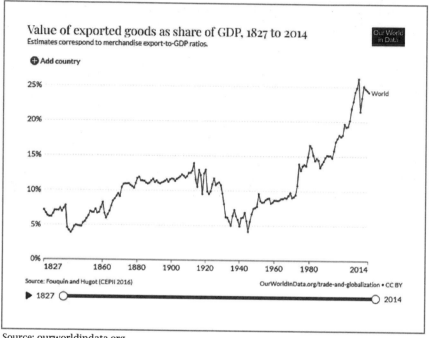

Source: ourworldindata.org
https://ourworldindata.org/trade-and-globalization

The Same Tides Lifts or Sinks All Nations.

Global prosperity and misery love company, and, for the most part, it's increasingly rare for certain parts of the world to endure hardship without it infecting other nations.

This was underscored by the events of 2020, more than any time since 1870, as 90% of the world's economics slipped into contraction at the same time.

This chart illustrates the history of economies with contractions in per capita GDP.

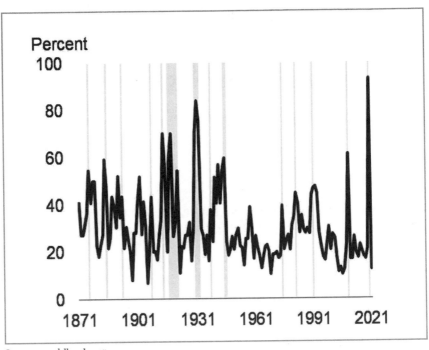

Source: worldbank.org
https://blogs.worldbank.org/opendata/understanding-depth-2020-global-recession-5-charts

Lessons of COVID-19

When the world locked down in 2020, global GDP contracted more than 6% — the largest since the end of World War II when much of the world was in physical and economic ruin and governmental budgets were being slimmed down from the need for military spending.

The chart below shows the contraction percentages since 1876.

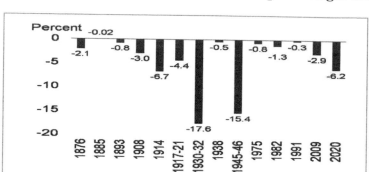

Source: weforum.org
https://www.weforum.org/agenda/2020/06/
coronavirus-covid19-economic-recession-global-compared/

At the end of the Second World War, the United States came to the rescue with the Marshall Plan to help Europe get on its feet.

During COVID-19, massive government intervention was provided through fiscal aid and central bank policies.

It turns out that too much money was printed and distributed to populations that couldn't go outside but could still spend that money.

Demand Shock

Commerce erupted in the digital world, which created a dilemma for the territorial world.

We saw global supply chains become unmoored during the global COVID-19 pandemic, which triggered shortages throughout the four corners of the planet.

Even as most of the world began to unlock their doors and go back outside, China retained a restrictive policy that saw cities of millions of people locked down after a single reported new case of COVID-19.

China didn't need U.S. products and services, so ship containers piled up at American ports.

The cost to ship products around the world became prohibitively expensive. This played a pivotal role in the spike in inflation to a forty-year high.

This chart shows the impact of the pandemic and the resulting breakdown of the supply chain due to the cost of moving goods globally.

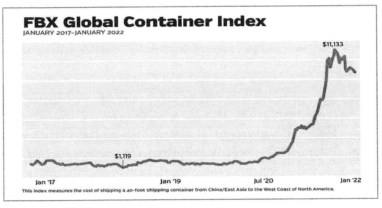

FBX Global Container Index
JANUARY 2017–JANUARY 2022

$11,133

$1,119

Jan '17   Jan '19   Jul '20   Jan '22

This index measures the cost of shipping a 40-foot shipping container from China/East Asia to the West Coast of North America.

Source: prospect.org
https://prospect.org/economy/hidden-costs-of-containerization/

This negatively impacted the U.S. economy. It's remarkable that a city you never heard of thousands of miles away could order everyone to stay home and it would cost U.S. workers jobs and investors portfolio losses.

Make no mistake when foreign nations are suffering through recessions, America feels the chill as well.

Central Bank Policies

There are five major central banks in the world.

    Federal Reserve (USA)

    European Central Bank

People's Bank of China
Bank of Japan
Bank of England

Because the roles these banks play in their own domestic economies has increased, moves made by one often influence potential moves of their global brethren.

For the United States, the Federal Reserve Bank has a major impact on the overall economy in general and the stock market in particular. The Fed is such an important influencer that I have devoted an entire chapter later in this book (Chapter 8) to understanding it and how it impacts market movement.

When the European Central Bank (ECB) sees inflation risk, the Federal Reserve will be on guard for similar conditions. The stock market sniffs these things out and reacts. Investors who are unaware of the current state of the global economy and rate policies put themselves at an unnecessary level of risk.

Below is a chart of the impact the global pandemic and economic shutdown had on bank policies around the world.

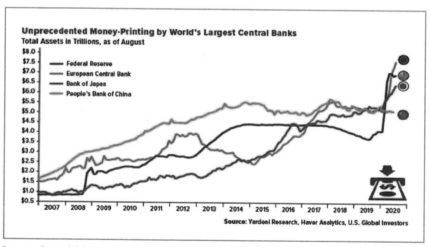

Source: thetradable.com
https://thetradable.com/charts/
federal-reserve-and-european-central-bank-print-money-like-never-before

Geopolitical Policies, Wars, & Conflicts

The Unbreakable Investor needs to be aware of the world as a whole. Decisions and actions from halfway around the world can have an impact on your portfolio. Here are just some of the examples.

Governments in Europe, China, and Japan can block potential mergers of two U.S. companies.

Governments can enact trade policies that would influence stocks in your portfolio.

Wars heighten risks, deplete resources, and trigger urges of protectionism.

The drumbeats of war have raged on for a long time, and it's hard to imagine conflicts will be avoided indefinitely.

Currently the lines are being blurred between commerce and the military in several industries including technology, and this becomes a focus of national policies.

We are looking at a future of increased protectionism and changing dance partners on the global stage. Trading partners today could become mortal enemies tomorrow.

There is also an ongoing effort to dislodge the U.S. dollar as the world's reserve currency.

Meanwhile, in the United States there is an onshoring phenomenon.

So, does this mean you should not invest? Of course not! It does mean that you need to become a student of the world. You need to pay attention to global situations and understand how they might impact you and your money.

Seasonality

There is another intriguing phenomenon in the world of investing known as seasonality. It's the recurrence of events over and over again to the point long-term trends are established.

There are so many of these seasonal trends it could make your head spin, but the more you know the better armed you are for investing especially during turbulence.

By the way, I am learning about different seasonality trends all the time.

Here are a few that I find most intriguing.

Typical Year

It's not unusual for the first part of the year to edge higher and then pick up speed on to the upside and while this is happening for the VIX (fear index and volatility gauge) to move lower. Things that might contribute to this are year-end tax loss harvesting that has created oversold individual stocks.

Often political programs that send money to households begin at the start of the calendar year.

Higher minimum wage kicks in as well.

I'm sure there are other rationale and theories out there, but the bottom line is these paths are uncannily accurate.

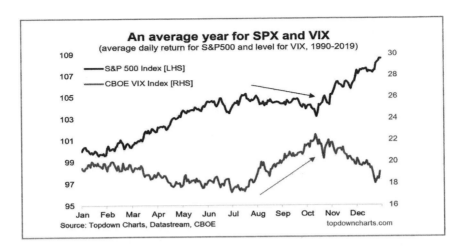

Understanding the time frame of seasonal trends is also important. I think it's better to look at trends over the past twenty to thirty years as most of the same participants are in the market, which means the same human reactions can be anticipated.

Elections years also have their own seasonality.

There are great sources for seasonal trends including:

· Stock Charts

· Ryan Detrick

· Bespoke

· Top Charts

Incorporating With 3 Pillars

Remember with the 3 pillars we learn what positions we want to own, how long we want to own those positions, and when we should buy and sell positions.

Seasonal trends help with holding and closing positions based on factors beyond that have no tangible bearing on the underlying companies.

Quiz: Chapter 2

1. What is the difference between Fundamental Changes and Technical Moves?

2. What do we use Technical Moves to do?

3. Why is it important to understand and control your emotions when investing?

4. What is the "average year" myth and why can it be misleading?

Answers to Quiz - Chapter 2

1. Fundamental Changes looks at the current situations within a company, like current financial statements. Technical Moves examines the trends of the stockholders and looks for support and resistance trends.

2. We use Technical Moves to determine when to open or close a position.

3. There are times when the market will react based almost solely on emotion. It can create a buying or selling frenzy for a particular stock that has nothing to do with the company's fundamentals. An Unbreakable Investor needs to understand this and be able to control emotions so he doesn't get caught.

4. Brokers can use this to compare the performance of a stock over a short period of time rather than looking at the performance over a more realistic time frame. It can distort the actual performance of the stock.

3

Foundational Principles

In my opinion there are three things that move stock prices:

> Fundamental Changes
> Technical Moves
> Behavioral Reactions

Actively monitoring the stock market is much like watching a sporting event like football or basketball. There are statistics that can help the viewer understand the score, but there are other elements that inform fans and coaches as to what the outcome might be, regardless of who is winning at any given point in time. In those cases, things like a reversal of a call on the field or an outstanding individual play that doesn't show up on the stat sheet can turn the tide or cement victory.

While we find ourselves rooting for certain stocks and even getting into a great rush based on share price movement or other forms of hype, ultimately, like sports, the cream rises to the top, and, more often than not, the best stock wins. However, investors can "win" by using any one of the 3 pillars with discipline. However, with that being said, we want long-term wealth creation, so the game plan is to incorporate **all 3 pillars**.

Fundamental

This is the analysis of real-time facts and trends to assess future trends and outcomes. There are three levels of this analysis.

Macro: broad economic and cultural trends. In our interconnected world, events that happen in far-flung areas of the world can eventually impact what happens in our own world and within our stock portfolios.

Of course, macro doesn't mean we must look from outer space orbit to assess all risks and probabilities. Macro can be a bird's eye view of the domestic economy as well as political and cultural conditions. As investors, we want to understand how these factors affect the overall stock market and the companies in our own portfolios.

For instance, it's hard for any company to grow the business or make money when the economy is in recession. But what if that company is losing less than its rivals?

Macro Fundamental Tools

There are a number of regularly scheduled monthly economic reports that offer macro data for investors.

I've given these factors a score of 1-5 based on their importance, with 5 being very important. Keep in mind that these rankings can vary depending on other factors from the overall economy.

As I write this book, the rankings shown correlate to the high inflationary environment with active or potential Fed rate hikes we are in. Conversely, in environments of low Fed fund rates and non-inflationary growth, measures of inflation take on less impactful importance to the broad market and serve a greater role in the stock-picking discovery process.

ISM Manufacturing (Score: 3)

Although manufacturing is only 8% of the economy, it is extremely influential as a harbinger of the future. Case in point, manufacturing drives:

11% of employment

20% of cap-ex spending

35% of productivity

60% of exports

70% of research and development

The ISM Manufacturing report is posted once a month and covers the following areas.

- New Orders
- Production
- Employment
- Supplier Deliveries
- Inventories
- Customers' Inventories
- Prices
- Backlog of Orders
- New Export Orders
- Imports

Of these, the "new orders" component is the most important and during times of higher inflation prices and limited inventories command extra attention.

ISM Non-Manufacturing (Score: 2)

This report covers the service side of the economy. Although the service economy is larger than manufacturing, there are a number of other gauges that carry more weight and influence for investors.

Jobs Report (BLS) (Score: 5)

For the most part, this is the most important of all regularly released economic reports. This report reverberates beyond the stock market and can even make or break presidential campaigns. There are a number of moving parts to this monthly survey from the Bureau of Labor Statistics (BLS).

The report is actually two surveys.

Comparison of survey concepts, definitions, and methodologies
The major features and distinctions of the two surveys are shown below.

Comparison of:	Household Survey (CPS)	Payroll Survey (CES)
Scope	Civilian noninstitutional population age 16 and over	Nonfarm wage and salary jobs
Data source	Monthly sample survey of approximately 60,000 eligible households	Monthly sample survey of approximately 122,000 businesses and government agencies, representing about 666,000 individual worksites
Major outputs	Labor force, employment, unemployment, and associated rates with demographic detail	Employment, hours, and earnings with industry and geographic detail
Reference period	Generally the calendar week that includes the 12th of the month (see note below)	Employer pay period that includes the 12th of the month (could be weekly, biweekly, monthly, or other)
Employment concept	Estimate of employed people (multiple jobholders are counted only once). Includes people on unpaid leave from their jobs.	Estimate of jobs (multiple jobholders are counted for each nonfarm payroll job). Includes only people who received pay for the reference pay period.
Employment inclusions and exclusions	Includes the unincorporated self-employed, unpaid family workers in family businesses, agriculture and related workers, workers in private households, and workers on unpaid leave. Excludes workers on furlough for the entire reference week, even if they receive pay for the furlough period (they are considered unemployed, on temporary layoff).	Excludes all of the groups listed at left, except for the logging component of agriculture and related industries. Includes furloughed workers if they receive pay for any portion of the pay period that includes the furlough.
Approximate size of over-the-month change in employment required for statistical significance at the 90-percent confidence level	± 600,000	± 130,000
Benchmark adjustments to survey results	No direct benchmark for employment. Adjustments to underlying population base made annually using intercensal population estimates, and every 10 years using the decennial census.	Employment benchmarked annually to universe employment counts derived primarily from unemployment insurance (UI) tax records.

source: zenfires.com

Household Survey (Score: 4)

For me, the most important component of the jobs report is participation. This reflects the grit of a nation, which, for me, is a crucial component of a nation's determination. The report gives us the unemployment rate, which is vital to politicians and the Federal Reserve.

"Employment to population ratio" is also important, though rarely mentioned in the financial media.

The Real Unemployment Rate (Score: 5)

HOUSEHOLD DATA
Summary table A. Household data, seasonally adjusted
[Numbers in thousands]

Category	May 2022	Mar. 2023	Apr. 2023	May 2023	Change from: Apr. 2023- May 2023
Employment status					
Civilian noninstitutional population	263,579	266,272	266,443	266,618	175
Civilian labor force	164,278	166,731	166,688	166,818	130
Participation rate	62.3	62.6	62.6	62.6	0.0
Employed	158,299	160,892	161,031	160,721	-310
Employment-population ratio	60.0	60.4	60.4	60.3	-0.1
Unemployed	5,979	5,839	5,657	6,097	440
Unemployment rate	3.6	3.5	3.4	3.7	0.3
Not in labor force	99,400	99,541	99,755	99,800	45
Unemployment rates					
Total, 16 years and over	3.6	3.5	3.4	3.7	0.3
Adult men (20 years and over)	3.4	3.4	3.3	3.5	0.2
Adult women (20 years and over)	3.4	3.1	3.1	3.3	0.2
Teenagers (16 to 19 years)	10.5	9.8	9.2	10.3	1.1
White	3.2	3.2	3.1	3.3	0.2
Black or African American	6.2	5.0	4.7	5.6	0.9
Asian	2.4	2.8	2.8	2.9	0.1
Hispanic or Latino ethnicity	4.4	4.6	4.4	4.0	-0.4
Total, 25 years and over	3.0	2.9	2.9	3.0	0.1
Less than a high school diploma	5.2	4.8	5.4	5.7	0.3
High school graduates, no college	3.4	4.0	3.9	3.9	0.0
Some college or associate degree	3.4	3.0	2.9	3.2	0.3
Bachelor's degree and higher	2.0	2.0	1.9	2.1	0.2
Reason for unemployment					
Job losers and persons who completed temporary jobs	2,732	2,949	2,642	2,960	318
Job leavers	766	845	790	765	-25
Reentrants	1,944	1,665	1,761	1,821	60
New entrants	530	492	531	508	-23
Duration of unemployment					
Less than 5 weeks	2,052	2,272	1,866	2,083	217
5 to 14 weeks	1,771	1,733	1,915	1,865	-50
15 to 26 weeks	687	734	679	858	179
27 weeks and over	1,349	1,104	1,156	1,188	32
Employed persons at work part time					
Part time for economic reasons	4,317	4,102	3,903	3,739	-164
Slack work or business conditions	3,000	2,873	2,760	2,582	-178
Could only find part-time work	984	682	817	824	7
Part time for noneconomic reasons	20,822	21,433	21,796	21,864	68
Persons not in the labor force					
Marginally attached to the labor force	1,477	1,289	1,480	1,508	28
Discouraged workers	418	351	364	422	58

NOTE: Persons whose ethnicity is identified as Hispanic or Latino may be of any race. Detail for the seasonally adjusted data shown in this table will not necessarily add to totals because of the independent seasonal adjustment of the various series. Updated population controls are introduced annually with the release of January data.

Source: U.S. Bureau of Labor Statistics
https://www.bls.gov/news.release/empsit.a.htm#

The media has anointed the most flawed of all the components to be the most important. Citing the U-3 unemployment rate is nuts because it doesn't count people who aren't looking for work.

If ten people are looking for work and nine are successful, the U-3 unemployment rate is 10%, but let's say one person stops looking and drops out of the workforce while the other nine continue working. In that case the U-3 unemployment rate is 0%.

But the person who dropped out of the labor force still needs to eat, needs shelter, still needs to be clothed. That person is a strain on the economy. While this might seem like an oversimplification, the reality is that the jobs data can be misinterpreted in the financial and general media. Why either gets it wrong is beyond me, although there are nefarious reasons.

I've seen record job growth portrayed as bad news because the U-3 unemployment number edged higher, which simply means more people came into the labor force than found jobs. But we want people willing to work. When there is an avalanche of folks looking for jobs and 99% of those looking find them in a given month, that is encouraging.

Conversely, when people are dropping out of the labor force and the unemployment rate is going down, it's terrible news for the nation beyond economics. It means Americans are giving up.

I prefer the U-6 unemployment rate and urge everyone to look into it, as well as other aspects of the report, to counter knee-jerk narratives and market reactions.

HOUSEHOLD DATA
Table A-15. Alternative measures of labor underutilization
[Percent]

Measure	Not seasonally adjusted			Seasonally adjusted					
	May 2022	Apr. 2023	May 2023	May 2022	Jan. 2023	Feb. 2023	Mar. 2023	Apr. 2023	May 2023
U-1 Persons unemployed 15 weeks or longer, as a percent of the civilian labor force........	1.3	1.2	1.3	1.2	1.2	1.1	1.1	1.1	1.2
U-2 Job losers and persons who completed temporary jobs, as a percent of the civilian labor force....................	1.4	1.4	1.6	1.7	1.5	1.7	1.8	1.6	1.8
U-3 Total unemployed, as a percent of the civilian labor force (official unemployment rate)................................	3.4	3.1	3.4	3.6	3.4	3.6	3.5	3.4	3.7
U-4 Total unemployed plus discouraged workers, as a percent of the civilian labor force plus discouraged workers..................	3.6	3.3	3.6	3.9	3.6	3.8	3.7	3.6	3.9
U-5 Total unemployed, plus discouraged workers, plus all other persons marginally attached to the labor force, as a percent of the civilian labor force plus all persons marginally attached to the labor force.........	4.2	3.9	4.3	4.5	4.2	4.4	4.2	4.2	4.5
U-6 Total unemployed, plus all persons marginally attached to the labor force, plus total employed part time for economic reasons, as a percent of the civilian labor force plus all persons marginally attached to the labor force...............	6.7	6.1	6.4	7.1	6.6	6.8	6.7	6.6	6.7

NOTE: Persons marginally attached to the labor force are those who currently are neither working nor looking for work but indicate that they want and are available for a job and have looked for work sometime in the past 12 months. Discouraged workers, a subset of the marginally attached, have given a job-market related reason for not currently looking for work. Persons employed part time for economic reasons are those who want and are available for full-time work but have had to settle for a part-time schedule. Updated population controls are introduced annually with the release of January data.

Source: U.S. Bureau of Labor Statistics
https://www.bls.gov/news.release/empsit.a.htm#

Then there's the consensus game, which has cost Wall Street a ton of credibility (although there was little left to lose).

Establishment Survey (Score: 5)

This survey dominates the headlines with the change in total non-farm payrolls, hourly wages, and workweek.

I suspect in the future, with the advent of artificial intelligence and robots, we may use this data differently.

For now, it's the most important report card on the economy.

ESTABLISHMENT DATA
Summary table B. Establishment data, seasonally adjusted

Category	May 2022	Mar. 2023	Apr. 2023[p]	May 2023[p]
EMPLOYMENT BY SELECTED INDUSTRY (Over-the-month change, in thousands)				
Total nonfarm	364	217	294	339
Total private	343	157	253	283
Goods-producing	61	-19	28	26
Mining and logging	2	2	5	3
Construction	38	-9	13	25
Manufacturing	21	-12	10	-2
Durable goods[1]	8	-5	11	3
Motor vehicles and parts	-6.4	4.8	9.0	6.8
Nondurable goods	13	-7	-1	-5
Private service-providing	282	176	225	257
Wholesale trade	18.3	3.5	2.4	1.1
Retail trade	-51.4	-18.9	10.0	11.6
Transportation and warehousing	45.3	16.2	3.7	24.2
Utilities	0.7	1.7	1.5	0.1
Information	32	3	1	-9
Financial activities	6	-5	25	10
Professional and business services[1]	72	45	65	64
Temporary help services	3.6	-3.3	-6.9	7.7
Private education and health services[1]	76	70	85	97
Health care and social assistance	56.9	55.9	69.1	74.6
Leisure and hospitality	73	46	30	48
Other services	10	14	2	10
Government	21	60	41	56
(3-month average change, in thousands)				
Total nonfarm	344	312	253	283
Total private	231	234	201	231
WOMEN AND PRODUCTION AND NONSUPERVISORY EMPLOYEES AS A PERCENT OF ALL EMPLOYEES[2]				
Total nonfarm women employees	49.7	49.8	49.8	49.8
Total private women employees	48.3	48.3	48.3	48.3
Total private production and nonsupervisory employees	81.5	81.4	81.4	81.4
HOURS AND EARNINGS ALL EMPLOYEES Total private				
Average weekly hours	34.6	34.4	34.4	34.3
Average hourly earnings	$32.06	$33.20	$33.33	$33.44
Average weekly earnings	$1,109.28	$1,142.08	$1,146.55	$1,146.99
Index of aggregate weekly hours (2007=100)[3]	112.8	114.8	115.0	114.9
Over-the-month percent change	0.3	-0.2	0.2	-0.1
Index of aggregate weekly payrolls (2007=100)[4]	173.0	182.2	183.2	183.7
Over-the-month percent change	0.6	0.1	0.5	0.3
DIFFUSION INDEX (Over 1-month span)[5]				
Total private (250 industries)	70.6	57.0	58.8	60.2
Manufacturing (72 industries)	68.1	43.8	44.4	47.2

Source: U.S. Bureau of Labor Statistics
https://www.bls.gov/news.release/empsit.a.htm#

Regional Federal Reserve Manufacturing Surveys (Score: 3)

The Philadelphia Fed and Empire Fed Manufacturing surveys are the two most important of the regional Fed reports on local economies.

Manufacturing Business Outlook Survey

The *Manufacturing Business Outlook Survey* is a monthly survey of manufacturers in the Third Federal Reserve District. Participants indicate the direction of change in overall business activity and in the various measures of activity at their plants: employment, working hours, new and unfilled orders, shipments, inventories, delivery times, prices paid, and prices received. The survey has been conducted each month since May 1968.

Source: Federal Reserve Bank Philadelphia
https://www.philadelphiafed.org/surveys-and-data/regional-economic-analysis/manufacturing-business-outlook-survey

Investors can use these reports to understand the direction of the overall economy and to help make investment decisions.

- New orders underscore general strength, particularly looking six months out.
- Unfilled orders and delivery times give us insight to supply chains.
- Inventories declining means replenishing, while builds means less demand.
- Prices paid impact gross margins.
- Prices received can impact earnings.
- Cap-ex is huge — these are major investments that underscore confidence or lack thereof.

MANUFACTURING BUSINESS OUTLOOK SURVEY June 2023	June vs. May					Six Months from Now vs. June				
	Previous Diffusion Index	Increase	No Change	Decrease	Diffusion Index	Previous Diffusion Index	Increase	No Change	Decrease	Diffusion Index
What is your evaluation of the level of general business activity?	-10.4	19.5	44.9	33.2	-13.7	-10.3	32.6	43.9	19.9	12.7
Company Business Indicators										
New Orders	-8.9	23.3	39.1	34.4	-11.0	-2.3	36.3	38.6	22.2	14.1
Shipments	-4.7	31.2	45.2	21.2	9.9	4.5	37.8	51.1	9.5	28.3
Unfilled Orders	0.8	6.7	66.7	25.2	-18.5	-10.1	16.2	56.6	26.0	-9.8
Delivery Times	-9.3	1.0	80.2	17.1	-16.1	-31.0	12.0	64.9	22.7	-10.6
Inventories	6.4	14.1	65.3	17.6	-3.5	-2.2	16.8	44.8	36.3	-19.5
Prices Paid	10.9	22.0	65.5	11.5	10.5	28.3	34.0	53.7	10.5	23.5
Prices Received	-7.0	18.7	59.2	18.6	0.1	24.1	33.2	49.6	15.8	17.4
Number of Employees	-8.6	11.1	74.8	11.4	-0.4	12.6	22.8	66.7	9.8	13.1
Average Employee Workweek	-7.7	1.9	86.6	10.1	-8.2	-0.2	10.7	79.1	10.1	0.6
Capital Expenditures	--	--	--	--	--	2.5	26.7	54.8	16.8	9.9

NOTES:
(1) Diffusion indexes represent the percentage indicating an increase minus the percentage indicating a decrease.
(2) All data are seasonally adjusted.
(3) Percentages may not sum to 100 because of rounding, omission by respondents, or both.
(4) Survey results reflect data received through June 12, 2023.

Source: Federal Reserve Bank Philadelphia
https://www.philadelphiafed.org/-/media/frbp/assets/surveys-and-data/mbos/2023/bos0623.pdf

Leading Economic Indicators (Score: 3)

As the name implies, this data point attempts to measure the economy for the next six to twelve months. It's an especially important tool for those trying to anticipate the beginning or conclusion of a recession.

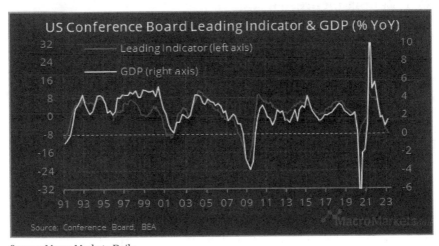

Source: Macro Markets Daily

The report uses ten components to come to its conclusions.

	Financial Components
	Leading Credit Index ™*
	S&P 500® Index of Stock Prices
	Interest Rate Spread, 10-year T-bonds less Fed Funds
	Non-Financial Components
	Avg. Consumer Expectations for Business Conditions
	ISM® Index of New Orders
	Building Permits, Private Housing
	Average Weekly Hours, Mfg.
	Manufacturers' New Orders, Nondefense Capital Goods excl. aircraft**
	Manufacturers' New Orders, Consumer Goods & Materials**
	Average Weekly Initial Claims, Unemp. Insurance*

Source: The conference board

PCE Report (Score: 5)

What is the Personal Consumption Expenditures Price Index?

This is a measure of the prices that people living in the United States, or those buying on their behalf, pay for goods and services. The PCE price index is known for capturing inflation (or deflation) across a wide range of consumer expenses and reflecting changes in consumer behavior. Remember the consumer is close to 70% of the economy (GDP).

Bureau of Economic Research (Score: 3)

The PCE is seen as a complement to the Consumer Price Index (CPI), although, in recent years, it has actually edged out its rival inflation gauge because the current Fed Chairman Jerome Powell has mentioned that it's his preferred gauge (his preferred measure within the gauge is the so-called core PCE excluding shelter).

	Bought by consumers	Bought by businesses & governments	Produced in U.S.	Imported to U.S.	Exported from U.S.	
PCE Price Index Personal Consumption Expenditures Price Index	✓	✗	✓	✓	✗	• Closely watched by the Federal Reserve • Similar to the BLS Consumer Price Index; the formulas and uses differ • Captures consumers' changing behavior and a wide range of expenses
Core PCE Price Index PCE Price Index, Excluding Food and Energy	✓	✗	✓	✓	✗	• Closely watched by the Federal Reserve • Excludes two categories prone to volatile prices that may distort overall trends

Source: Bureau of Economic Analysis
https://www.bea.gov/taxonomy/term/621

Note: *Core PCE ex-shelter isn't a traditional component of the PCE report, but it's widely available moments after the PCE release all over the internet and social media. Jerome Powell is admitting to flaws in how data is acquired for this report, especially housing information, which can be six months or more behind what's happening in real time.*

Consumer Price Index (CPI) (Score: 4)

Generally, this is considered the leading gauge for the level of inflation in the economy. It's quoted by folks on Main Street as much as the number crunchers on Wall Street.

Consumer Price Index: *Overview*

The Consumer Price Index (CPI) is a measure of the average change over time in the prices paid by urban consumers for a representative basket of consumer goods and services. The CPI measures inflation as experienced by consumers in their day-to-day living expenses. Indexes are available for the United States and various geographic areas. Average price data for select utility, automotive fuel, and food items are also available. CPI indexes are used to adjust income eligibility levels for government assistance, federal tax brackets, federally mandated cost-of-living increases, private sector wage and salary increases, poverty measures, and consumer and commercial rent escalations. Consequently, the CPI directly affects hundreds of millions of Americans.

Quick Facts: Consumer Price Index	
Subject areas	Prices
Key measures	Average prices Consumer price indexes Consumer prices
How the data are obtained	Survey of businesses, Survey of households
Classification	Commodity
Classification system	CPI entry level items (ELIs)
Periodicity of data availability	Bimonthly, Monthly
Geographic detail	Census region, Metro area
Scope	Urban consumers
Sample sizes	CPI survey collects about 94,000 prices and 8,000 rental housing units quotes each month
Reference Period	Monthly
Revision Information	Final when issued, except for C-CPI-U
Key products	• Consumer Price Index news release • Consumer Price Index factsheets • Databases • Tables • Interactive charts
Program webpage	www.bls.gov/cpi

Source: U.S. Bureau of Labor Statistics
https://www.bls.gov/opub/hom/cpi/

Note: *I like to comb the CPI report to see which industries have pricing power. It's a great tool, especially for short-term trading and investing (up to six months buy and hold).*

Producer Price Index (PPI) (Score: 3)

Businesses have costs, too. These are measured by the government through the PPI report. This report can give insight into potential corporate profits or help assess the direction of future consumer prices.

Consumer Confidence (Conference Board) (Score: 3)

Generally strong consumer confidence is positive,

although in high inflationary environments (there has only been one in the past forty years) the goal is to make consumers less confident.

Consumer Sentiment (University of Michigan) (Score: 3)

Measuring sentiment is a great way to discern where the economy is going. Often where consumers think the economy is going becomes self-fulfilling. This is especially true for prices. When people expect to pay higher prices, they tend to pay higher prices for the goods and services they want. On the other hand, when they expect to pay lower prices, they tend to hold off making purchases, which, eventually, tends to drive prices lower.

Productivity (Score: 2)

Productivity

| OPT Home | OPT Publications ▾ | OPT Data ▾ | OPT Methods ▾ | About OPT ▾ | Contact OPT |

Search Productivity [GO]

The **Office of Productivity and Technology (OPT)** measures how efficiently the U.S. converts inputs into the outputs of goods and services. Measures of labor productivity compare the growth in output to the growth in hours worked and measures of total factor productivity (TFP), also known as multifactor productivity (MFP), compare growth in output to the growth in a combination of inputs that include labor, capital, energy, materials, and purchased services.

Source: U.S. Bureau of Labor Statistics
https://www.bls.gov/productivity/

Interestingly, this report doesn't move the market and yet it's the key to America's success. It's the key to better lives for everyone. The ability to produce more with the same or less labor means higher wages and greater profits, which means greater investments.

Earlier I lamented about labor participation, which peaked as productivity was peaking. I suspect the so-called "productivity miracle" can be rekindled soon as part of the Roaring 2020s, which I outline later in the book.

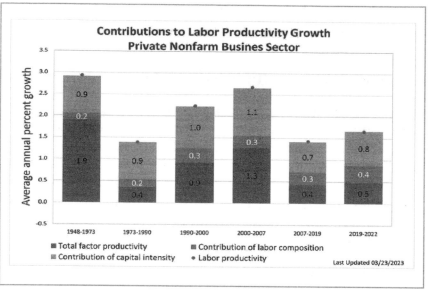

Source: U.S. Bureau of Labor Statistics
https://www.bls.gov/productivity/graphics/2022/graphic-3.htm

Durable Goods (Score: 2)

Durable goods reflect investments in items that last three years or longer. For consumers, think refrigerators, and for businesses, think factories.

Housing Starts and Permits (Score: 3)

This is a great report for Main Street since housing demand represents household formation and we must always root for greater household formation.

There are implications for the housing market and building trades as well.

Federal Reserve Consumer Surveys (Score: 1)

These reports do not move the market but influence the Federal Reserve so it's important to monitor them.

Gross Domestic Product (Score: 4)

What is the Gross Domestic Product or GDP report? This quarterly report is seen as a report card on the health and direction of the overall economy. It's still a backward-looking report, but it is important to assess whether the economy is as strong as it should be or, maybe, not as weak as assumed. There are a number of parts to this report that provide separate macro umbrellas.

GDP Report First Quarter 2023

Table 1. Real Gross Domestic Product and Related Measures: Percent Change from Preceding Period
Seasonally adjusted at annual rates

Line		2020	2021	2022	2019 Q2	Q3	Q4	2020 Q1	Q2	Q3	Q4	2021 Q1	Q2	Q3	Q4	2022 Q1	Q2	Q3	Q4	2023 Q1	Line
1	Gross domestic product (GDP)	-2.8	5.9	2.1	2.7	3.6	1.8	-4.6	-29.9	35.3	3.9	8.3	7.0	2.7	7.0	-1.6	-0.6	3.2	2.6	1.1	1
2	Personal consumption expenditures	-3.0	8.3	2.7	2.6	3.4	2.4	-6.2	-32.1	43.0	3.9	10.8	12.1	3.0	3.1	1.3	2.0	2.3	1.0	3.7	2
3	Goods	5.2	12.2	-0.5	5.5	5.8	2.8	0.0	-10.7	55.2	0.3	25.3	11.6	-7.9	2.3	-0.1	-2.6	-0.4	-0.1	6.5	3
4	Durable goods	10.0	18.5	-0.4	8.9	10.3	7.7	-11.3	0.4	103.6	0.6	44.7	10.6	-22.0	5.1	7.6	-2.8	-0.8	-1.3	16.9	4
5	Nondurable goods	2.7	8.8	-0.5	3.8	3.6	0.4	6.2	-15.9	33.7	0.1	14.9	12.2	1.7	0.7	-4.4	-2.5	-0.1	0.6	0.9	5
6	Services	-6.6	6.3	4.5	1.3	2.3	2.1	-8.9	-40.4	37.1	5.7	4.0	12.3	9.2	3.5	2.1	4.6	3.7	1.6	2.3	6
7	Gross private domestic investment	-5.3	9.0	4.0	2.4	2.6	-8.0	-5.1	-48.4	91.8	18.0	-5.4	0.9	10.4	32.0	5.4	-14.1	-9.6	4.5	-12.5	7
8	Fixed investment	-2.3	7.4	-0.2	6.2	4.1	-1.3	-3.0	-28.9	29.2	16.8	9.7	5.8	-1.1	0.6	4.8	-5.0	-3.5	-3.8	-0.4	8
9	Nonresidential	-4.9	6.4	3.9	6.2	4.1	-1.6	-8.2	-29.4	20.2	11.5	8.9	9.9	0.6	1.1	7.9	0.1	6.2	4.0	0.7	9
10	Structures	-10.1	-6.4	-6.6	15.4	17.9	-5.8	-3.4	-42.9	-10.4	0.9	1.9	-2.5	-6.7	-12.7	-4.3	-12.7	-3.6	15.8	11.2	10
11	Equipment	-10.5	10.3	4.3	0.8	-5.5	-8.3	-23.9	-38.0	57.1	21.1	6.1	14.0	-2.2	1.6	11.4	-2.0	10.6	-3.5	-7.3	11
12	Intellectual property products	4.8	9.7	8.8	7.3	7.3	9.3	7.9	-9.3	9.5	8.3	15.6	12.6	7.4	8.1	10.8	8.9	6.8	6.2	3.8	12
13	Residential	7.2	10.7	-10.6	6.5	4.2	0.0	17.4	-27.4	61.6	33.4	11.6	-4.9	-5.8	-1.1	-3.1	-17.8	-27.1	-25.1	-4.2	13
14	Change in private inventories																				14
15	Net exports of goods and services																				15
16	Exports	-13.2	6.1	7.1	-2.3	0.0	0.8	-15.3	-60.9	59.5	24.2	0.4	4.9	-11.1	23.5	-4.6	13.8	14.6	-3.7	4.8	16
17	Goods	-10.1	7.4	6.3	-7.2	1.9	-0.2	-3.6	-66.2	103.2	25.5	-0.7	3.4	-3.7	23.4	-7.2	15.5	17.8	-7.4	10.0	17
18	Services	-18.8	3.3	8.7	7.6	-3.4	2.5	-33.7	-49.1	1.4	21.2	2.5	7.7	4.7	23.6	1.6	9.9	7.5	5.0	-5.5	18
19	Imports	-9.0	14.1	8.1	0.7	-1.7	-8.0	-12.2	-53.7	88.2	32.9	7.6	7.9	6.6	18.6	18.4	2.2	-7.3	-5.5	2.9	19
20	Goods	-5.8	14.5	6.9	-0.4	-1.6	-9.4	-7.8	-49.3	103.7	29.3	10.9	4.0	0.2	19.6	20.4	-0.4	-8.6	-5.9	3.7	20
21	Services	-22.0	12.3	14.2	5.3	-2.3	-2.0	-28.9	-69.3	25.7	53.6	-8.8	31.9	45.3	14.0	9.1	16.6	-0.8	-3.7	-0.2	21
22	Government consumption expenditures and gross investment	2.6	0.6	-0.6	6.3	3.4	2.4	3.3	7.3	-5.9	-0.1	6.5	-3.0	-0.2	-1.0	-2.3	-1.6	3.7	3.8	4.7	22
23	Federal	6.2	2.3	-2.5	6.3	4.9	1.8	3.7	31.5	-10.9	1.8	17.3	-6.9	-7.2	0.0	-5.3	-3.4	3.7	5.8	7.8	23
24	National defense	2.9	-1.2	-2.8	0.0	6.8	1.8	2.1	1.8	1.3	11.8	-9.0	-2.6	-3.2	-5.3	-8.5	1.4	4.7	2.3	5.9	24
25	Nondefense	11.2	7.3	-2.2	16.6	2.2	1.8	6.1	86.5	-24.7	-10.8	64.8	-11.9	-12.1	7.4	-1.1	-9.2	2.5	10.6	10.3	25
26	State and local	0.4	-0.5	0.7	4.7	2.4	2.7	3.0	-5.5	-2.5	-1.3	0.1	-0.4	4.5	-1.6	-0.4	-0.6	3.7	2.6	2.9	26

Source: U.S. Bureau of Economic Analysis
https://www.bea.gov/sites/default/files/2023-06/gdp1q23_3rd.pdf

Personal Consumption Expenditures (Score: 4)

The U.S. consumer is now more than 70% of the total economy up from just over 60% two decades ago. Americans spending money is critical to economic growth, but that also ultimately means more debt and, at some point, periods of default.

Strong and steady consumption is the most desired outcome in any GDP report.

Under PCE we get a glimpse of where consumers are spending.

Goods include durable (stuff that last at least three years or longer) and nondurable goods.

Services are the bulk of the economy and support the largest share of the labor force.

In the first quarter of 2023 (1Q23), overall GDP growth decelerated for the third consecutive quarter. Consumption, however, was robust, coming in at the highest level since 2Q21, when $1.9 trillion in aid was approved and began making its way into the economy. What was even more surprising was the spike in durable goods, which might have been explained by supply chain relief and the availability of such products.

Meanwhile, services growth continued at a healthy pace.

Table 1. Real Gross Domestic Product and Related Measures: Percent Change from Preceding Period

Seasonally adjusted at annual rates

Line		2020	2021	2022	2019			2020				2021				2022				2023	Line
					Q2	Q3	Q4	Q1	Q2	Q3	Q4	Q1	Q2	Q3	Q4	Q1	Q2	Q3	Q4	Q1	
1	Gross domestic product (GDP)	-2.8	5.9	2.1	2.7	3.6	1.8	-4.6	-29.9	35.3	3.9	6.3	7.0	2.7	7.0	-1.6	-0.6	3.2	2.6	1.1	1
2	Personal consumption expenditures	-3.0	8.3	2.7	2.6	3.4	2.4	-6.2	-32.1	43.0	3.9	10.8	12.1	3.0	3.1	1.3	2.0	2.3	1.0	3.7	2
3	Goods	5.2	12.2	-0.5	5.5	5.8	2.8	0.0	-10.7	55.2	0.3	25.3	11.6	-7.9	2.3	-0.1	-2.6	-0.4	-0.1	6.5	3
4	Durable goods	10.0	18.5	-0.4	8.9	10.3	7.7	-11.3	0.4	103.6	0.6	44.7	10.6	-22.0	5.1	7.6	-2.8	-0.8	-1.3	16.9	4
5	Nondurable goods	2.7	8.8	-0.5	3.8	3.6	0.4	6.2	-15.9	33.7	0.1	14.9	12.2	1.7	0.7	-4.4	-2.5	-0.1	0.6	0.9	5
6	Services	-6.6	6.3	4.5	1.3	2.3	2.1	-8.9	-40.4	37.1	5.7	4.0	12.3	9.2	3.5	2.1	4.6	3.7	1.6	2.3	6

Source: U.S. Bureau of Economic Analysis
https://www.bea.gov/sites/default/files/2023-06/gdp1q23_3rd.pdf

Gross Private Domestic Investment (Score: 2)

Investments are a proxy for our faith in the future, especially when it pertains to enabling that future. There are two areas of fixed investments. The first is nonresidential, which speaks to the building blocks of the future. Are we building factories? Are we making equipment needed to improve the future? Are we investing in technology that will open paths to better living and new dreams?

In 1Q23 fixed investments were negative for the fourth consecutive quarter, but there were bright spots that helped to inform investors.

I want to underscore here that a lot of macro data trends have counterintuitive impacts on the stock market. Let me give you an example.

Residential investments were spiraling lower for years, but in early 2023 homebuilder stocks were on fire. The homebuilders Exchange Traded Fund (ETF) whose trading symbol is ITB" was truly ablaze, rallying 28% through early May.

So, how can that be explained?

The Counterintuitive Nature of Investing

With trillions of dollars in "free money" sloshing around from 2020 to 2023 all assets soared and housing was no exception.

Adding even more oomph to what became a sizzling housing market was:

A) the initial exodus from big cities where people decided they didn't want their children pushing elevator buttons, unsure about who may have touched it moments prior;

B) the ability to work from home pushed the housing market farther into suburbia.

So, the housing market was on fire, but homebuilder stocks began to lurch into freefall in 2022.

Yikes!

Housing prices were higher, but so too was the cost of lumber and workers (for those lucky enough to be able to find them) as well as other costs, including getting necessary permits and other administrative costs.

By 2023 there were so few houses for sale that prices continued to climb. However, at the same time lumber costs began plummeting, along with other input costs.

That meant fatter profits, and profits are the mother's milk of stock market rallies.

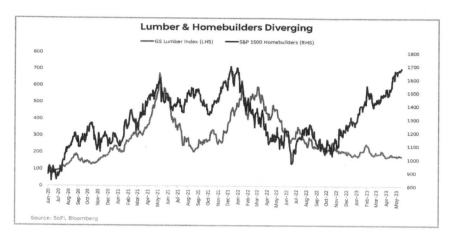

The larger homebuilders came out of the fog with more land and more pricing power.

All of this was informed by micro information, which tends to be updated more frequently for greater decision-making applications.

So, homebuilder stocks lagged during the good times because they lacked pricing power, but these stocks came to life as conditions for fatter profit margins and improved bottom lines emerged.

There are things that can influence stock prices at a more local, or micro level.

Microeconomic Indicators

There are a number of reports that inform on the micro level including:

Retail Sales

This is a direct gauge of the strength and appetite of

consumers. The report is important for deciphering the strength of the economy, but it is also great for idea-discovery, as the trends are usually durable for three to six months.

Personal Income and Spending

This report calculates total incomes and spending. It is a great gauge for the overall health of the economy and it's important to judge the pace of change between spending and income. A steady economy will see income outpace spending and savings holding up.

Changes in savings give us a glimpse into the confidence or concerns of households.

Line		2022				2023				Line
		Sept.	Oct.	Nov.	Dec.	Jan.	Feb.	March	April	
1	Personal income	22,096.4	22,201.9	22,240.1	22,281.9	22,422.0	22,496.7	22,559.0	22,639.1	1
2	Compensation of employees	13,856.1	13,826.8	13,822.8	13,832.7	13,949.4	13,981.5	14,026.1	14,083.5	2
3	Wages and salaries	11,450.6	11,420.4	11,408.7	11,412.7	11,516.1	11,541.8	11,573.4	11,628.0	3
4	Private industries	9,818.5	9,785.8	9,763.9	9,762.3	9,855.5	9,874.3	9,899.4	9,948.0	4
5	Goods-producing industries	1,797.4	1,795.8	1,793.7	1,789.6	1,813.1	1,810.2	1,818.4	1,828.5	5
6	Manufacturing	1,064.8	1,061.4	1,055.5	1,046.9	1,063.4	1,057.5	1,062.0	1,068.2	6
7	Services-producing industries	8,022.1	7,990.0	7,970.1	7,972.7	8,042.2	8,064.1	8,080.9	8,119.5	7
8	Trade, transportation, and utilities	1,762.3	1,757.7	1,749.7	1,745.6	1,774.0	1,780.4	1,775.0	1,785.0	8
9	Other services-producing industries	6,259.8	6,232.2	6,220.4	6,227.2	6,268.2	6,283.7	6,305.9	6,334.4	9
10	Government	1,631.1	1,634.6	1,644.8	1,650.4	1,660.6	1,667.5	1,674.1	1,680.0	10
11	Supplements to wages and salaries	2,405.5	2,406.5	2,414.1	2,420.0	2,433.3	2,439.7	2,446.6	2,455.5	11
12	Employer contributions for employee pension and insurance funds [1]	1,625.6	1,630.6	1,637.1	1,642.9	1,647.1	1,652.1	1,657.1	1,662.5	12
13	Employer contributions for government social insurance	779.9	777.9	777.0	777.1	786.2	787.7	789.5	793.0	13
14	Proprietors' income with inventory valuation and capital consumption adjustments	1,874.4	1,877.2	1,882.7	1,888.6	1,894.7	1,892.5	1,890.2	1,883.5	14
15	Farm	97.1	99.0	100.9	102.8	99.3	95.8	92.4	88.4	15
16	Nonfarm	1,777.4	1,778.3	1,781.9	1,785.8	1,795.4	1,796.7	1,797.8	1,795.1	16
17	Rental income of persons with capital consumption adjustment	797.0	804.7	810.6	820.0	830.1	841.4	853.3	866.5	17
18	Personal income receipts on assets	3,367.7	3,413.8	3,424.7	3,433.5	3,447.0	3,454.0	3,467.9	3,502.6	18
19	Personal interest income	1,745.2	1,766.6	1,788.7	1,811.6	1,810.4	1,808.9	1,807.0	1,830.3	19
20	Personal dividend income	1,622.6	1,647.2	1,636.0	1,622.0	1,636.6	1,645.1	1,660.9	1,672.3	20
21	Personal current transfer receipts	3,892.9	3,961.6	4,002.2	4,010.8	4,028.0	4,857.9	4,862.1	4,044.6	21
22	Government social benefits to persons	3,623.5	3,912.2	3,932.8	3,941.2	3,957.1	3,986.6	3,990.5	3,972.7	22
23	Social security [2]	1,216.9	1,229.1	1,224.3	1,223.6	1,335.0	1,339.9	1,344.2	1,345.3	23
24	Medicare [3]	926.7	933.8	941.5	949.7	955.8	960.9	964.7	967.4	24
25	Medicaid	783.6	791.2	796.9	800.6	819.5	832.3	840.0	839.3	25
26	Unemployment insurance	18.0	18.9	20.6	21.6	21.9	22.8	23.6	23.7	26
27	Veterans' benefits	162.5	163.2	164.0	164.8	165.4	166.3	167.0	168.1	27
28	Other	716.6	776.0	785.4	780.9	699.3	664.5	651.0	628.9	28
29	Other current transfer receipts, from business (net)	69.4	69.4	69.5	69.6	71.0	71.3	71.6	71.9	29
30	Less: Contributions for government social insurance, domestic	1,707.7	1,704.3	1,703.1	1,703.8	1,727.2	1,730.6	1,734.6	1,741.6	30
31	Less: Personal current taxes	3,248.6	3,232.7	3,213.6	3,202.1	2,920.5	2,901.3	2,895.8	2,896.5	31
32	Equals: Disposable personal income	18,831.7	18,969.2	19,026.5	19,079.7	19,501.5	19,595.4	19,663.2	19,742.6	32
33	Less: Personal outlays	18,257.4	18,391.8	18,362.3	18,377.4	18,727.8	18,760.2	18,784.4	18,940.4	33
34	Personal consumption expenditures	17,556.8	17,778.2	17,735.0	17,736.5	18,078.7	18,101.5	18,116.0	18,267.7	34
35	Goods	5,995.6	6,064.4	5,974.1	5,901.5	6,103.0	6,096.6	6,090.5	6,115.3	35
36	Durable goods	2,200.2	2,238.9	2,167.3	2,134.9	2,288.1	2,258.5	2,232.0	2,268.1	36
37	Nondurable goods	3,795.4	3,825.6	3,806.8	3,766.5	3,814.9	3,838.1	3,818.5	3,847.2	37
38	Services	11,661.2	11,713.7	11,760.9	11,835.0	11,975.7	12,004.9	12,085.5	12,152.4	38
39	Personal interest payments [4]	375.6	389.1	402.6	416.1	425.5	434.9	444.2	448.3	39
40	Personal current transfer payments	225.0	224.5	224.7	224.8	223.6	223.9	224.1	224.4	40
41	To government	116.7	116.9	117.1	117.2	117.5	117.8	118.0	118.3	41
42	To the rest of the world (net)	108.3	107.6	107.6	107.6	106.1	106.1	106.1	106.1	42
43	Equals: Personal saving	574.4	577.4	664.1	702.3	773.7	835.2	878.8	802.1	43
44	Personal saving as a percentage of disposable personal income	3.0	3.0	3.5	3.7	4.0	4.3	4.5	4.1	44
	Addenda:									
45	Personal income excluding current transfer receipts, billions of chained (2012) dollars [5]	14,653.2	14,618.1	14,607.0	14,604.2	14,815.3	14,606.3	14,637.3	14,661.2	45
	Disposable personal income:									
46	Total, billions of chained (2012) dollars [5]	15,172.2	15,218.9	15,238.7	15,250.6	15,495.3	15,522.5	15,560.3	15,566.4	46
	Per capita:									

Source: U.S. Bureau of Economic Analysis
https://www.bea.gov/sites/default/files/2023-06/gdp1q23_3rd.pdf

Initial Jobless Claims

For years this report didn't matter. But when the labor market is strong and when the Federal Reserve is trying to slow the economy, the report picks up additional importance as a real-time scoreboard.

Weekly Petroleum Inventories

Investors need to be aware that every industry has a number of associations, surveys, and vital data that are regularly updated.

Micro Metrics

The term "micro", for me, means a closer look at the industry. Let's call it a ground floor view. Beyond broad economy and cultural trends, industries can be especially influenced by a number of things that aren't affecting other industries or the overall economy.

Demand is a key micro metric that can be influenced from macro events but ultimately is distinctive from industry to industry.

Micro factors can also include or be influenced by other factors such as:

- · Rules
- · Regulations
- · Locations
- · Taxes
- · Supply

In addition, certain taxes, as well as shifts in public norms and developments within their specific industries, can change the fortunes of individual companies.

Of course, there is also good old-fashioned competition, where a better mouse trap replaces a former standard bearer.

This phenomenon is known as "creative destruction." As the name implies, it means one business is destroyed but it also means a new (better) business has emerged.

Creative Destruction

Austrian economist Joseph Schumpeter (1883-1950) coined the term "creative destruction," 'In Capitalism, Socialism, and Democracy' published in 1942. In the six-page chapter titled "The Process of Creative Destruction" Schumpeter described capitalism as "the perennial gale of creative destruction."

The key passage:

The opening up of new markets, foreign or domestic, and the organizational development from the craft shop to such concerns as U.S. Steel illustrate the same process of industrial mutation—if I may use that biological term—that incessantly revolutionizes the economic structure from within, incessantly destroying the old one, incessantly creating a new one. This process of Creative Destruction is the essential fact about capitalism. (p. 83)

Micro analysis gets us closer to making our final decision based on fundamentals. It allows us to narrow the field of potential investments, but now, to find just the right idea, we need to become even more granular in our investigations. We have moved from the global and national events that can impact stocks through the local events and trends. Now we need to look at specific companies.

Company-Specific Research & Company-Specific Fundamentals

To understand the business direction, economic condition, and ability to reach individual potential (living up to the hype), we use a number of publicly accessible materials including industry periodicals and websites, news articles, and Wall Street research. But the number one source for decision-making is quarterly financial reports starting with the most recent release.

Income Statement

Revenue growth gives insight into product and service demand, pricing power, and market share gains.

Margins underscore management's ability to maximize growth without sacrificing research and development. This is sort of a "report card within a report card" on execution.

Margin expansion is one of my top "buy and sell" measures.

Note: *It's best to use the past five quarters of income statements to understand execution against the company's own history and against rivals. This also smooths out seasonal factors.*

Cash Flow Statement

"Cash Rules Everything Around Me, CREAM, get the money, dollar, dollar bill, ya'll."

There is an old saying about following the money for the answers. The same is true for investing. How cash goes in and goes out is of utmost importance to investors. This is where you may find the financial shenanigans, if there are any. It is also the place that can indicate whether a business has the ability to pull off business plans and pay hefty dividends without borrowing.

There are three components of a cash flow statement.

Cash from operating activities

Cash from investing activities

Cash from financing activities

Balance Sheet

In the previous chapter I gave you an overview of my 3 Pillars. In this chapter we have been looking at the things that can impact the fundamental analysis of a company. I think it might be helpful if we had a real-life example to show you what that might look like.

I want to present a case study that gives investors an insight into how to incorporate my pillars for successful investing.

Case Study: Cisco (CSCO)

I'm going to take you on a walk down memory lane with one of the most remarkable stock stories in history. The great technology bubble of the 1990s finally imploded in early 2000-2001, and, when the dust cleared, what was left were lessons that could guide us for a lifetime.

There were a number of stocks that gained infamy during the tech bubble like pets.com, and others that were shining stars that plunged into darkness only to reemerge as great investments more than a decade later (see MSFT).

Fundamental Pillar

Note: *There are several components of fundamental research that include income statement, balance sheet, and cash flow statements. In addition, there are industry trends, reports and regulatory issues that alter the dynamics of the company's products and services.*

These are not arranged as a checklist that must see all boxes marked for the all clear to buy or sell. The importance varies against different macro backdrops, but, by far, the most important in most instances is the income statement.

At the end of 2020 these are the stocks you would have wanted to own if stock prices only move on the size of profits. The last name on this list makes for a great case study of investing and how you can glean investing clues for your own portfolio.

Most Profitable Companies: 2020

SYMBOL	PROFITS	SYMBOL	PROFITS
BRK.A	$81.4	PFE	$16.3
AAPL	$55.3	JNJ	$15.1
MSFT	$39.2	WMT	$14.9
JPM	$36.4	XOM	$14.3
BAC	$27.4	FNM	$14.2
INTC	$21.0	T	$13.9
WFC	$19.5	UNH	$13.8
C	$19.4	CMCSA	$13.1
VZ	$19.3	V	$12.1
FB	$18.5	**CSCO**	**$11.6**

The profits listed above are in billions USD.

In 2020 only nineteen publicly traded companies were as profitable as Cisco Systems (CSCO), and yet you would be hard pressed to find any talk about the company either online or in traditional financial media. It was, at one time, a darling that drove the entire market. Yet, even as an economic powerhouse today, it's a stock market afterthought.

When the hot company still makes big-time money but doesn't grow as fast as it once did, it can hit a wall and never recover. This is important since there are six names that have single-handedly carried the stock market. But, at some point, not only did their magic no longer lift the S&P 500, their own shares limped into a stage of limbo that became a "purgatory."

Cisco Systems

In 1984 Cisco Systems was formed by computer scientists Len Bosack and Sandy Lerner. These two set up cables between two different buildings on the campus of Stanford University, creating the first computer router. This initial development immediately led to more innovations and growth.

In 1985 the company created an ethernet interface subsystem. The company had two employees.

In 1986 they developed a multi-protocol router and grew to four employees.

In 1987 things really began to happen quickly for this startup. The company received $2 million in funding from Sequoia and grew to nine employees.

In 1988 John Morgridge became the CEO and the company expanded to twenty-nine employees. This was the jumping off point for tremendous growth in both the size of the company and the revenue generated. By 1989 the company saw revenue grow to $27.0 million and the number of employees expand to 111. 1990 saw revenues grow to $69.0 million and the company go public with a market cap of $224.0 million and 251 employees.

In 1991 revenues grew to $183.0 million and the market cap hit $1,000,000,000. This was also the year that the company announced its first stock split. By this time, it had grown to 503 employees. In a period of seven years this company had grown from two guys stringing cables between buildings on a college campus to one with annual revenues in excess of $180 million dollars and employing more than 500 people. But the best was yet to come!

The stock had become a juggernaut when, in 1995, John Chambers took over as CEO or "Chief Excitement Officer."

A regular on financial television, John Chambers would come on television and, with his enthusiasm and optimism, not only move his stock but the entire market! The chart below demonstrates the incredible sustained growth Cisco showed for an entire decade.

YEAR	BEGINNING PRICE	ENDING PRICE	PERCENT GAIN OR LOSS
1991	44.875	132.50*	195.26%
1992	66.25	157.25*	137.36%
1993	78.625	129.25*	64.39%
1994	64.625	70.25*	8.70%
1995	35.125	74.625	112.46%
1996	74.625	127.25*	70.52%
1997	63.625	83.625*	31.43%
1998	55.75	139.21875*	149.72%
1999	92.8125	214.25*	130.84%

What a Ride!

From 1991 to March of 2000 shares of Cisco (CSCO) climbed 40,000%, peaking when the company announced its ninth stock split in nine years.

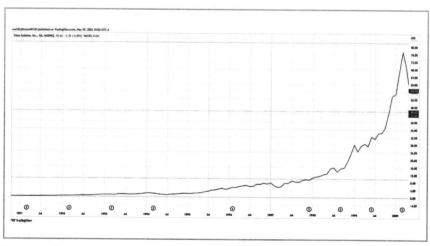

Source: tradingview.com

Ran Out of Oxygen

It was easy to believe the ride could go on forever, although everyone knew it was in an orbit where there was no breathable air. It was the most expensive of a bunch of very expensive names that led the technology and communications bubble to unfathomable heights.

This was four years after Alan Greenspan's remarks that the stock market was running on "irrational exuberance" and yet the rally didn't skip a beat. But the market finally buckled in March 2000, and soon it would collapse in a heap and would take years to recover.

These stocks were expensive in general, especially those with no earnings, poor management, and nothing beyond hype and a sexy story.

But even for those companies that were making money many were expensive. I'm not big on high PE ratios, but the PE at which Cisco changed hands wasn't like being on top of a mountain but more like floating in outer space.

TECH BUBBLE PEAK MARCH 2000	CSCO	MSFT	INTC	ORCL	AAPL	HPQ	IBM
PE	222	66	27	21	35	42	28
Yield	0	0	0.01	0	0	0.42	0.38
Market Cap ($B)	591	620	341	135	27	148	230
% Of S&P 500	4.5%	4.8%	2.6%	1.0%	0.2%	1.1%	1.8%
Revenue ($B)	17	23	34	10	8	49	88
Earnings ($B)	2.7	9.4	10.5	6.3	0.8	3.6	8.1

The Run Is Over

The company posted fourth quarter fiscal 2000 results on August 8, 2000. The stock traded higher the next day but the following session shares were hit...and never looked back. An article in the *New York Times* the next day gave subtle clues the party was over. Headlines and storylines from that month seemed to indicate that everything was fine. But there were cracks that a careful observer might have begun to see.

Cisco Sales Rise 61% in Quarter as Company Continues to Gain from Internet Growth

Headline heralds another quarter of accelerated growth...

SAN FRANCISCO, Aug. 9 -- Cisco Systems Inc. reported a 61 percent gain in sales for its fiscal fourth quarter today, as the company continued to be the leading supplier of the necessary hardware for the build-up of the Internet. It was the company's 10th consecutive quarter of accelerating year-over-year revenue growth.

Wall Street fawned over the results...

"The quarter, as expected, looks very strong," said Greg Geiling, an analyst with J. P. Morgan. Revenue growth of 61 percent year over year, and 16 percent over the immediately previous quarter, "are tremendous numbers for a company this size," he said. "And it looks like very balanced growth across all the business lines, which is just what you like to see."

But the number of acquisitions were a serious red flag...

During the quarter, Cisco completed the acquisitions of Atlantech Technologies Ltd., JetCell Inc., PentaCom Ltd., Qeyton Systems and Seagull Semiconductor Ltd. for a combined purchase price, including assumed liabilities, of approximately $1.39 billion, and took one-time charges of $461 million, or approximately 6 cents a share, on an after-tax basis, as write-offs of purchased in-process research and development. Additionally, Cisco completed the acquisitions of ArrowPoint Communications Inc., the InfoGear Technology Corporation and SightPath Inc., which were accounted for as pooling of interests.

John Chambers puts on the pom-poms...

"We predicted five years ago that we were in the midst of a second Industrial Revolution that would determine the prosperity of companies, countries, and individuals. Today, the Internet continues to drive the strongest U.S. economy in history," John Chambers, Cisco's president and chief executive, said in a statement. "We see no indications in the marketplace that the radical Internet business transformation in practices like customer service, supply-chain management, employee training, empowerment, and e-commerce that is taking place around the world today is slowing -- in fact, we believe it is accelerating globally."

But John Chambers also gets serious...

But Mr. Chambers also said that Cisco is experiencing some of the problems that come with explosive growth. Particularly in new product areas, the company has been constrained by shortages of crucial components and is taking steps to increase order volume with its major suppliers. Lead times on its own products reached what Mr. Chambers called "an undesirable peak" in June, but he added that he expected improvements in manufacturing management to return these times to normal by the end of the calendar year.

I remember watching John Chambers come on CNBC just about every week during the late 1990s. He always had a smile; he was always comfortable and even cocky.

Then all of a sudden, he smiled less and admitted to hurdles more. His unbridled optimism morphed into constant doubt. His tentative appearances would send shares of CSCO lower unlike the time when his statements were instant gold.

Chambers actually didn't have a lot to work with and should be applauded for not hyping missteps the company began to make as they grappled to maintain torrid growth and lofty expectations.

One of my favorite metrics is operating margins. I've always believed that as margins expanded, share prices could climb higher.

Cisco (CSCO) gross margins peaked in fiscal 1998, but the stock remained on autopilot. It was only a matter of time before the receding numbers would weigh on the stock.

Stock Loses Altitude

The delayed reaction to the August 8, 2000, earnings release was missed by a lot of people for sure. There was a growing chorus of folks complaining about the market in general, and lots of cracks in the veneer were emerging. But this specific moment is something we all must be on the lookout for since there will be a time when some of the hottest stocks in the market today quietly peak.

This is critical as we move deeper into the fourth industrial revolution that has already begun and already has certain stocks moving into outer space orbit. A ton of money is going to be made, and investors that catch the wave, and then get out in time, are going to change their lives.

I'll have more to say about these industries and stocks in "The Roaring 20s" chapter.

I'm going to show how the 3 Pillars could have gotten you into the CSCO trade and out before it flew completely off the rails.

FUNDAMENTAL PILLAR

Buy Signal (Aug 1995)

Cisco (CSC) began making waves in the early 1990s. In the mid-1990s the company had become the number one network equipment provider, as the internet was taking the nation by storm and businesses were racing for the best and fastest equipment to get connected.

One reason for the hesitation to buy sooner was that after peaking on March 8, 1994, the share price tumbled 51% by July 15, 1994.

The super growth seemed to be slowing as FY95 only grew 67.3% versus the 105.6% growth in FY94. It's true no company is expected to grow 100% year after year, but early in this rapid growth phase there were large expectations.

Fiscal Year End	Revenue	Change	Growth
Jul 27, 2002	18.92B	-3.38B	-15.15%
Jul 28, 2001	22.29B	3.37B	17.78%
Jul 29, 2000	18.93B	6.76B	55.49%
Jul 31, 1999	12.17B	3.68B	43.40%
Jul 25, 1998	8.49B	2.04B	31.57%
Jul 26, 1997	6.45B	2.36B	57.52%
Jul 28, 1996	4.10B	1.86B	83.46%
Jul 30, 1995	2.23B	898.22M	67.31%
Jul 31, 1994	1.33B	685.40M	105.60%
Jul 25, 1993	649.04M	-	-

Alternate Source: Stock Analysis
https://stockanalysis.com/stocks/csco/revenue/

Back then, if an active investor wasn't in the stock, they were certainly spying it for an entry point. That came after the close on August 17, 1995, when the company reported its financial results.

Press Release

SAN JOSE, Calif., August 17, 1995 -- Cisco Systems, Inc., (NASDAQ: CSCO), the leading global supplier of internetworking solutions, today reported its fourth quarter and annual results for the period ending July30, 1995. Net sales for the fourth quarter were $621,184,000, an increase of 72% compared to last year's results for the same period of $361,159,000.Net income was $143,723,000, or $.51 per share, an increase of 60% and 50% respectively, versus $89,566,000 or $.34 per share during the fourth quarter last year.

Net sales for the 1995 fiscal year were $1,978,916,000, an increase of 59% compared to fiscal 1994 revenues of $1,242,975,000. Net income was $421,008,000, or $1.52 per share, an increase of 34% and 28% respectively, compared to the previous year's $314,867,000 or $1.19 per share.

The fiscal 1995 results include a one-time pretax charge of $95,760,000, or $.21 per share, incurred by the company upon acquisition of the assets of LightStream Corporation in the second quarter.

Cisco Systems' fiscal year is a 52- or 53-week year ending on the last Sunday of July. The 53rd week in fiscal 1994 was included in the second quarter that ended January 30, 1994. Fiscal 1995 was a 52-week year.

"We are pleased to report that in addition to a strong financial performance, Cisco continues to grow faster than our traditional competitors," said John Chambers, president and CEO of Cisco. "Revenue in the fourth quarter increased 22% over the previous quarter. Overall, fiscal1995 was an outstanding year for us."

The July quarter that was reported on August 17, 1995, was also the fourth quarter showing the kind of growth that made it easy to extrapolate the kind of business momentum that buy and hold investors seek.

Buy signals from the press release:

Quarterly sales +72% versus FY sales +59%.

Net income +60% versus FY net income +34%.

FY pre-tax charge of $95.7 million or 21.0% John Chambers announced the company was taking more of the market share — we love to hear that!!!

Beyond the press releases, the results pointed to renewed quarter-to-quarter revenue momentum.

Jan 1995 +18.9%

Apr 1995 +12.7%

Jul 1995 +20.6% (buy signal)

And there was volume — one of the best corroborating factors in investing:

The week before posting those fourth quarter results, 63 million shares, on average, changed hands each session. On August 17 more than 115 million shares changed hands ahead of the financial release scheduled for after the close. The next session the stock traded 213 million shares, finishing up +8.6% (huge buy signal).

(In thousands, except per-share amounts)								
	July 30, 1995	Apr. 30, 1995	Jan. 29, 1995	Oct. 30, 1994	July 31, 1994	May 1, 1994	Jan. 30, 1994	Oct. 24, 1993
Net Sales	$621,184	$509,910	$454,897	$392,925	$361,159	$331,193	$302,166	$248,457
Gross margin	418,727	344,388	306,693	264,956	242,755	222,052	200,644	164,700
Operating income	222,076	190,876	78,316	151,671	138,718	131,587	119,924	97,887
Income before provision for income taxes	231,812	201,661	86,266	159,307	144,929	136,479	125,359	102,726
Net income	$143,723	$125,030	$ 53,485	$ 98,770	$ 89,566	$ 84,344	$ 77,472	$ 63,485
Net income per common share	$ .51	$ .45	$ .19	$ .37	$ .34	$ .32	$ .29	$ .24

Source: Securities and Exchange commission Archives
https://www.sec.gov/Archives/edgar/data/858877/0000950149-96-001640.txt

Sell Signal (Aug 2000)

Before Cisco's shares crashed, the internals were already collapsing. Some indications were evident in financial releases posted earlier in 2000. But the August 8, 2000 report should have jarred even the most ardent lover of the stock.

Income Statement

Years Ended	July 29, 2000	July 31, 1999	July 25, 1998
NET SALES	$ 18,928	$ 12,173	$ 8,489
Cost of sales	6,746	4,259	2,924
GROSS MARGIN	12,182	7,914	5,565
Operating expenses:			
Research and development	2,704	1,663	1,052
Sales and marketing	3,946	2,465	1,579
General and administrative	633	381	247
Amortization of goodwill and purchased intangible assets	291	61	23
In-process research and development	1,373	471	594
Total operating expenses	8,947	5,041	3,495
OPERATING INCOME	3,235	2,873	2,070
Net gains realized on minority investments	531	--	5
Interest and other income, net	577	330	196
INCOME BEFORE PROVISION FOR INCOME TAXES	4,343	3,203	2,271
Provision for income taxes	1,675	1,180	940
NET INCOME	$ 2,668	$ 2,023	$ 1,331
Net income per common share--basic	$ 0.39	$ 0.30	$ 0.21
Net income per common share--diluted	$ 0.36	$ 0.29	$ 0.20
Shares used in per-common share calculation--basic	6,917	6,646	6,312
Shares used in per-common share calculation--diluted	7,438	7,062	6,658

✳Revenue Red Flag

Source: Securities and Exchange commission Archives
https://www.sec.gov/Archives/edgar/data/858877/000109581100003692/f65797e10-k.txt

Revenues are obviously critically important as a proxy for the demand of a company's goods and services and a gauge into the willingness of how much the public is willing to pay for those goods and services.

Years Ended	July 29, 2000	July 31, 1999	July 25, 1998
NET SALES	$ 18,928	$ 12,173	$ 8,489
Cost of sales	6,746	4,259	2,924

Source: Securities and Exchange commission Archives
https://www.sec.gov/Archives/edgar/data/858877/000109581100003692/f65797e10-k.txt

But it must be viewed on an organic basis. In other words, when making comparisons an investor needs to make sure it's the same "apples to apples" comparison for a true reflection of a company's health and demand for its products and services.

When businesses buy additional businesses or open new locations over the course of a year, we expect revenues should be higher, but that doesn't mean there is organic growth.

Notice for Cisco (CSCO) there was a surge in topline sales, $18.9 billion from $12.2 billion a year earlier and $8.5 billion two years earlier. Surely this company was a juggernaut, and everyone had to own it, right?

Not so fast!

In the one-year period between these four quarter filings the company went on an acquisition spree. The company bought thirteen additional companies during that period.

The blistering pace of these deals not only pointed to the "wild west" nature of the tech boom but, for me, created suspicion about Cisco's ability to keep up with competition.

When that's the case, management normally overpays for such deals. It also suggests management is too focused on the stock and not the substance. These actions are more commonplace than anyone might imagine and happen more frequently in runaway bull markets. Some of the motivation is greed but, I suspect just as much, is ego.

I liken this action to the creation of a financial Potemkin Village.

Potemkin Villages

Named after the Russian Nobleman and suitor of Catherine the Great (Tsarina) who was charged with building up newly acquired Crimea in 1873. He was totally inept at the task and when the Tsarina decided to check his progress, he arranged a river cruise to view several villages. The problem was these villages didn't exist.

So, Potemkin had pasteboards created to look like thriving villages from the riverbank and had serfs dressed in prosperous clothing to meet the Tsarina at various stops. Fireworks displays and other festive events were arranged to distract her. She was then rushed back onto her ship to continue the journey.

As the ship was making its way down the river to the next stop the boards were disassembled and taken down and rushed ahead to be positioned before Catherine the Great arrived.

In the stock market, media hype and stock prices serve the same purpose as those pasteboard towns and fireworks. For those investors willing to actually take a closer look, the truth is right out in the open.

Cisco Builds Its Villages

Grigory Potemkin came from a middle-income family of noble landowners but wanted to be so much more. Having helped Catherine fend off a coup and later being the military commander in the Russo-Turkish War, he gained her favor, became her lover and later governor-general of newly acquired southern provinces.

By this time, he and Catherine were no longer lovers, and he would have to prove his worthiness for the job through those fake villages.

Investors fell in love with Cisco, but to keep that warm embrace management had to do something.

The burden of having one of the hottest stocks in the market is keeping up and also looking busy. Non-stop acquisitions were a way to satisfy the notion of frenzied success and non-stop action, but also bolster the income statement — at least at the top end.

The following table summarizes the significant assumptions underlying the valuations for our significant purchase acquisitions completed in fiscal 2000 and 1999 (in millions, except percentages):

Acquired Company	Acquisition Assumptions	
	Estimated Cost to Complete Technology at Time of Acquisition	Risk-Adjusted Discount Rate for In-Process R&D
Fiscal 2000		
Monterey Networks, Inc.	$ 4	30.0%
The optical systems business of Pirelli S.p.A.	$ 5	20.0%
Aironet Wireless Communications, Inc.	$ 3	23.5%
Atlantech Technologies	$ 6	37.5%
JetCell, Inc.	$ 7	30.5%
PentaCom, Ltd.	$ 13	30.0%
Qeyton Systems	$ 6	35.0%
Fiscal 1999		
Summa Four, Inc.	$ 5	25.0%
Clarity Wireless, Inc.	$ 42	32.0%
Selsius Systems, Inc.	$ 15	31.0%
PipeLinks, Inc.	$ 5	31.0%
Amteva Technologies	$ 4	35.0%

✳Margins Red Flag

Source: Cisco Annual Report 2000 pg.20
https://www.cisco.com/c/dam/en_us/about/ac49/ac20/downloads/annualreport/ar2000/pdf/Cisco_00_AR.pdf

Gross margins are important but mostly reflect input costs, which are often out of the control of management. There are ways to hedge raw materials and build independent supply chains, which should be recognized by the market, but we really want to focus on operating margins.

We get operating margins by dividing operating income by total revenue.

July Quarter Op Margins

2000 17.1%

1999 23.6%

1998 15.7%

Operating expenses:			
Research and development	2,704	1,663	1,052
Sales and marketing	3,946	2,465	1,579
General and administrative	633	381	247
Amortization of goodwill and purchased intangible assets	291	61	23
In-process research and development	1,373	471	594
Total operating expenses	8,947	5,041	3,495
OPERATING INCOME	3,235	2,873	2,070

Source: Securities and Exchange commission Archives
https://www.sec.gov/Archives/edgar/data/858877/000109581100003692/f65797e10-k.txt

It's clear in 1999 the company was firing on all cylinders because the operating margins erupted to 23.6% from 15.7%, but the share decline in 2000 from a year earlier was the kind of red flag that cannot be ignored. It would take enormous faith in management to continue holding.

On a more granular level it was clear there were issues from the top line to the bottom line, as net income peaked in Jan 2000 quarter at $816.0 million.

SUPPLEMENTARY FINANCIAL DATA(1) (Unaudited)
(In millions, except per-share amounts)

	July 29, 2000	April 29, 2000	Jan. 29, 2000	Oct. 30, 1999	July 31, 1999	May 1, 1999	Jan. 23, 1999	Oct. 24, 1998
Net sales	$ 5,720	$ 4,933	$ 4,357	$ 3,918	$ 3,558	$ 3,172	$ 2,845	$ 2,598
Gross margin	3,662	3,172	2,818	2,530	2,297	2,059	1,857	1,701
Net income	$ 796(2)	$ 641(3)	$ 816(4)	$ 415(5)	$ 605(6)	$ 632(7)	$ 279(8)	$ 507(9)
Net income per common share--basic*	$ 0.11	$ 0.09	$ 0.12	$ 0.06	$ 0.09	$ 0.09	$ 0.04	$ 0.08
Net income per common share--diluted*	$ 0.11(2)	$ 0.08(3)	$ 0.11(4)	$ 0.06(5)	$ 0.08(6)	$ 0.09(7)	$ 0.04(8)	$ 0.07(9)

* Reflects the two-for-one stock split effective March 2000.

Source: Cisco Annual Report 2000
https://www.cisco.com/c/dam/en_us/about/ac49/ac20/downloads/annualreport/ar2000/pdf/Cisco_00_AR.pdf

This income statement was one of the brightest red flags ever. Study it and try to put yourself back in the shoes of investors at the time.

It's easy to look back and think you would have been the exception, but, without knowing a similar lesson prior to Cisco's runaway peek and spectacular decline, more than likely you would have been a buyer not a seller.

Fundamental Conclusion

The story of Cisco was always in plain sight via the income statement but it meant peeling lots of layers. And as the company became larger, and the stock a proxy for all of tech, those layers became more complicated and byzantine-perhaps on purpose.

We are going to see this replayed over the next three to five years as new technology becomes ubiquitous in our daily lives.

TECHNICAL PILLAR

Charts Reflect & Anticipate Fundamentals.

One of the more interesting aspects of investing is how often charts seem to predict fundamentals before they are revealed. A stock begins breaking down without any "news" and then, a few days later or even farther down the road, there is a bombshell.

There are a number of reasons this occurs.

A) The fundamental breakdown has begun and is available in public filings and other news but it's not large enough to ring any bells. When it's a popular stock, more than likely, it will not be reported at all. Essentially it happens in the dark.

B) If the breakdown is happening on greater than average volume, someone knows something. This is important for all investors to understand. Nothing happens by accident. When a stock trades at 50% to 100% greater than average daily volume in an otherwise placid market, something is going on and there will be news to that effect shortly.

Many times, that news will be something like an upgrade or downgrade of the shares by a major Wall Street firm. At other times it will be something even more impactful. Remember, I began this book acknowledging that the stock market isn't fair. There are select people who get the information first and they act on that information. It's reflected in a number of ways including things like changes in daily volume, or in option activity.

Note: *There are also power players out there with large teams of experienced analysts and experts looking through the data as well. It's not all Bud Fox looking for insider stuff* *for Gordon Gecko. The great news is you can piggyback off their actions or, at least, use it to mitigate mistakes in your own portfolio.*

Buy Signal

Remember the press release on August 17, 1995 that was a screaming fundamental "buy" signal? Well, the technical buy signal had already occurred.

That happens to be the beauty of technical moves analysis — overwhelmingly stocks move long before investors have concrete evidence the fundamentals are changing. I think that's because there are investors out there with greater access to business channels and executives. Some of that might be considered "insider information" but I began this book with a reminder that nobody said this would be fair.

The great news is those entities with the edge still have to buy and sell stocks and options and we can see that action in price movement and filings.

After tumbling more than 50%, shares of Cisco began rebounding and eventually formed a cup (arrow) and handle (circle) formation. Shares took out the March 8 high on April 28 and were off to the races.

Upon breaking out, the stock formed a perfect trading channel that should have given buy and hold investors reasons to stay long since support held over and over, and, at the same time, traders made a fortune buying the bottom of the channel and selling the top of the channel.

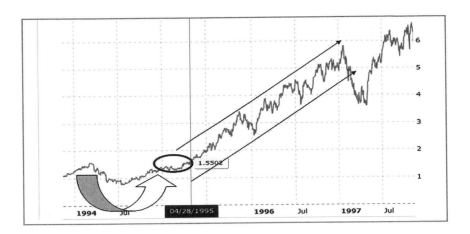

Other Technical Buy Signals

I'm a big believer of buying double bottoms but those are mostly trading buy signals whereas breakouts (See the arrows in the chart below) above long foundations and staunch resistance points tend to be long-term buy signals.

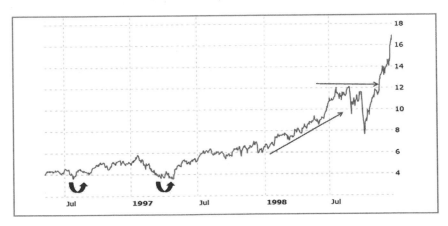

Technical Sell Signals

The Story from Cisco's Chart at the Top

The company reported earnings on August 8, 2000, where shares closed at $65.50.

The next day, August 9, 2000, the shares popped to $67.80, but the next session the stock tumbled to $63.38. One year later, on August 10, 2001, the shares were changing hands at $17.51.

Let's take a look at how the action might have felt back then.

From September 1999 to March 2000 shares of CSCO were up 122% and it felt like the sky was the limit. There were lots of macro events in March 2000 that nudged the overall market lower and CSCO shares dipped as well.

After that initial pullback, the subsequent rebound attempt ran out of steam before the stock could re-test the old highs. (See dash line as this becomes a key resistance point and the main technical tool that could have helped investors pocket cash or not lose a bundle.)

Later in the month, the stock rallied back to that same resistance point and failed. That proved to be the ultimate sell signal, followed by other signals when key support points failed to hold.

The stock, that was up 122% from Sept 1999 to March 2000, wound up being down 61% from Sept 1999 to April 2001.

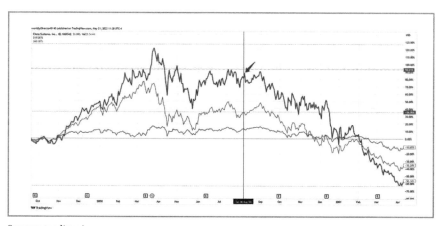

Source: tradingviews.com

BEHAVIORAL PILLAR

These days you hear a lot of FOMO and YOLO when it comes to the stock market. While these are newer terms, there is nothing new under the sun except different ways to make the same mistakes humans have always made.

Fear of Missing Out (FOMO)

When it seems like everyone is having fun, making money, and loving life, it's only natural that you want a piece of the action as well.

The key word there is "natural"

We all succumb to emotions in some form or another. It's not unusual to see the coolest professional poker player have the messiest personal life. Or a top CEO getting fired for doing something others would consider dumb.

These self-inflicted wounds in life are tough to avoid, but, when it comes to the stock market, they certainly can be minimized. We can take it a step further and actually profit when the masses are feeding off each other's exuberance.

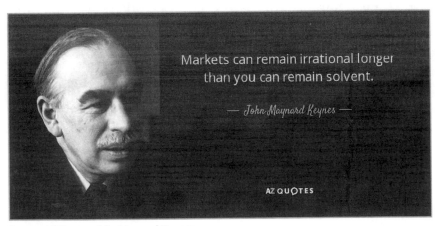

Source: AZ Quotes, John Maynard Keynes

Here's the thing about these periods of mass excitement when the world is more afraid of missing out than of losing money — they can last a long time and they can be hugely profitable.

This is the part that Wall Street always seems to miss, and, upon sitting out gargantuan moves, these experts morph into cheerleaders for destruction.

You hear stuff like:

"This isn't going to end well."

"When the bottom falls out its going to be ugly."

"There will be a lot of bodies out there."

Those comments and more are a mixture of sour grapes and defending their own work. Remember that pride and ego probably hurt professional investors more than retail investors. It's tough to look into a mirror and admit you made a mistake.

It's even tougher to look into a camera or audience of your peers and investors who used your approach and admit fault. Instead, some just try to buy time.

All along, there is this extended period of waiting and inaction from the experts who are wagging their fingers, and the novice, who didn't wait and is making a fortune. It's such a pompous charade.

You Only Live Once (YOLO)

In recent years there has been a change in how Americans approach life. Gone are the days of waiting your turn. So too is the notion of working for years and counting promotions until you are near the top or saving up for that dream home. Now it's about making videos in your garage and cashing in on clicks.

Household formation is delayed or just not considered.

Many investors take this same approach in the stock market. The problem for them is when they go through the history cycle of market emotions, they tend to sell it all at a loss (capitulation) and vow never to return.

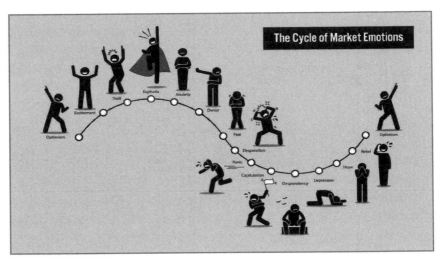

Source: Adobe Stock

It is true we only live once. With that in mind, we need to make time an asset, not a liability. I'm not in the camp of blindly buying and holding.

I know the market has never had a down twenty-year stretch and a 200-year chart looks like a perfect 45-degree angle from left to right where the crashes are hard to pick up with a quick glance.

But that look is disingenuous since market indices change and the stocks that led the way in 1900 weren't the leaders in the 1920s and those winners were not the winners in the 1950s.

With that said, there are names you want to own for as long as the underlying fundamentals story keeps appreciating.

Irrational & Emotional

So, what's my secret to dealing with the pitfalls of an irrational and emotional market?

Acknowledge it!

Yes...don't try to convince yourself a stock or a market that is on fire isn't or that there is not an element of hype of excessive exuberance.

By the same token, don't fall for the notion that there is a greater fool out there. This will have you buying in the eighth inning of a market run rather than the second or third inning.

The Cisco Behavioral Example

I'm not a fan of buying and selling stocks based mostly on valuations, especially price to earnings ratios. Wall Street experts normally won't touch a stock trading with a PE north of twenty times. But the gamechanger winners each year normally rally up to PEs of thirty, forty or even above 50 times earnings.

With that in mind, I'm well aware that risk increases exponentially the higher the PE. But when the underlying company is growing and capturing the attention of the general public, that risk is worth the ride.

This is why we use behavioral analysis along with fundamental and technical analysis. A great earnings release (fundamentals) that attracts Wall Street upgrades and technical breakouts (technical) to new highs on convincing volume fuel enthusiasm (behavioral).

Back to the PE ratio...remember we got a fundamental buy signal in August 1995 and the technical buy signal when shares of CSCO were trading below fifty times earnings after peaking at ninety times? For me, that ninety threshold reveals how much tolerance for risk investors in the stock could be willing to accept.

With this in mind, I would have been a seller in 1999.

Note: *The stock rallied hard in 1999 and early 2000 before peaking on March 24, 2000, at $55.50.*

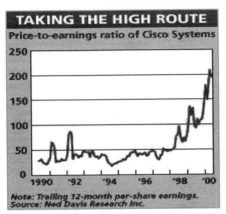

TAKING THE HIGH ROUTE
Price-to-earnings ratio of Cisco Systems
Note: Trailing 12-month per-share earnings.
Source: Ned Davis Research Inc.

Source: The Wall Street Journal
https://www.wsj.com/articles/
SB955485845794159366

Also, in 1999 the overall hysteria was outrageous, and it was only a matter of time but most of these stocks (below) had already made mindboggling gains. It was tough for those late to the game since they had already missed out but many still bought.

Unsustainable Values
Large-cap companies with price/earnings ratios over 100

COMPANY	MARKET CAP (3/7/00, in bil.)	1999 P/E	EST. GROWTH	P/E IN 5 YRS.	P/E IN 10 YRS.
Cisco Systems	$452	148.4	29.5%	73.9	40.9
AOL/Time Warner	232	217.4	31.5	100.0	51.1
Oracle	211	152.9	24.9	91.3	60.5
Nortel Networks	167	105.6	20.7	74.5	58.4
Sun Microsystems	149	119.0	21.1	82.8	64.0
EMC	130	115.4	31.1	54.0	28.1
JDS Uniphase	99	668.3	44.0	195.5	63.5
Qualcomm	91	166.8	37.3	61.8	25.5
Yahoo!	90	623.2	55.9	122.6	26.8
15 non-tech	2,361	30.4	13.7	23.8	20.3
S&P 500	11,281	28.6	12.5	23.8	21.3

Source: Bloomberg

Source: New Low Observer

Another sign it's almost time to sell is when Wall Street starts to chase and finds intriguing ways to justify new bullishness.

Interestingly, this transformation happens just as CEOs are becoming more circumspect. I began noticing a more somber John Chambers in 1998 after years of laying it on thick as chief excitement officer.

On November 10, 1999, Cisco posted financial results that beat the street (official estimates) but missed the whisper number (what they really expected).

Analysts were unfazed and even tried to downplay a serious warning from John Chambers that he was experiencing a "healthy level of paranoia."

Technology   The New York Times ON THE WEB

| Home | Site Index | Site Search | Forums | Archives | Marketplace |

November 10, 1999

Cisco Systems's Sales Surge and Profit Meets Forecasts

Excluding the charge, Cisco earned 24 cents a share. Analysts had expected the company to report earnings of 23 cents a share, according to First Call/Thomson Financial. The whisper number, communicated verbally between analysts and fund managers, was 25 cents.

It was Cisco's 39th earnings report since going public, and the company has never missed analysts' forecasts since its initial public offering.

"I think the best indicator was that receivables were flat at 32 days, and that inventory turns improved," said Al Tobia, an analyst with Bank America Securities. "This is seasonally their worst quarter, so that is a positive."

Chambers, he said, "has used the phrases 'healthy level of paranoia,' and 'cautiously optimistic' for the last 17 calls, but relative to expectations, this was a very clean quarter."

Source: The New York Times

Another sign of excess is a lot of stock splits. Stock splits do not make a stock cheaper even though the share price is lower.

100 shares of XYZ at $100 a share = $10,000

200 shares of XYZ at $50 a share = $10,000

But there is no doubt the public buys into the notion the stock is cheap when it just had a forward stock split. Keep that in mind because this ploy is designed to take advantage of Main Street. (By the way, reverse splits that make the share prices higher with less ownership are far more problematic and potentially disastrous for investors.)

Splits

Shareholders of Record	Original Price	Price Before Split	Price After Split	Expected Distribution Date	Split Ratio
Feb 16, 1990	18.00				
Mar 1, 1991		57.00	28.50	3/15/91	2 for 1
Mar 6, 1992		78.00	39.00	3/20/92	2 for 1
Mar 5, 1993		92.00	46.00	3/19/93	2 for 1
Mar 4, 1994		79.00	39.50	3/15/94	2 for 1
Feb 2, 1996		89.00	44.50	2/16/96	2 for 1
Nov 18, 1997		80.13	53.42	12/16/97	3 for 2
Aug 14, 1998		96.63	64.42	9/15/98	3 for 2
May 24, 1999		123.12	61.56	6/21/99	2 for 1
Feb 22, 2000		144.38	72.19	3/22/00	2 for 1

Source: Cisco stock information
https://investor.cisco.com/stock-information/dividends-and-splits/default.aspx

Quiz: Chapter 3

In this chapter we have focused on my 3 Pillars. I believe these tools are essential to be an Unbreakable Investor.

1. **What are the three levels of fundamental analysis an investor needs to study and take into account when considering a stock?**

2. **What do the acronyms FOMO and YOLO stand for and how might they influence an investor negatively?**

3. **Identify how John Chambers may have been able to control Behavioral Reactions for CISCO.**

<u>Answers</u>

1. The three levels are (1) Macro, (2) Micro, (3) Company level.

2. The acronyms stand for Fear of Missing Out and You Only Live Once. Both of them can cause an investor to make emotional decisions about stocks, which is NOT what we want to be doing.

3. For this question I want you to recognize the impact that a CEO can have by being a capable spokesperson for his or her company. John Chambers was very good at not only moving stock prices for his company but for the whole industry.

Chapter

4

Finding Ideas

A Universe of Stocks

"Space: the final frontier. These are the voyages of the starship *Enterprise.* Its five-year mission: to explore strange new worlds; to seek out new life and new civilizations; to boldly go where no man has gone before!"

Captain James Tiberius Kirk of the USS Enterprise (played by actor William Shatner)

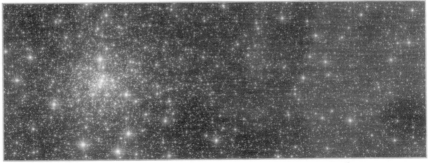

Source: esahubble.org
https://esahubble.org/images/potw/page/3/

In May 2022 the Hubble Space Telescope sent back the magnificent image (previous page) of Global Cluster NSC 6558 in the Sagittarius constellation, which lies 23,000 light years away from Earth. For many would-be stock market investors, finding stocks seems as bewildering as looking at all the stars in the sky.

It isn't.

It's not even close.

Yet, investing will take you on a journey not unlike the Hubble Space Telescope. A journey of discovery, a journey of knowledge, a journey of major surprises and occasional pain. This is a journey through the universe of stocks in search of those with the most upside potential at various levels of risks.

I love it.

I have been blessed to make this my own personal journey. The process of discovery is why I will always consider myself a student of the market.

I actually spend more time seeking fresh ideas than I do managing my current portfolio positions.

Assembling and Managing Your Watch List & Potential Buy List

Once you are even slightly interested in a company add it to your watch list. From there you would begin to apply the evaluation process using the 3 pillars approach (we go deeper into the process later in the book).

Once you've whittled down the stocks on your watch list, the ideas that seem more enticing are moved to your potential buy list. From there you can decide to buy them based on other factors, including macro backdrop and individual signals.

Discovery Journey:
The Stuff You Know (paying yourself)

Buy What You Know

As I said earlier in the book, people should buy stock in companies they know. It's a philosophy I subscribe to with respect to the discovery process as well.

In fact, in the first few years of coming on television, and before I had my own daily show, I would run into people who told me how much they admired my work and the stances I took on various issues. However, more often than not, they would also tell me they were not in the stock market.

That's when I would launch into my "you-are-in-the-stock-market" routine. Scanning their clothes immediately several publicly traded names would jump out.

- Nike
- Under Armour
- Calvin Klein (PVH)
- Lululemon
- Gap Stores
- Ralph Lauren
- Uggs (Deckers)
- Crocs

And nothing jumped out more than logos on baseball caps, like Caterpillar and Deere or any number of other companies you can think of.

Upon seeing these things, I would ask how or why they picked that brand of clothing or baseball cap. Turns out they liked the product. Then I would ask what kind of vehicle they drove and why. Turns out they like the vehicle they drive and invariably they have been buying that model or brand for years.

Now we are five minutes into the conversation and the watch list has gotten pretty long. I'm talking a dozen or even a couple of dozen names.

Then I would present this to them. I would make the point that they are in the stock market. They are the most important part of the stock market — the consumer who drives the profits that shareholders dine on for a much more lavish life.

Yep, everyone is in the stock market. As I did earlier for you, I would make the point that even when they were sleeping, they were in the stock market. Each minute of our daily lives powers the stock market.

That revelation always floored them. And they would always reply: "I never thought of it like that."

Then the final comment from me to bring down their self-imposed barriers for not being investing in the stock market:

> *"So, let's get this straight. There are these wonderful products and services out there that you put your own hard-earned cash into and tell your friends and family about and yet you never considered that maybe you should be part owner of these companies?"*

A moment of silence, or as they call it in the media business the "pregnant pause", would follow. And then would come the epiphany, "Wow, you're right," would be one of the next responses. Sometimes I might hear "I don't have an account."

I would swat those down like a slow horsefly.

I hope by this time I'm "preaching to the choir." But this idea and overcoming the hesitancy that seems to be so much a part of the population that isn't investing is so very important that I felt I needed to say it one more time.

New Investor Revolution

I started appearing on television more than thirty years ago after my research business began to ramp up. The proverbial hockey stick path to success saw me start in a one-bedroom apartment in Harlem NYC at the height of the crack cocaine epidemic. Rent was cheap, but danger was rampant and everywhere.

I was a one-man show. I did the research in the evenings and cold called brokerage firms during the day. To say that this was tedious is an understatement. Exciting is an even greater understatement. I was chipping away and making a name for myself, albeit, very slowly.

Soon I had my first hire and not long after was able to get my first office on Wall Street (50 Broad to be exact). The march continued over the couple of years that saw me move into a larger space and hire more employees. And then the phone rang one morning and it was a CNBC producer. They heard about my work and wanted me to come on and discuss.

At some point I will write a separate book about growing my business against so many odds but wanted to point out that back then the masses had to be convinced to buy stocks.

When I was a broker, prospects had to be sold on hype. They never asked about things like earnings, or valuations, or growth potential.

Honestly, trying to go too deeply into fundamentals could cost you the order.

This mentality was already prevalent when the tech bubble began to inflate in the 1990s. Entire generations had been brought up on a future of technological wonders. The Silent Generation had Buck Rogers and Baby Boomers had The Jetsons.

We were all enthralled. Books, movies, and television shows started to morph into real life with the widespread distribution of the personal computer and internet. It was a wonderful time to be alive.

And then the phone would ring and it would be me on the other end and my pitch was simple:

Hi, Mr. Jones?

This is Charles Payne calling from Wall Street.

I have a great stock investment idea I would like to share with you.

You have a minute?

Mr. Jones, XYZ is a company that plans to sell pet food on the internet.

This is a great time to be in the stock because this is the ground floor.

Someday everyone will be using the internet.

I would like you to open an account today.

How much could you afford to invest right now?

After a month in the business a pivotal call got me to toss the script and just have conversations with people, but it was still about the hype. It wasn't what I wanted. It was what the person on the other end of the line wanted to hear in order to buy the stock.

Here's the thing, always start your investing journey with the idea of owning the things you put your own hard-earned money into. I always have the Cheshire cat grin on my face when I'm buying something when that company's stock is in my portfolio.

Follow the money, in this case your own money, and then do the work you are learning in this book.

Discovery Journey:
Financial Media & Pundits

Today, retail investors are more sophisticated but that pendulum may have swung over too far. Many retail investors are being "talked out of" great ideas based on current stock valuations, which are misplaced on great stocks and companies. They are adhering to "rules" they have heard or read in the financial media. Using information is vital. But using information wisely is even more important. Let's look at some of the potential pitfalls.

Print Media

Unfortunately, the print side of financial media has gotten far too political and mostly champion ideas and causes of the left. There has always been bias in journalism. But the outright rooting for policy when it may not be in the best interest of investors is unfair.

I have my own personal political beliefs but think it's crazy to let them override trading and investing opportunities. When it comes to making money in the stock market, I'm not red or blue. It is true I feel better when I invest in companies that are helping people. For example, I have never invested in cigarette stocks, but I wouldn't tell anyone else not to if they wanted to own them. At my first brokerage firm as a stockbroker I discovered a company named Burroughs Welcome, which was working on a new drug called AZT for a new disease called AIDS. I found the stock from an article and subsequent research I did and was the only person at my firm getting investors to buy the stock. I was opening new accounts with the stock. In my first full month as a broker, I opened more new accounts than anyone else in the office.

When payday rolled around, I got the smallest check in the office.

I learned that because AZT wasn't a house stock that the firm held in inventory and had significant markups on, I got paid very little. With a new wife and one-year-old baby I immediately switched to selling the house stock, even though, in my heart, I knew Burroughs Welcome was a better investment. That wasn't something I wanted to be doing and now I don't. But it did teach me an important lesson. Knowledge is power, and, at the same time, I needed to be aware of the source of my information. That source might have an agenda that was different from mine.

I'm interested in learning about everything I can when it comes to the stock market. I also try to understand the viewpoint of the information source.

Television

Investors need to understand that there are different interests in the stock market, even within the same firm, and those competing interests can often be seen playing out on any given day in the financial media. Part of the issue is that there are different players on Wall Street with different jobs and concerns.

First you have to understand the players:

Sell-Side Analysts work at Wall Street brokerage firms. They analyze companies and industries and write in-depth research that generally boils down to the question of whether the public should buy, sell, or hold.

Buy-Side Analysts work for funds like Fidelity, institutions like insurance companies and hedge funds. Their work covers a wider swath of names and is distributed within the firm.

There are independent analysts who are my favorite. This is, in part, because I have been an independent analyst for more than thirty years. I know the special pressure to be right more often than everyone else because there are no other sources of revenue, like those that can be found in large firms where the analytical team could be a lost leader and the mistakes can be covered by other revenue streams.

There are also macro analysts and economists and strategists.

These folks are treated like the superstars of Wall Street and their words carry enough influence to move stocks and markets.

Interestingly, I'm not very impressed with most of them because they get to be wrong for long stretches and are hardly ever taken to task by a fawning media.

I have a greater affinity for independent macro economists, but they also don't face day-to-day pressure of sell side analysts and active money managers. Moreover, retail investors cannot hold positions that are sinking for as long as those strategists can remain confident.

You have money managers who are being relegated to a "paint-by-numbers" approach to investing.

You have folks who own brokerage firms who want you to trade but not too much (wink).

There are hedge funds that don't need your money so they aren't trying to sell anything per se. But it doesn't hurt if they can get the crowd to buy stock(s) they already have long positions on or get sellers to stampede stocks they already have massive short positions against.

There are also CEOs of companies who get to come on and regale the anchor(s) with wonderful stories and predictions.

The bottom line is that just as with print media, you need to understand the position of the person talking before you begin to take what they are saying to heart.

There is generally one rule for guests on financial television — they are talking about their own book. Recognize that what is being said is based on the speaker's view of the market. Just because he is on television doesn't necessarily make him or her right.

Still, I get some ideas from financial television, although I get more from watching the tickertape at the bottom of the screen, which captures the most active trading at that particular time.

I actually begin each day on a new page in my spiral notebook. I put the date on the top lefthand side and then begin to take notes.

Under the date I have two columns for earnings reactions (moving higher or moving lower).

In the middle I have columns for upgrades for that morning — I'm mostly looking for new symbols. I'm attracted naturally to names making big moves. I also pay attention when I see anomalies, like a stock moving in the opposite direction from the rest of the industry names.

On the right side of the page, I have a column for positions my Wall Street Strategies subscribers own.

My handwriting is suspect, but the notes and shorthand are precise and become a great tool in my journey to find fresh names with the potential to outperform the broad market.

By the way, financial media has played a dastardly role in one of the greatest rip-offs of the American public in history: The initial public offering circus. I want to talk more about Initial Public Offerings (IPOs).

Discovery Journey: Initial Public Offerings

Wall Street and Silicon Valley have watched and learned. Now they have hijacked your enthusiasm for the stock market. They have taken the art of stealing from the public to levels that have old snake oil salesmen sitting up in their graves applauding in approval.

The investing public continues to be duped by IPOs and SPACs that leverage the Peter Lynch mantra. Not only do you know and love these products and services, you have been hearing about them going public and, of course, you want to get in on the ground floor.

But the ground floor happened years earlier when entrepreneurs with bright ideas and little money began knocking on the doors of venture capitalists.

The New IPO — Cashing Out

The IPO process is the liquidity event where everyone on the inside gets paid when the public is now given a chance to take a bite of the apple.

Sadly, by then the stock is overvalued — significantly. The IPO process has become a greed festival to rival Roman banquets where the elites of society would over indulge and then purge themselves by vomiting through a hole in the table.

It's so grotesque. The public is being played like this. The hubris of financial television is also hard to stomach when they are complaining even when the stock's initial offering goes up on the first day of trading and trades much higher during the session.

They lament how money was left on the table and chastise the Wall Street firms for not being smart enough to get every single nickel from the dupes in the general public. That makes me want to scream.

I've been watching and hearing them talk about this for a couple of decades, and I wish I had a table with a puke hole.

The Investing Public Is Being Played Like Chumps

Some might ask, "Isn't that one of your top investing axioms — buy what you know?"

The answer is yes, but these days nobody is getting in anywhere near the ground floor anymore. When I talk about buying what you know I'm referring to companies that have been publicly traded for years and have simply come up with a better mousetrap or have a track record of innovation and execution that's worthy of owning.

Buy what you know but only get in on the ground floor if you can be an early investor in names before they are public. Otherwise, you have to be prepared to watch for at least a year, but often longer, to buy stock in those hot products and services because even a great company can have an overvalued stock.

Incidentally, one of the main reasons you think the product or service is great is because it seems like such great value. That's where your investor hat must differ from your consumer hat. Perhaps the greatness of the company is it's NOT making money while it lures in your loyalty.

When companies are raising billions of dollars privately it's used for two things:

- Build out the business and create or take market share and that means it has to be unprofitable.
- Build out a product and service reputation through public relations, including making the CEO well known to investors.

The origins of this great heist evolved innocently enough. A few company founders became household names like JD Rockerfeller and Henry Ford, but for the most part the general public knew little to nothing about the folks behind the greatest brands and most popular innovations.

That all changed during the technology bubble fueled by companies based out of Silicon Valley or funded by Silicon Valley firms.

With all due respect to Ozzy Osborne and others, the CEOs of tech companies with sizzling stocks became modern day rock stars.

Restaurants and bars began switching wall-mounted televisions from sports to financial television. And soon enough everyone wanted in on the action.

You Left Money on the Table

IPO days were huge and CNBC laid it on thick with countdown clocks, reporters on the floor, reporters outside, man on the street reporters, and all-star guests all building up anticipation.

Then the stock would begin trading. Invariably, shares would skyrocket upon trading and the chorus of commentators would lament that management left money on the table. Talk about hubris. The process is supposed to be about the public getting a bite at the apple.

But the assumption was that management could have raised more money at the peak trading level achieved on the first day of trading.

The shaming was so intense that it helped craft a new line of thinking: squeeze every nickel out of the general public and give them no chance of making money with the stock.

That mindset hasn't gone away (see reaction to SNOW IPO

below). Amazingly, these folks still think it's a sin if the public buys a stock on the first day of trading and has a legit shot at making money.

MARKETS

Snowflake's first-day pop means IPO left $3.8 billion on the table, the most in 12 years

PUBLISHED THU, SEP 17 2020·1:07 PM EDT | UPDATED THU, SEP 17 2020·5:05 PM EDT

Source: cnbc.com
https://www.cnbc.com/2020/09/17/snowflakes-first-day-pop-means-ipo-left-3point8-billion
-on-the-table-the-most-in-12-years.html%23

Face Plant (The Infamous Facebook IPO)

A great example of a company that did it right, according to Wall Street and media enablers, was Facebook.

Armed with the knowledge that it was a sin to leave money on the table, Mark Zuckerberg took full advantage of investor IPO demand.

The IPO price changed three times: $28 to $35 to $38

The IPO size was increased 25% to 421 million

Insiders were 57% of sellers

Bad news like a ratings downgrade and lost advertising contracts were not disclosed.

Like a ship that took on too much water, the first day of trading saw the shares barely budge as all the potential aftermarket buyers had already bought the IPO but at much elevated levels.

The stock sank like a stone as the company lost $50 billion in value over the next six months.

Of course, this disaster was forgotten as Facebook eventually regained its balance and became a hot stock.

Initial offerings have been getting more expensive for years but took a turn for the worse in 2020. The IPO ETF declined 46% from February 2021 to February 2022 - no other investing approach fared worse.

IPOs Too Damn High

Initial public offerings have become so rich the events mint new billionaires, but you are not one of them. The good news is these are normally really good to great companies, and at some point, if the market does its job of adjusting share price to fair value, the stock(s) will get to a point where you must own many of these names.

Meanwhile, look how much has been raised in recent IPOs. When I started in the business, a hot IPO might raise $100.0 million.

COMPANY	MARKET VALUE AT THE TIME OF THE IPO	PRICING DATE
AT&T Wireless	$68.15 billion	April 2000
Kraft Foods Inc	$53.79 billion	June 2001
Blackstone	$34.15 billion	June 2007
Visa Inc	$44.32 billion	March 2008
General Motors Co	$49.50 billion	Nov. 2010
Facebook Inc	$81.25 billion	May 2012
Uber Technologies Inc	$75.46 billion	May 2019
Airbnb Inc	$40.97 billion	Dec. 2020
Rocket Companies Inc	$35.98 billion	Aug. 2020
Snowflake Inc	$33.96 billion	Sept. 2020
Rivian Automotive Inc	$66.5 billion	Nov. 2021
Didi Global Inc	$60.96 billion	June 2021
Coupang Inc	$60.03 billion	Mar. 2021

The enthusiasm and excitement that came with the new investor revolution was hijacked by the richest people who ever walked the planet and whose only goal is to become even richer.

Many of these masters of the universe would lobby Congress to bar individuals from trading in the stock market, but this approach is much more lucrative.

Layer on all the money the government dished out during the pandemic, and even after the financial crisis was over, the billionaire class saw a chance to play the equivalent of three-card-monte with the general public.

An Aside

My high school was in a very prestigious part of Manhattan: Sutton Place. That's where old Astor and Vanderbilt money lived. Around the corner was the flagship Bloomingdales department store — at the time it was considered the best in the world.

There were a few students at Art & Design from Harlem, the South Bronx, and the more dangerous parts of Brooklyn. They had some serious skills, including one of my buddies who was great at running three-card monte games. He would turn over all the cards revealing two kings and a red queen.

Then he would shuffle those cards face down and stop and ask the folks watching to pick out the red card. It was nuts, two high school kids and all these businessmen and rich people placing bets — and losing. There was a technique to the game but the biggest trick was playing on greed.

You Are the Red Card

The longer investors have to wait for these IPOs the more expensive these stocks will become. Using price to sales ratios, tech IPOs in 2021 were 276% more expensive than those debuting in 2016.

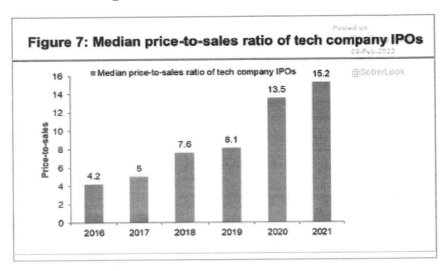

Figure 7: Median price-to-sales ratio of tech company IPOs

While the street is fixated on the bottom line and price to earnings ratio, investors have to remember that it all starts at the top of the income statement with sales. How much are they growing, how much is organic, and how much is being done with the company exercising outsized pricing power?

Like everything else about the stock market, there is a debate over what constitutes excessive price to sales ratio although most would agree 10 x sales is a lot. This is why growth stocks generally trade at higher valuations and why investors are willing to overlook unprofitability — at least for some time.

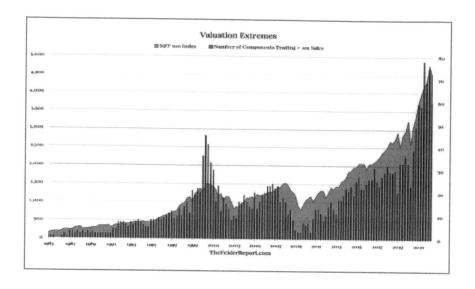

Spankings from SPACs

Special Purpose Acquisition Companies have been around for decades. One version used to be called "blind pools." This is where certain investors pour cash into a public shell with no operating company in hopes of buying one later.

The sales pitch is simple enough. These brilliant folks will find the best companies (like the folks on "Shark Tank") and get them for the best price. Initially I loved the idea. Investors would be getting in closer to the ground floor instead of waiting a decade.

Then Came the Hype

The number of IPOs and SPACs (Special Purpose Acquisition Company) were the equivalent of looting during the Great 1977 NYC Blackout. It became a simply free-for-all of greed.

Each day financial media, with countdown clocks to whet the appetite of viewers, would lay it on thick for the next sizzling IPO or SPAC.

The excitement and sense of urgency would make a travelling snake oil salesman blush.

These companies were hyped for weeks before they officially began to trade and then they would take off like they were shot out of a cannon.

Initially the first day of trading was always exhilarating but soon enough people got hip. Many IPOs and SPACs were dead on arrival.

The hubris and greed, however, will always leave a lasting memory.

It's no longer good enough to simply know the company and love the products and services.

You have to educate yourself on risk and valuations and know who in the company or among their financiers is selling. Read the offering prospectus or, at least, the shorter version.

I know it seems like a great bother and looks like a laborious task to read an offering prospectus cover to cover. It's laborious for a reason. You just have to know the details more than ever these days because even the best companies can be overvalued stocks.

You want a piece of the action. You must take action.

Meanwhile, be wary of the hype machine that has the investing public lining up to "buy, buy, buy" as some guy on TV implores us to do moments after the first trade.

For newbies, those "hot" new issues can seem extremely exciting, especially when you've waited so long to own the company after singing its praises for years. Many times, newbies feel compelled to put their money where their mouths have been after discovering the company before anyone else in their circle.

In an odd way they have already become "invested," taking credit and pride when the product or service serves their friends well. How could they not be a buyer of the stock being touted as a hot IPO. I hope Wall Street and Silicon Valley are reconsidering their rip-off scheme.

I've been told that's not the case. But at some point, if individual investors start ignoring the hype and falling for the pitch, there will be no choice except to give folks a real chance.

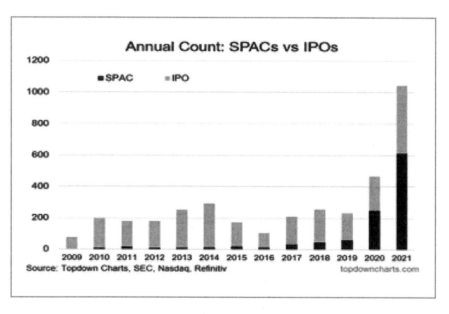

Silicon Valley and Wall Street saw all the money gushing into society via fiscal programs designed to counter the negative economic effects of COVID-19 followed by bald-faced attempts to win elections and they took advantage.

The rest was a tidal wave of offers...

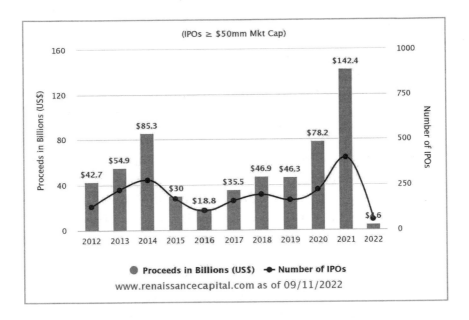

...of far crappier stocks.

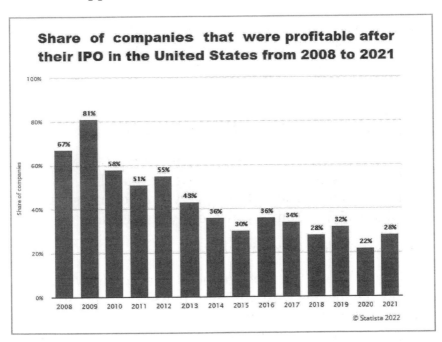

We'll Get It Back

With the vast majority of new offerings coming to market at insane and unfair valuations, the best move is to let them go public, ignore the hype, stop assuming you would have put in a buy ticket at $30 and not gotten filled at $60, and just stay on the sidelines.

I think the best way now, other than occasionally, is for trading investors to wait a year or two before buying a new listing — at much lower entry prices than the first day of trading when the snake oil folks from Silicon Valley and Wall Street invited the public into the castle for a feast.

You Were the Meal!

In reality, you don't need IPOs or SPACs to have great opportunities. Opportunities are around you all the time. You just need to look for them. That might mean that you need to view the world around you in a slightly different way. We have talked about "buying what you know" and that is important. Really looking at what you "know" opens up a whole world of new possibilities.

Discovery Journey:
The Stuff You Don't Know You Know

There are so many great investing ideas out there — some seem obvious but others might not, even when they are right under your nose. Let me give you an example of what I'm talking about from my own daily activities.

Discovering New Investing Ideas

Each day I go to the Fox Business and Fox News studio, and my day begins with studying news from all corners of the spectrum, from business to geopolitical to individual companies that might be reporting earnings, etc. Then I meet with my show team as we map out the show and put together the rundown. When we have that all wrapped up, I make a mad dash downstairs to get a late breakfast or early lunch (or dinner, since it's the only time I will eat until the evening).

I go to a spot on the ground floor of the building called Fresh & Co.

It's a nice spot, even if they have too many healthy offerings and no hamburgers. The staff is fantastic but very young and severely underpaid. For that reason, turnover is high but they always seem to hire more, nice people — young adults trying to make it in life. For years there was a tip jar at the cash register and, sadly, many folks didn't tip even though some of them were earning millions of dollars a year. To add to the "tipping dilemma" was the credit card system the owners used. It was slow and inconsistent at best. Folks using credit cards had to manually add the tip to the receipt. Many of these people were under a time crunch and simply didn't take the time. Because the credit card system was so slow and clunky, I always paid cash. But even paying cash, the tips I left were not always representative of the effort and hustle of these young hard workers. Let's say the total came to $19.00, (I know it sounds like I'm overeating but this is New York City. That might be a bagel and cup of tea.) If all I had was a twenty-dollar bill I would, of course, leave the dollar in the tip jar but it was not enough.

My tip ranges would generally range from 20% to 50%, so one dollar on $19.00 is only a 5% tip.

Then Fresh & Co rolled out a new system. Initially I didn't think much of it but I did notice more people used it than used the last system and they were in and out of the store faster. One day I was running later than usual and decided to give it a try, thinking I would pay them the tip on my next visit.

I tapped the square box with my card instead of having to slide the card inside an unanchored box and trying to make sure it didn't slide all over the place before clicking in. After tapping, a screen appeared offering tip options. I saw a screen that allowed me to choose 5%, 10%, 15%, 18%, or custom.

I tapped 18% and then tapped one more time (declining a receipt) and I was out the door. Initially I didn't even think about asking who made this new system. Then one day I asked the manager how the system was working out. She told me it was great. As we spoke, I looked closer and saw the system was from a company called Toast (TOST).

"Wow, I've heard of this company because it just went public," I blurted out.

She asked if she should buy the stock. I said no, not yet, even though she gave the product a huge thumbs' up. I was sure Toast was overvalued at IPO time but I began my research because there is a chance, I would want to own the stock in the future.

Let's use this company as an example of how you might choose to add something to your own watch list and what you should be doing with that company while it is on the list.

Founders & Ethos

Step One: Learn about the company and the industry.

The company was formed a decade earlier in the basement of one of the three co-founders, a trio of MIT graduates. Initially the company's goal was to provide a mobile payments app for restaurants.

Since then, the software expanded beyond handling point-of-sale transactions to encompass features including online ordering, delivery management, and marketing.

So, now I knew a little something about the background of the company and its founders. But that was just the starting point. I want to know more.

True Grit

My favorite thing about finding new companies to follow as potential investments is learning about the history, including struggles of the founders and company ethos. I know it's a hip thing these days to say younger investors are focused on "values," which is cool. The fact of the matter is things like the Environmental, Social and Governance or ESG movement have been hijacked and manipulated.

It's better to look into actions and not rely on words or platitudes. Moreover, company initiatives that check boxes without heart or real commitment are shallow and shouldn't be rewarded by potential investors.

What I'm looking for is grit. I'm looking for vision. I'm looking for the ability to turn an idea into usable products and services. Don't tell me all the wonderful things you're going to do, show me. Show me you have the ability and determination necessary to take a service or product and make it profitable.

Toast was launched out of the basement of Aman Narang with co-founders Steve Fredette and Jonathan Grimm in 2011. The trio of MIT graduates had previously worked together at e-commerce search software company Endeca, which was acquired by Oracle.

The three co-founders had business success and startup success. In addition, they were able to expand the company beyond its initial mission.

The COVID-19 pandemic was a major hurdle where management had to lay off workers. I cannot say I got much on the ethos of the company, but I like what I've seen thus far.

And I will keep trying to learn more about the folks driving the company.

So, I have some preliminary information on the company. I would want more, but I have a start. What about the industry in which they are competing? What is the market like for their product? Below is some information they provide along with some additional information about the scope of the product.

Market Potential

"The restaurant industry is massive; in the U.S. alone there are over 800,000 restaurants. We're thrilled about this milestone, but we've got 48,000 restaurants on our platform and we see so much potential to grow."

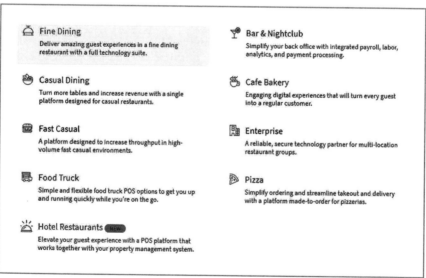

Source: toasttab.com
https://pos.toasttab.com/

The company's products menu is vast.

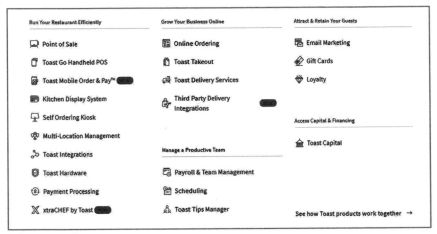

Source: toasttab.com
https://pos.toasttab.com/

Covering the entire store

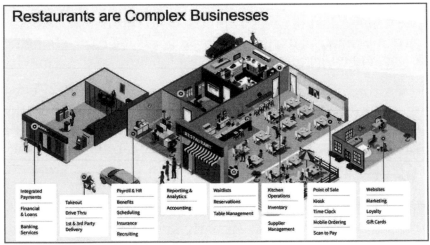

Source: toasttab.com
https://pos.toasttab.com/

This is all interesting and useful information. We also need to take a hard look at the financial information available.

Price to Sales

Third quarter 2021 revenues came in at $486 million, up 105% from a year earlier. Consequently, the Price to Sales Ratio declined to 9.7% from 18.7%. In this regard the stock is getting cheaper but nowhere near what I would consider a bargain.

Money Maker?

Since the late 1990s more and more publicly traded companies have not made any money. They trade up and down but have yet to find a way to bring any cash to the bottom line. Some haven't brought much money to the top line either.

You can invest in these companies for sure, but what we are looking for are earnings that will justify higher share prices. Back in the 1990s, when the biotech boom began, there was an avalanche of biotech IPOs with noble goals of curing everything. Most of those companies, to this day, have never earned a dime. Many are still trading, raising cash, changing focus, and enriching insiders. Shareholders?...not so much.

When considering a potential buy you want to know what the path to profitability is, if it's a new listing, or what the path to greater profitability is if it's already a name that's traded publicly for years. Let's continue our look at Toast.

Toast Revenue Trends

Toast booked $823 million in revenue in 2020, up 24% from 2019. To be frank, an early-stage company ready to go public should be seeing high double-digit or even triple-digit revenue gains.

But there was the pandemic — the company did report revenues of $704 million for the first six months of 2021 — a 70% increase.

But the company was not profitable when it went public.

They reported net losses of $248 million in 2020 and $235 million for the first six months of 2021.

When asked about the lack of profits, Narang was reportedly "cagey" saying "there's many ways to build a great business" and that the company would "continue to invest in product and innovation."

Those are cool buzz words, but when the founders become instant billionaires from their IPOs, it's important that those folks buying the stock aren't treated like stooges and fools.

This is an example of a company worth putting on a watch list. Let's look at another example with a little more history that functions in the same market.

I was telling my twenty-five-year-old son about this passage of the book when he called to see what I was up to. As I explained to him the premise, he interrupted with a eureka kind of moment to say he knew exactly what I was talking about because something like that just happened with him.

He told me about a company named Equinix (EQIX) that has a point-of-sales system that was really impressive. In addition to asking how much you want to tip, it gives you the chance to have the receipt sent to your email address and you do not even have to input your email address. The system already knows.

My son found that to be amazing. He also remarked about the footprint of the company. He saw the system at a very popular NYC restaurant called Sarah Beth, but he also saw the same system in a tiny hole-in-the-wall pizza shop in SoHo. As he told me the story, I had to interrupt with my own eureka kind of moment.

Equinix?

"Oh, my goodness," I said with a mix of pride and excitement.

I knew this company very well. Not only had I featured the stock on my Hotline service on October 28, 2010, but I also invited the company's CEO on Fox Business in 2011. We got out of the stock too soon for a profit. If we had held, it would have been an 800%+ winner by October 2021. But all this happened after the stock tumbled 99% amid the dot. com bubble crash. From more than $400 a share in 2000 to $2.40 in April 2003.

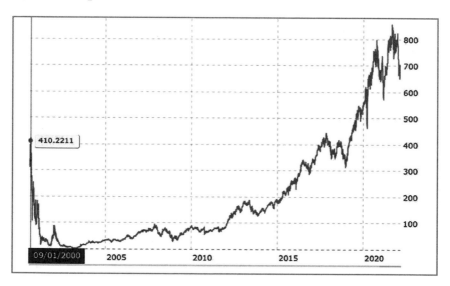

Wipeout

When I was a broker, we had an inside, and somewhat cruel, joke when going back to the same clients to ask for more money. Yes, that is the real job of a broker and all of the folks I mentioned on Wall Street, no matter the title, is to get more assets under management, otherwise known as AUM.

We would go back to ask them to buy stocks they already owned under the guise of "averaging down," so their cost would be cheaper. When a stock is down more than 50% in less than a year, management is not going to turn it around fast, if it's even possible to turn around at all.

There are special circumstances when a stock is extremely overvalued and the drawdown is a proper and an overdue adjustment. But when it's just a stock collapsing on its own, more than likely it's warranted and not a short-term situation.

That said, very volatile stocks can be worth a trade after massive drawdowns, but that's a different kettle of fish.

So, the joke would go something like this:

Mr. Jones, I think now is the time to buy more XYZ

I know it's down a lot and that's the point

If you liked it at $20.00 you have to love it at $7.00

Every company has potential, but it takes the right management to bring it to fruition.

That's what happened at Equinix.

Management merged with another company, restructured its debt, and reimagined its business model. Interestingly, management also decided not to file for bankruptcy protection, which would have wiped out shareholders that were still holding the stock.

As I lamented not holding the stock to my son, he said to me, "Maybe it's still a buy," and that's when I said to myself, "I raised this kid right." It's still on my screens and, if the stars align in the future, I will not hesitate.

I share this example of a company that has been around for a while and had some difficult times but has made a comeback. We've briefly looked at two different companies in the same market. They would certainly need more research using the 3 Pillars before any decisions were made, but they deserve to be on a watch list. Potential investments are all around you every day. They might be things you interact with or things family and friends find exciting. The point is that they are out there and all you need to do is be open and watchful.

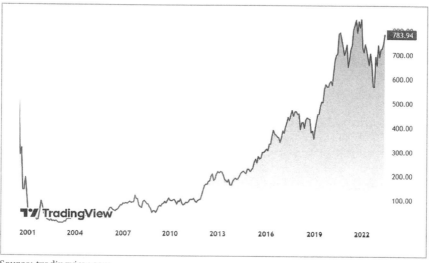

Source: tradingview.com
https://www.tradingview.com/symbols/NASDAQ-EQIX/

Chapter 4 Assignment

At the end of most of the chapters I have provided a quick quiz to review some of the key points. In this chapter I am going to do something different. Creating a watch list is so important, and something I am afraid isn't done often enough, that I am going to give you a "homework" task. I think you'll have a lot of fun with this, and I expect it will be very eye opening for you. I want you to find five products or services you engage with daily or weekly but they never caught your eye before. In addition, I want you to identify five companies you think are boring as hell and follow them too.

Look closely at all the names that pop up on your screen when you turn on your computer.

Check out the hottest stuff in your own industry.

Check out the hottest stuff in your hobbies.

I just want you to get in the habit of immediately thinking after seeing something cool or groovy:

- Is the company publicly traded?
- What makes it tick?
- Is there something proprietary to the company (patents, approach, uniqueness)?
- Can it have a larger audience (and make sure you are open minded — not everyone shares your taste)?
- Can the company be profitable?
- Can management grow the business (the answer is most often no, so beware)?

The one thing you are going to learn quickly is just how many things in your everyday life are made by publicly traded companies.

Then, as you dig deeper, you will find the components of these goods and services are also from publicly traded companies.

The reason this is important is because sometimes it's better to sell picks and shovels than dig for gold. Back in the gold rush era it was the folks who sold picks and shovels to miners that made the real money on a consistent basis rather than those that used the picks and shovels and staked everything on striking it rich and finding gold in California.

Take some time and build your Watch List. I think you will find it both fun and informative.

Chapter

5

Populating and Managing your Portfolio

It's time to begin populating your portfolio. For portfolios up to $500,000 I think the maximum number of positions is twenty spread over eleven S&P 500 sectors and including cash. The reasoning for this is you need a large enough position to have meaningful impact when they are profitable, but not be ruinous when they are losers.

STAPLES	DISCRETIONARY	TECHNOLOGY	TELECOMM	HEALTH CARE	MATERIALS
INDUSTRIALS	REAL ESTATE	FINANCIALS	UTILITIES	ENERGY	CASH

I'm not a fan of diversification for the sake of balance and safety as it just means owning stocks that are not working while eschewing those that are or will be soon. That defeats the purpose of this endeavor. I know Wall Street has sold the public on this would-be "barbell" approach, which means more assets under management for them and fewer gains for you.

The idea is to buy and hold for a period of three to six months with the underlying objective of a double-digit return. Closing positions are determined by several factors:

Value Proposition — when the share price moves the story changes, and you have to determine if the underlying fundamentals continue justifying holding.

Technical Challenges — risks the downside increase when stocks fail to breakout after big moves higher or key support points are breached.

Sector in Retreat — bad news and developments in specific sectors or industries will bring all stocks down, even the best companies, and, while these moves create buying opportunities, they can be a signal to take profits on a name that is also becoming stretched, based on other factors.

Mitigate Loss — avoid, at all times, the trap of thinking you are right, and the market is wrong because the market doesn't care about your facts.

Don't be afraid to be overweight and underweight in some sectors but be careful. Often there are sectors and industries with great potential, but, when the work is done, only a few names have the actual potential, and the rest are riding their coattails.

Going for the Grand Slams

There is a difference between great long-term success in the stock market and phenomenal long-term success in the stock market.

The difference is Generating Windfalls. So, how do you do that?

I think everyone needs a few stocks over time that make

outsized returns. I used to publish a list of four never-sell stocks. For a long time, they were:

· AAPL

· AMZN

· BA

· NKE

These stocks were to be held and not count against your more active investment portfolio. I will resume these updates very soon. And while the name suggests "set it and forget it," my work makes assumptions over five-year intervals.

When considering these "never-sell" stocks it's easy to imagine they would be the next Apple, but there are a number of reasons stocks climb for years that go beyond having killer apps.

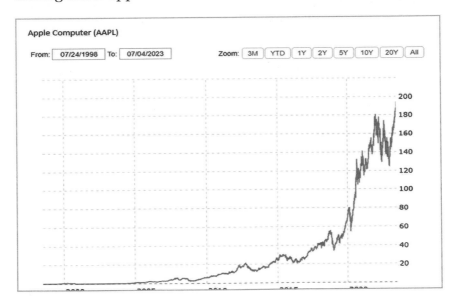

Owning National Instruments (NATI), chart shown on the next page, over the past thirty years would have been a great investment that could have been that life-changing windfall.

The key is to really know the company.
- Read everything on the founder(s)
- Read all the filings
- Understand the industry
- Listen to conference calls

Try not to become a zealot, but every great stock in history has endured major setbacks and while it's easy to say, "I wish I bought and held XYZ" in real life you may have sold during one of those periods of distress.

Bottom Line:

This should not be your primary approach but there are names you should hold for a long time. More than likely these will come out of your active portfolio. Names that are up triple-digit percentage gains and still leading the pack can come out of your active portfolio and onto your never sell list.

More on this approach when I focus on the original Diamond Hands, Mr. Warren Buffett later in the book.

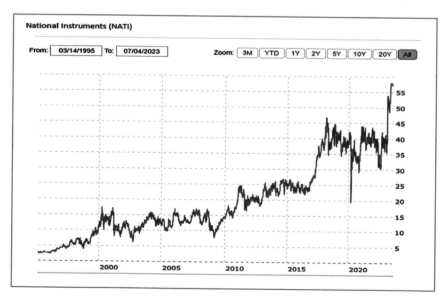

It Is Always a Stock Pickers Market

Wall Street calls buying stocks "risk on" and selling "risk off," which seems counterintuitive if the stock market is the greatest money machine in history.

They are referring to stocks versus treasury bills and bonds, which have guaranteed rates of return backed by the United States government.

With that in mind you should never invest for small returns.

With that in mind you should always be a stock picker.

Hendrik Bessembinder posted the most amazing research on the actual wealth creation in the stock market vis-à-vis treasury bills.

He studied 26,168 publicly traded stocks from 1926 to 2019 and found that 57.8% of them reduced wealth rather than increased shareholder wealth.

57.8%! My goodness that's nuts.

That means the $47.4 trillion in wealth created in the stock market during that time came from just 42.2% of publicly traded stocks.

Wealth Creation in the U.S. Public Stock Markets 1926 to 2019

23 Pages · Posted: 25 Feb 2020 · Last revised: 12 Nov 2020

Hendrik Bessembinder
W.P. Carey School of Business

Date Written: February 13, 2020

Abstract

This report quantifies long-run stock market outcomes in terms of the increases or decreases (relative to a Treasury bill benchmark) in shareholder wealth, when considering the full history of both net cash distributions and capital appreciation. The study includes all of the 26,168 firms with publicly-traded U.S. common stock since 1926. Despite the fact that investments in the majority (57.8%) of stocks led to reduced rather than increased shareholder wealth, U.S. stock market investments on net increased shareholder wealth by $47.4 trillion between 1926 and 2019. Technology firms accounted for the largest share, $9.0 trillion, of the total, but Telecommunications, Energy, and Healthcare/ Pharmaceutical stocks created wealth disproportionate to the numbers of firms in the industries. The degree to which stock market wealth creation is concentrated in a few top-performing firms has increased over time, and was particularly strong during the most recent three years, when five firms accounted for 22% of net wealth creation. These results should be of interest to any long-term investor assessing the relative merits of broad diversification vs. narrow portfolio selection.

The wealth was most abundant in technology, financials, and manufacturing stocks.

Wealth Creation by Industry

Industry	Lifetime Wealth Creation ($ millions)	Firm/Months for Industry	Industry % of Wealth Creation	Industry % of Firm/Months	Ratio, % of Wealth Creation to % of Firm/Months
1 Consumer Nondurables	3,590,411.9	281,215	7.58%	7.55%	1.00
2 Consumer Durables	1,587,804.0	122,321	3.35%	3.28%	1.02
3 Manufacturing	5,915,559.3	601,476	12.49%	16.15%	0.77
4 Energy	3,393,818.3	180,887	7.16%	4.86%	1.48
5 Technology	8,999,079.6	529,443	18.99%	14.21%	1.34
6 Telecommunications	1,749,579.2	77,588	3.69%	2.08%	1.77
7 Wholesale and Retail	4,074,656.9	368,757	8.60%	9.90%	0.87
8 Healthcare and Pharmaceuticals	4,638,915.5	245,398	9.79%	6.59%	1.49
9 Utilities	2,135,778.2	127,564	4.51%	3.42%	1.32
10 Finance	7,210,235.9	584,916	15.22%	15.70%	0.97
11 Other, incl. Bus Serv and Ent	4,085,124.2	605,853	8.62%	16.26%	0.53
Total	47,380,963.0	3,725,418			

Technology Beast

STOCK	YEAR TRADING	WEALTH CREATED
AAPL	1981	$1.64 trillion
MSFT	1986	$1.41 trillion
XOM	1926	$988 billion
AMZN	1997	$865 billion
GOOGL	2004	$718 billion

Forget Wall Street's Sour Grapes – Own the Winners

In the past ten years much has been made about the outsized role in a handful of stocks powering the stock market higher.

That's Wall Street sour grapes. By avoiding stocks with PE ratios above twenty and other artificial restrictions, the street continues to miss the grand slams.

From 1926 to 2022 only three stocks were responsible for 10% of wealth creation.

From 1926 to 2022 only seventy-two stocks were responsible for half the market's wealth creation — out of more than 26,000.

You must be in this market and moving and thinking on your own or you will not attain the goals you desire. Nothing is guaranteed, even the ideas and strategies in this book, but history shows you must own and manage a portfolio of individual stocks.

The flip side is if you own the right names, you can change your life.

Bear Markets

They are inevitable and they are painful. They also create the kind of opportunities that can change your life: Bear Markets.

I'm ever the optimist, even as I'm presently down 7.2% year-to-date in the Golden Capital Portfolio. Not the best start to a year, but also not my worst. I've survived many a market condition that proved bearish for seemingly months on end. In hindsight, the bear markets generally don't last that long, the 2020 bear market being the shortest anyone has ever experienced. So let's look at that for a second. I'm guessing we'll be focusing on "time" this week and as Edward offered atop our weekly Research Report via a quote from Warren Buffett: *"Time is an investors best friend"*.

Bear Market Recoveries
S&P 500 Index Length To Recover From A Bear Market

Month of Peak	Month of Low	Length of Bear (Months)	% Decline	Length of Recovery (Months)	Recession?
August-56	October-57	14	-22%	11	Yes
December-61	June-62	6	-28%	14	No
February-66	October-66	8	-22%	7	No
December-68	May-70	17	-36%	21	Yes
January-73	October-74	21	-48%	69	Yes
September-76	March-78	18	-19%	17	No
November-80	August-82	21	-27%	3	Yes
August-87	December-87	4	-34%	20	No
July-90	October-90	3	-20%	4	Yes
July-98	August-98	1	-19%	3	No
March-00	October-02	31	-49%	56	Yes
October-07	March-09	17	-56%	49	Yes
April-11	October-11	6	-19%	4	No
September-18	December-18	3	-20%	4	No
February-20	March-20	1*	-30%	1	?
Average For All Bear Markets		12	-30%	20	
Average Bear Market (In Recession)		18	-37%	30	
Average Bear Market (No Recession)		7	-24%	10	

Firstly, I'm not predicting or forecasting a bear market. This is a matter of having all the information at-hand, and considering all options given the aforementioned signals year-to-date combined with several other unmentioned market statistics like P/E ratios and rising rate environments during a midterm election year. We have to keep an open mind, as savvy investors, in order to remain flexible with our approach during treacherous price action.

Source: lplresearch.com
https://lplresearch.com/2020/03/18/how-quickly-can-stocks-recover-from-covid-19/

Year	Year End Return	Intra Year Drawdown	Year	Year End Return	Intra Year Drawdown	Year	Year End Return	Intra Year Drawdown	Year	Year End Return	Intra Year Drawdown
1928	43.8%	-10.3%	1951	23.7%	-8.1%	1975	37.0%	-14.1%	1999	20.9%	-12.1%
1929	-8.3%	-44.6%	1952	18.2%	-6.8%	1976	23.8%	-8.4%	2000	-9.0%	-17.2%
1930	-25.1%	-44.3%	1953	-1.2%	-14.8%	1977	-7.0%	-15.6%	2001	-11.9%	-29.7%
1931	-43.8%	-57.5%	1954	52.6%	-4.4%	1978	6.5%	-13.6%	2002	-22.0%	-33.8%
1932	-8.6%	-51.0%	1955	32.6%	-10.6%	1979	18.5%	-10.2%	2003	28.4%	-14.1%
1933	50.0%	-29.4%	1956	7.4%	-10.8%	1980	31.7%	-17.1%	2004	10.7%	-8.2%
1934	-1.2%	-29.3%	1957	-10.5%	-20.7%	1981	-4.7%	-18.4%	2005	4.8%	-7.2%
1935	46.7%	-15.9%	1958	43.7%	-4.4%	1982	20.4%	-16.6%	2006	15.6%	-7.7%
1936	31.9%	-12.8%	1959	12.1%	-9.2%	1983	22.3%	-6.9%	2007	5.5%	-10.1%
1937	-35.3%	-45.5%	1960	0.3%	-13.4%	1984	6.2%	-12.7%	2008	-36.6%	-48.8%
1938	29.3%	-28.9%	1961	26.6%	-4.4%	1985	31.2%	-7.7%	2009	25.9%	-27.6%
1939	-1.1%	-21.2%	1962	-8.8%	-26.9%	1986	18.5%	-9.4%	2010	14.8%	-16.0%
1940	-10.7%	-29.6%	1963	22.6%	-6.5%	1987	5.8%	-33.5%	2011	2.1%	-19.4%
1941	-12.8%	-22.9%	1964	16.4%	-3.5%	1988	16.5%	-7.6%	2012	15.9%	-9.9%
1942	19.2%	-17.8%	1965	12.4%	-9.6%	1989	31.5%	-7.6%	2013	32.2%	-5.8%
1943	25.1%	-13.1%	1966	-10.0%	-22.2%	1990	-3.1%	-19.9%	2014	13.5%	-7.4%
1944	19.0%	-6.9%	1967	23.8%	-6.6%	1991	30.2%	-5.7%	2015	1.4%	-12.4%
1945	35.8%	-6.9%	1968	10.8%	-9.3%	1992	7.5%	-6.2%	2016	11.8%	-10.5%
1946	-8.4%	-26.6%	1969	-8.2%	-16.0%	1993	10.0%	-5.0%	2017	21.6%	-2.8%
1947	5.2%	-14.7%	1970	3.6%	-25.9%	1994	1.3%	-8.9%	2018	-4.2%	-19.8%
1948	5.7%	-13.5%	1971	14.2%	-13.9%	1995	37.2%	-2.5%	2019	31.2%	-6.8%
1949	18.3%	-13.2%	1972	18.8%	-5.1%	1996	22.7%	-7.6%	2020	18.0%	-33.9%
1950	30.8%	-14.0%	1973	-14.3%	-23.4%	1997	33.1%	-10.8%	2021	28.5%	-5.2%
			1974	-25.9%	-37.6%	1998	28.3%	-19.3%			

Data Sources: NYU, Bloomberg (My Calculations)

Source: lplresearch.com
https://lplresearch.com/2020/03/18/how-quickly-can-stocks-recover-from-covid-19/

Grin & Bear It: Extending Holding Period

With the exception of the COVID-19 /global lock-down induced bear market in the spring of 2020, new investors are normally drawn to the stock market during up periods. Normally this occurs in the middle of a strong bull market run. The majority of these newbies say they want to be investors, which is easy to say when it seems stocks only go up.

But when the ride gets bumpy many:

A) are shaken out, often for a net loss;

B) are frustrated and, while holding, decide never to buy another stock;

C) see the opportunity.

I want to go over all these scenarios, starting with seeing opportunities. This is the tricky part because it's easy to "get in too soon" and find yourself joining the folks in group A (bailing at a loss). Here's what you need to remember — the stock market comes back in phases. There is the snap back phase from being oversold. That is then followed by the sideways period, where underlying fundamentals have to corroborate that the coast is clear.

Normally this period also sees exogenous factors, like major geopolitical disruptions or the economic cycle also dissipate. I need to point out that crude oil and the dollar react very violently to these types of events, so use them like "a canary in a coal mine" early-warning system. This same cycle mostly holds true for the majority of individual stocks as well. Before talking about buying the bounce, let's talk about how a bull market morphs into a bear and how and why it remains that way.

COMPARISON					NOTES

S&P 500 Breaks Below 200-Day Moving Average

	1-Month Return	3-Month Return	6-Month Return	12-Month Return
No. of Returns	34	34	34	34
Average Return	1.80%	3.30%	7.03%	9.99%
Median Return	1.97%	4.87%	8.30%	11.68%
Percent Positive	74%	76%	79%	82%
Std. Deviation	5.04%	6.34%	8.84%	17.44%

S&P 500 Anytime Since 1990

	1-Month Return	3-Month Return	6-Month Return	12-Month Return
No. of Returns	8018	7976	7913	7787
Average Return	0.79%	2.36%	4.75%	9.82%
Median Return	1.23%	3.05%	5.48%	11.14%
Percent Positive	64%	70%	74%	81%
Std. Deviation	4.47%	7.42%	10.70%	16.09%

NOTES

When the market or individual stock breaks the 200-day moving average it's in freefall – its not pretty and it hurts.

Study these two charts to see one, three and even six month returns from that point are actually higher on average than normal periods of the market.

But the pace of gains slows after six months from the snap back bounce as it takes six months to go from 7% gains to 9.9% gains. Normally that stretch sees 4.7% gains rocket to 9.8%.

Breaking Under 200-Day Moving Average

The year 2021 was very sanguine for the stock market, although there were early signs of weakness. A rolling bear market began early in the year, taking out one group at a time with the precision of a sniper. Since most of the market held up, it was hard to notice at first. I will go into further details but want to pick up on the macro story of trendlines and the 200-day moving average.

I'm a sucker for trendlines and trading channels. They are so simplistic and yet work so well.

People who trade for a living use the tops and bottoms of channels to make big money. Having complete faith in them allows buying into sharp declines and selling just as Wall Street starts cheering big rallies.

The S&P 500 was locked in a great channel in 2021 — surviving a noticeable decline in March. That coincided with the 10-year treasury yield spiking to 1.72% after beginning the year barely above 1.00%. This was a huge spike and a major yellow flag (or red, depending on your time horizon).

The ten-year yield worked its way back to 1.21% by late July and the stock market rebounded accordingly but found its upper trendline resistance. The ten-year yield began moving higher again and rallied to 1.61% by late October, triggering the stock market to sell off in a perfect correlation.

Once again yields eased and stocks rallied.

Sell Signal

The S&P 500 exited 2021 riding higher, but there were serious signs of erosion of the foundation of the rally (more on that later).

Trendline support finally failed on January 18, 2022. Purists might have sold immediately. But even if you gave it a couple of days, that first rally attempt failed at what had been a trendline support. There was another try and another failure, which was followed by a second failure at the 200-day moving average — that was the ultimate sell signal.

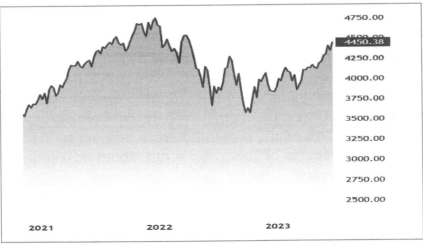

Source: tradingview.com
https://www.tradingview.com/symbols/CBOE-SPX/

The Market Swooned But Rebounded Quickly

But here's the thing — the S&P 500 failed to get back above what was the bottom of the previous trading channel. Remember, once failed support becomes resistance and, in this case, the inability to get back above the previous bottom, THAT was a serious red flag.

The S&P 500 got back above the 200-day twice but with little conviction and the dip on earlier April 2022 was decisive.

S&P 500 + Ten-Year Bond Yield

Source: tradingview.com

I have to point out that often when the market is breaking down, money will rotate into stronger names, which regularly have great weighting on the market. So even though the S&P 500 has a greater chance of being up 1.80% on average (74% of the time), the truth is most individual stocks are going to be lower. Let's talk about adjustments in a down market.

Managing Portfolio in Down Markets

It's fine to say you are going to "grin and bear it" because you own great stocks, but even great stocks eventually succumb to a market that is in the grips of a persistent downward spiral.

Moreover, great stocks often get ahead of themselves (overvalued) and can get even more crowded during initial drawdowns as they will be thought of as new value or new safe havens.

Be careful! At some point during the drawdown, after everything else has been hit, those new value stocks (even the more expensive ones) move into the crosshairs of major corrections and bear markets.

You are going to need patience, and, if you stay in the market long enough, you will see every scenario and develop a certain calm. You will recognize the cycles, trends, and warning signs. Things turn around and the stock market comes back.

Source: personalfinanceclub.com
https://www.personalfinanceclub.com/how-much-would-a-10k-investment-40-years-ago-be-worth-today/

Bear Market Bottoms

There are two types of bear markets: those associated with recessions and those that happen sans recession. There have been fourteen bear markets in the post-war era.

If you are lucky you will live through a dozen or more.

There is an old saying that millionaires are forged during bear markets not during bull markets and I agree.

It begins with staying the course since 90% to 95% of individual investors blink to some degree. Stocks can only get cheap when there are far more sellers than buyers.

Enduring bear markets is one thing and will come with some pain. That means closing out stocks along the way. But mostly it means being positioned for the turn.

The first twelve months after the end of a bear market sees the S&P 500 up an average of 43%. In fact, the first two years is where gobs of money are made, life-changing stuff.

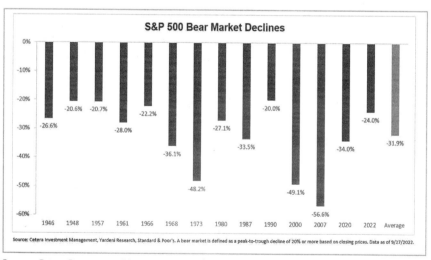

Source: Cetera Investment Management, Yardeni Research, Standard and Poor's

Average Non-Recession Bear

- · Duration six months
- · Decline -21%

Average Recession Bear

- · Duration twenty months
- · Decline -35%

Bear Market Bottom Check List: Valuations

Price to earnings ratios, using the trailing twelve months, is the most referenced valuation metric. I prefer the forward PE ratio, but it becomes more complicated considering forward-looking earnings are being adjusted lower during bear markets. Still, they will ultimately beat consensus, so keep that in mind. Stocks are usually hammered during bear markets, pushing all valuation metrics lower.

The average bear market bottom PE ratio going back to 1957 is 13.6. However, that is not the case in recent years (since 1987). The average PE ratio since 1987 has bottomed at 14.9.

I suspect this is because the Federal Reserve has become very active during times of market duress with rate cuts that turn the tide. Alan Greenspan was on the job for only a month when he began cutting rates and turning the market. His actions gained him the nickname: The Maestro.

© 2022 The Leuthold Group Date of S&P 500 Bear Market Low	S&P 500 P/E on 5-Yr. Normal EPS
October 22, 1957	12.5
June 26, 1962	16.2
October 7, 1966	16.3
May 26, 1970	12.5
October 3, 1974	9.3
March 6, 1978	9.4
August 12, 1982	7.4
December 4, 1987	14.6
October 11, 1990	14.7
October 9, 2002	17.0
March 9, 2009	9.9
March 23, 2020	18.1
Median	**13.6**
September 26, 2022	23.4

Source: The Leuthold Group

Bear Market Bottom Checklist: Sentiment

AAII

Below is the AAII chart on investor sentiment.

When individual investor bear sentiment minus bull sentiment is 20%+ its usually a sign of the market is oversold. When the ratio is north of 50% is often a sign of the end of the bear market.

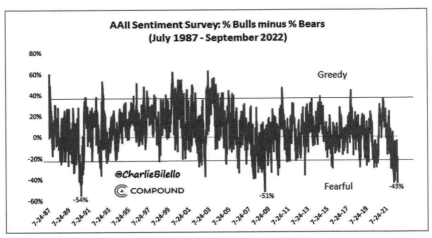

Source: nasdaq.com
https://www.nasdaq.com/articles/whats-in-store-for-q4-for-the-nasdaq-100

CNN *Fear & Greed*

This index uses several metrics and is pretty good for short-term moves. It's contrarian, which means that extreme fear = buying opportunity.

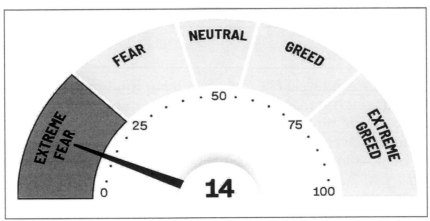

Source: cnn.com
https://www.cnn.com/markets/fear-and-greed

Bank of America Bull & Bear Indicator

I have seen this indictor rest in extreme bearishness for weeks before the market turned higher so it's not one I employ often and never solely rely on.

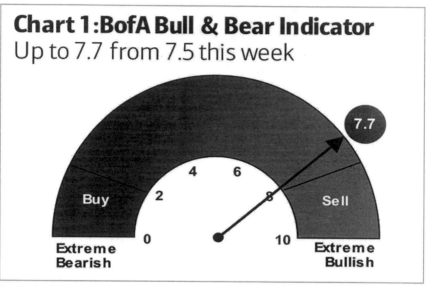

Source: bankofamerica.com

Fund Managers

Extreme cash levels (5% plus) by global fund managers are a sign a bottom is approaching. I find the number to be about three months ahead of reversals. Remember these fund managers must put that cash to work and you want to be positioned before they start to buy. By the way, cash under 2.0% is often a bearish signal.

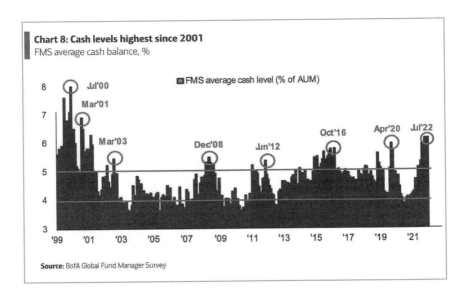

Chart 8: Cash levels highest since 2001
FMS average cash balance, %

Source: BofA Global Fund Manager Survey

Overweight stocks

When funds' overweight equities decline to negative, the market is approaching oversold territory.

Chart 1: FMS Asset Allocation to Global Stocks at All-Time Low
Net % of FMS investors that are overweight/underweight equities vs YoY change in S&P500 returns

Source: BofA Global Fund Manager Survey, Bloomberg.

BofA GLOBAL RESEARCH

Source: BofA Global Fund Manager Survey, Bloomberg
https://www.bloomberg.com/news/articles/2022-09-13/bofa-survey-shows-nadir-in-stock-al-locations-amid-recession-fear

Another metric from the FMS is risk appetite. When the professionals are afraid, it's usually smart to assume that soon thereafter the market will have found a bottom.

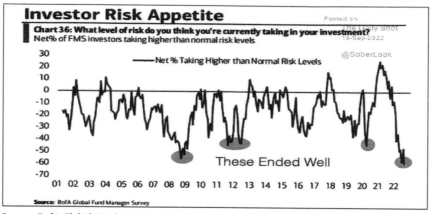

Source: BofA Global Fund Manager Survey
https://www.asiamarkets.com/data-sparks-fears-of-new-gfc/

Economy

The colloquial definition of recession has always been two negative quarters of GDP in a row. Later the NBER will time stamp the quasi-official start and end. The stock market will turn during a recession.

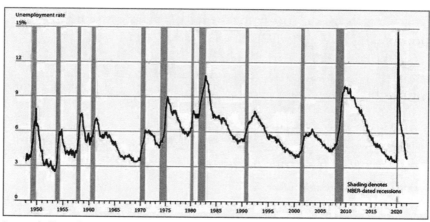

Source: hellenicshippingnews.com
https://www.hellenicshippingnews.com/explainer-what-is-a-recession/

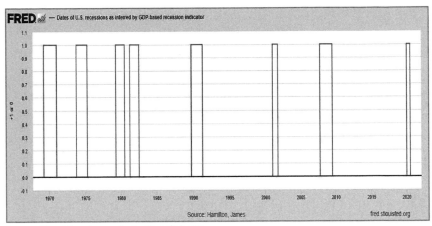

Source: Hamilton, James fred.stlouisfed.org
https://fred.stlouisfed.org/series/JHDUSRGDPBR

Bond Yields and Inflation Rate

It would be simple to say these numbers are your check list to mark the end of the bear market:

- · Decline 33%
- · Days 351
- · 10-year yield 5.0%
- · Inflation rate 4.8%

But that would be too simplistic. A lot depends on starting points. Moreover, the political will for aggressive Fed action has changed dramatically. According to Arthur Burns, Fed Chairman in 1978, there was huge congressional pressure on the Fed to halt rate hikes.

The higher the ten-year yield and inflation rate, the longer the bear market. As yields come down, a move under 3.0% is a buy signal and a move under 2.0% is a screaming buy signal. After a forty-year bull market marked by yields marching lower, I'm not sure where the new low level will be but think we could be moving into a secular bear market in bonds.

That means higher yields.

Keep in mind that bear markets usually do not end until the Federal Reserve has raised Fed funds above the inflation rate. I do not think there is political will to hike rates above 7% or 8%. If that is the case, it might mean hiking them to 5%, or a little higher during worst case scenarios, and waiting for inflation to drift lower.

The sign to watch for from the Fed is lowering the intensity of rate hikes. 75bps to 50bps to 25bps is a bullish trend and might mark a turn that you would want some exposure to.

Peak	Trough	% Decline	# of Days	10 Year Yield	Inflation Rate
5/29/1946	10/9/1946	-26.6%	133	2.2%	3.4%
6/15/1948	6/13/1949	-20.6%	363	2.4%	9.5%
7/15/1957	10/22/1957	-20.7%	99	3.9%	3.3%
12/12/1961	6/26/1962	-28.0%	196	4.1%	0.7%
2/9/1966	10/7/1966	-22.2%	240	4.8%	2.6%
11/29/1968	5/26/1970	-36.1%	543	5.7%	4.7%
1/11/1973	10/3/1974	-48.2%	630	6.5%	3.6%
11/28/1980	8/12/1982	-27.1%	622	12.7%	12.6%
8/25/1987	12/4/1987	-33.5%	101	8.8%	4.3%
3/24/2000	10/9/2002	-49.1%	929	6.3%	3.8%
10/9/2007	3/9/2009	-56.8%	517	4.5%	3.5%
2/19/2020	3/23/2020	-33.9%	33	1.5%	2.3%
1/3/2022	6/13/2022	-21.8%	161	1.7%	7.5%
Averages		-32.7%	351	5.0%	4.8%

Sources: YCharts, Shiller

*Yields and inflation rates from the month stocks peaked

Source: YCharts, Shiller
https://awealthofcommonsense.com/2022/06/increase-your-exposure-to-humility-during-a-bear-market/

Federal Reserve

When bear markets are spurred on by higher Fed fund rates, everyone is looking for the "pivot," which is a change to rate cuts. This is very important since market bottoms often come after the Federal Reserve cuts rates.

Note, this also means the economy is probably still in recession. There will be a major disconnect between the stock market and the economy and many will question out loud "how can the market be moving higher when the economy is still in so much pain?"

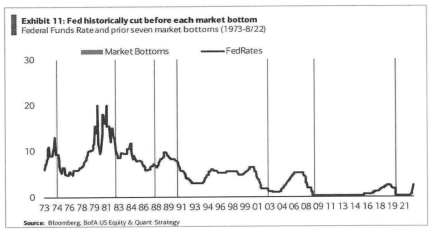

Exhibit 11: Fed historically cut before each market bottom
Federal Funds Rate and prior seven market bottoms (1973-8/22)

Source: Bloomberg, BofA US Equity & Quant Strategy

Source: Bloomberg, BofA US Equity & Quant Strategy
https://seekingalpha.com/article/4543589-high-dividend-yield-is-leading-edge-of-defense-for-us-shares

Why not wait for the bottom to occur and then start buying?

Great question. But it's easier said than done.

Looking back at the 2008-2009 market meltdown, there are important things to note.

Volume peaked during the more dramatic part of the decline. After the low was established in March 2009, volumes proceeded to decline to 2014.

In 2014 the old highs were finally taken out (see the lightning bolt in the chart on the next page) and buyers remerged.

If you had been a buying near the bottom, there would have been some pain. However, by the time the crowd began to buy again your positions would have been substantially higher.

Right now, I think maximum risk near term is 10%, but that's not guaranteed.

I think maximum gain over the next two to three years is 100%+.

I like those odds. Depending on your risk tolerance level you might choose to act sooner rather than wait. If you choose to wait to move, be sure you are zeroing in on some individual stocks of interest so that you are ready to act when the time is right for you.

Some will pop like Albemarle (ALB), which rallied 28% in two weeks, and some might initially languish.

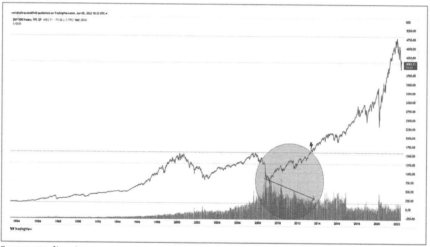

Source: tradingview.com

After doing this for more than three decades, I know most people who cannot endure another 10% decrease in stock market pain are not going to miraculously pick the bottom. On the contrary, they will be on constant guard for the other shoe to drop. Substantial gains will have to be made before they are in their comfort zone.

Inspiration & Motivation

MS & Co. S&P 500 Price Target: Year-End 2022

LANDSCAPE	EARNINGS	PRICE/EARNINGS MULTIPLE	PRICE TARGET	UPSIDE/ DOWNSIDE
Bull Case	$265	18.8	5,000	14.0%
Base Case	$245	18.0	4,400	0.4%
Bear Case	$225	17.2	3,900	-11.1%
Current S&P 500 Price			4,385	

Posted on

ISABELNET.com

Note: Price targets are based on estimated 2023 earnings.
Source: MS & Co. Research as of Feb. 25, 2022

Source: MS & Co. Research as of Feb. 25, 2022

Market Breadth: Measuring Foundational Strength & Weakness

There are several ways to measure market breadth and get a truer read on overall strength than simply looking at the change on major indices.

2021 is one of the worst years ever for one-sided trading as stocks mostly traded in unison. Opening bell rallies fizzled and there were decidedly more daily decliners than advancers.

Advancers Versus Decliners

52-week Highs & Lows

This is the easiest and fastest way to dicern the underlying health of the stock market. It's simple: when there are more 52-week new highs than lows, the market is healthy, and the overall bias is to the upside. When there are more new lows than highs, the underlying health of the market is weak and vulnerable.

Understanding the true health of the market is very important. There are times when just a handful of stocks (less than ten) can rally big and lift major indices like the S&P 500 higher because the indices are weighted to overreact to the stocks with the largest market capitalization.

Be careful when the market is "up" but most stocks are down.

You also want to be on the lookout for extremes. When there are 1000 more new highs or lows rather than lows and highs, it points to extreme fear and anxiety. This is a contrarian indicator of sorts but can last a long time. So, in these circumstances, you want to aggressively sharpen your potential buy list.

But do not force the action.

When there is a shift it's time to start moving on your ideas. I prefer to see two straight weeks of reversals where new highs eclipse new lows. This means the market has already climbed off the lows, but it keeps you from trying to guess the bottom, which is a dangerous proposition.

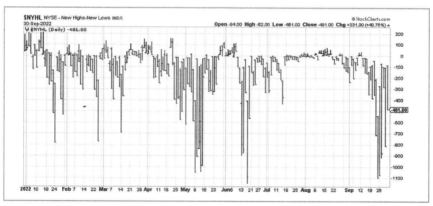

Source: stockcharts.com

Market Volume

I'm a huge fan of volume spikes in individual stocks, coupled with compelling chart formations. But volume is also a very important macro tool. It's ideal for monitoring niches, sectors, and the overall market.

If you are a trader, and not looking at fundamentals at all, then all you would have to do is follow and react to volume. It takes a lot of discipline, but, like professional poker players, this can be easy money. If you are looking to take more substantial, long-term positions or looking for signs to lower risk and even sell, volume-direction is important.

When stocks, sectors, or the broad market is moving higher on increasing volume, you want to be long. If the market is down on lighter than average volume, you might hold onto positions (this is where fundamentals matter). By the same reasoning, if volume is decreasing but the price is moving higher, it's not automatically bullish or bearish, so other factors are important — especially when you have pondered closing a position. Below is a quick reference chart.

Volume Analysis

VOLUME	PRICE	IMPLICATION
Increasing	Rising	Bullish
Decreasing	Falling	Neutral
Increasing	Falling	Bearish
Decreasing	Rising	Neutral

Buying in Bull Market

Buying in a bear market is hard for most investors and impossible for most fence-sitters. It's a dream scenario for the procrastinator and perpetual whiners.

While the most widely known axiom on Wall Street is buy low, sell high, market "pros" are petrified during a bear market.

Ironically, market pros are also petrified during bull markets. Sadly, this overthinking has spread to individual investors who have no professional reputation to worry about but now fear actually being the "dumb money investor" the financial media tries to label them each day.

What many don't understand is that the pros still get paid a lot of money even as they are botching call after call.

What Is a Bull Market?

The textbook definition of a bull market is one that sees the market or an individual stock climb 20% off a recent low. Typically bull markets are sustained periods of upside movement in the underlying market or security.

Note: a security or stock can still be lower over a longer period and still technically be in a bull market. There is a school of thought that likes to see all-time highs before affixing the bull market label.

It's important to know that bull markets last a lot longer than bear markets, and, over a couple hundred years, every bear market has been followed by a bull market and, eventually, new all-time high milestones.

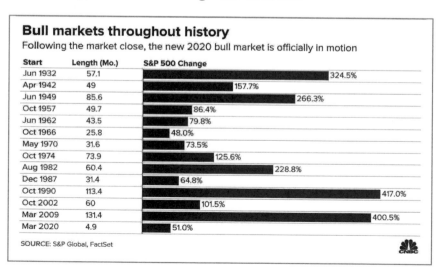

Bull markets throughout history
Following the market close, the new 2020 bull market is officially in motion

Start	Length (Mo.)	S&P 500 Change
Jun 1932	57.1	324.5%
Apr 1942	49	157.7%
Jun 1949	85.6	266.3%
Oct 1957	49.7	86.4%
Jun 1962	43.5	79.8%
Oct 1966	25.8	48.0%
May 1970	31.6	73.5%
Oct 1974	73.9	125.6%
Aug 1982	60.4	228.8%
Dec 1987	31.4	64.8%
Oct 1990	113.4	417.0%
Oct 2002	60	101.5%
Mar 2009	131.4	400.5%
Mar 2020	4.9	51.0%

SOURCE: S&P Global, FactSet

CNBC

There is no doubt that bear markets are painful. But, outside the 1980 bear market, they are simply a function of the market getting ahead of itself and these events are very short-lived. Moreover, the ensuing rally after is typically strong and robust.

Bear markets associated with the implosion of the overall economy are deeper and last longer. These require more investing finesse but at the same time create the best opportunities as stocks become extremely oversold.

The real trick is to avoid being human.

Study after study reveals people feel much more pain from losses than joy for gains. Mitigate the pain of losses with the knowledge the more the market goes down, the richer you could possibly become when the market rebounds.

Focus on the future and how it could change your life.

Bear markets throughout history
The 2020 decline is officially the shortest on record

Start	Length (Mo.)	S&P 500 Change
Sep 1929	32.8	-86.2%
Mar 1937	61.8	-60.0%
May 1946	36.5	-29.6%
Aug 1956	14.7	-21.5%
Dec 1961	6.5	-28.0%
Feb 1966	7.9	-22.2%
Nov 1968	17.8	-36.1%
Jan 1973	20.7	-48.2%
Nov 1980	20.4	-27.1%
Aug 1987	3.3	-33.5%
Jul 1990	2.9	-19.9%
Mar 2000	30.5	-49.1%
Oct 2007	17	-56.8%
Feb 2020	1.1	-33.9%

SOURCE: S&P Global

CNBC

Historically bull markets were tied to an improved and expanding economy. And there is still a correlation to the start of bull markets and the end of recessions.

It is important to remember that the stock market anticipates the economic cycle, which means it begins to move higher during the end of recessions.

RALLY BEGINS	MONTHS PRECEDING END OF RECESSION
March 2020	1
March 2009	3
October 2002	10 after
October 1990	5
August 1982	3

This seems like a nice and easy guide to buy and believe in new bull markets. The only problem is the timestamping of recessions.

It is not done in real time.

The National Bureau of Economic Research (NBER) is tasked with timestamping the business cycle, which includes determining peaks and troughs.

The problem is they always make this determination after the peaks and troughs have been established. There are ways to incorporate the NBER methodology to make assumptions before the actual news, but I haven't seen any real long-term success at that game.

This is why assessing economic data and trends is so important. Yet, keep in mind buying a great stock that is under pressure only means short-term pains.

NBER | NATIONAL BUREAU OF ECONOMIC RESEARCH

Business Cycle Dating Committee Announcements

July 19, 2021 Determination of the April 2020 Trough in US Economic Activity

June 8, 2020 Determination of the February 2020 Peak in US Economic Activity

September 20, 2010 Announcement of June 2009 business cycle trough/end of last recession

April 12, 2010 Memo from the Business Cycle Dating Committee

December 1, 2008 Announcement of December 2007 business cycle peak/beginning of last recession

January 7, 2008 Memo from the Business Cycle Dating Committee

October 21, 2003 Memo from the Business Cycle Dating Committee

July 17, 2003 Announcement of November 2001 business cycle trough/end of last recession

November 26, 2001 Announcement of March 2001 business cycle peak/beginning of last recession

December 22, 1992 Announcement of March 1991 business cycle trough/end of last recession

April 25, 1991 Announcement of July 1990 business cycle peak/beginning of last recession

December 21, 1990 Memo from the Business Cycle Dating Committee

July 8, 1983 Announcement of November 1982 business cycle trough/end of last recession

January 6, 1982 Announcement of July 1981 business cycle peak/beginning of last recession

July 8, 1981 Announcement of July 1980 business cycle trough/end of last recession

June 3, 1980 Announcement of January 1980 business cycle peak/beginning of last recession

But this all gets back to the key problems with buying in a bull market. In the past, one would simply buy during economic expansions. But that means you would be a buyer in the months ahead of economic contraction.

And these days the greatest wildcard is the Federal Reserve. As the Fed moves away from rate hikes, the market will rally. When the Fed initially cuts rates the market will sag, as it's clear there is an economic emergency that won't be built into share prices.

That said, be ready to pounce because corporate America and the stock market love free money — it's like ambrosia for bull markets.

The chart below by Nick Maggiulli highlights how the market initially moved lower in response to rate cuts before moving higher. That's because during those early rate cutting cycles the Fed was trying to put out economic fires (that they often set).

It usually takes three to six months before the economy reacts and before the market shifts gears and direction.

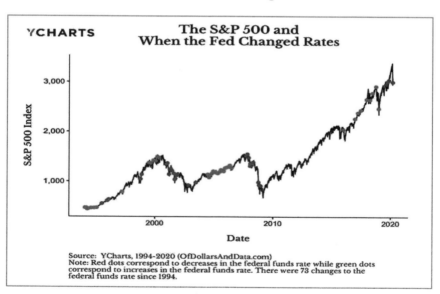

Source: YCharts, 1994-2020 (OfDollarsAndData.com)
Note: Red dots correspond to decreases in the federal funds rate while green dots correspond to increases in the federal funds rate. There were 73 changes to the federal funds rate since 1994.

Rules for Buying in Bull Markets

- You must be in the market - don't get cute and wait for dips or write off the message of the market

- You want to be overweight in parts of the economy that are turning higher

- You want to focus on stocks that are ready to rally hard — forget the foxholes

- You can be nimble when markets are parabolic — going up more than 1% a day several times a week

- You want to avoid over diversification at the start of bull markets — there will be clear leadership

The bottom line is you are never completely out of the market. You will own stocks during bear markets and you will own a lot more during bull markets.

Quiz: Chapter 5

1. **What is a quick and simple way to evaluate the overall health of the market?**

2. **During bear markets it is necessary to avoid being human. Why is that?**

3. **When looking to find a "Windfall" stock there were four things I said you would want to do to know everything about the company. What were they?**

<u>Answers</u>

1. Use the 52-week highs and lows. If there are more highs, the market is generally healthy.

2. Studies show that people react more strongly to the pain of loss than to the pleasure of gain. In bear markets, overreacting to the downside can cause you to miss opportunities as the market begins to turn.

3. Read everything on the founder(s). Read all the filings. Understand the industry. Listen to conference calls.

Investment Vehicles Beyond Stocks

Introduction

In this chapter, I'll introduce you to five investment vehicles that go beyond the stocks in our model portfolio. These strategies do NOT replace the model portfolio approach.

Ideally you should have a diverse investment portfolio. The following mix works for me but, from time to time, I fine-tune it.

- 50% stocks
- 15% Real Estate
- 10% dividends
- 5% Options
- 4% precious metals

- 1% digital
- 5% collectibles (art, antique cars, rare stamps and rare items)
- 10% cash

They're presented here to potentially provide additional diversity to your portfolio. They all have their pros and cons, and before you jump in to any one of these investing vehicles, it's important for you to be educated and to learn if they have a place in your portfolio or not.

The short answer is they do have a place, although the percentages should be on a sliding scale depending on your overall financial well-being and overall goals.

The American Dream, But...

It has been sold as the American dream and there is no denying the feeling of owning a home. It is not the best investment vehicle, however.

Middle-class success is based in debt, which, for the most part, can be the ultimate trap that stops you from attaining real wealth. All those things that say to the world that you have arrived will trip you up for years to come. Borrowing money for the house, car, wedding, vacation rentals, kid's education... those payments are making the 1% richer.

That's not where they have their investments. They have close to 80% of their wealth in financial assets and less than 10% in their primary residence. I want you to be more like the wealthy. It's okay to put off the purchase of your primary home when interest rates are too high or the housing market has been on fire. That said, avoid rent traps. A good FICO score is fine as it points to financial discipline but it is not financial freedom. Not by a long shot.

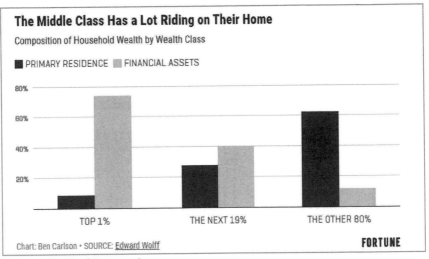

The Middle Class Has a Lot Riding on Their Home

Composition of Household Wealth by Wealth Class

■ PRIMARY RESIDENCE ▨ FINANCIAL ASSETS

Chart: Ben Carlson • SOURCE: Edward Wolff   **FORTUNE**

Source: A Wealth of Common Sense
https://awealthofcommonsense.com/2021/08/how-to-hedge-the-housing-market/

I'm not going to delve into real estate because that is a special investment that has lots of variables and I would do it an injustice. I do urge care as there is no area of investing with more charlatans than in this field (an old tradition that goes back to the selling of swamp land in Florida or the Brooklyn bridge to a million people).

Here's a short overview of the five strategies that will be covered in this chapter:

Options — Options are contracts where a trader either has the right to buy or to sell stock. Option traders can make money in up, down, and sideways markets. Options can be used for speculation, for protection, or for income.

Dividends — A dividend is a sum of money paid from a company's profits or reserves. Not all companies pay dividends. Some investors use dividends to create cash flow. An investor, focused on companies paying dividends, can also be focused on how the companies' stock values are changing. They don't need to focus only on dividend payments, which many do.

Why not double dip and get both stock appreciation and dividends, or even triple dip and get the stock appreciation, the dividends, and income from options?

Precious Metals — Precious metals, such as gold, are scarce, meaning they're finite. There's only so much of it in the world. A country can't just create more like they may do with their own currency. Scarcity makes it useful as a long-term store of value. Investing in precious metals has traditionally been used to hedge portfolios against risks created by war, or by monetary and fiscal policies. The devaluation of a currency or hyperinflation may rapidly reduce the purchasing power of a portfolio, whereas precious metals may bring some stability to the portfolio in these situations.

Digital Assets — Digital assets, including digital currencies such as Bitcoin, are still relatively new. They have the appeal of not being tied to the risks of any country nor its currency. Currently, digital assets are considered speculative and highly volatile. They've been compared to precious metals and to currencies. They may offer similar benefits, too. They have the potential to disrupt the way we currently look at money and so, even if you're not planning on using them, it's important to have a basic understanding.

Antiques & Collectibles

You should never have "old junk" laying around the house. I have never minded spending a lot on liquor, handbags, and toys if I know they would be kept in great condition. This is an area of investing that will only grow exponentially with consignment stores and companies bringing the notion of value to everyday items we once were told had to be thrown away some day. Warning: there is a line between collecting and hoarding. LOL.

- Wine
- Whisky

· Handbags

· Stamps

· Trainers

· Toys

Options

When I began in the business the options market was orderly. Now it is anything but orderly. I suspect the overarching use of options will always be driven by two components.

A) The aftermath of market crashes where investors are trying to get it all back on one swing.

B) The emergence of a sizzling play where it seems their upside will go on forever.

I want to begin with the emergence of the sizzling, can't-miss investment that captures the imagination of the world.

In the 1600s the Netherlands, recently freed from the Spanish empire, began their own efforts to grow wealth and might. The Dutch East India Company was formed and soon began to bring back tulips from Turkey. (Tulips originated in Kazakhstan and were brought to Turkey by the Ottoman Empire.)

Originally, tulips were seen as status symbols for wealthy aristocrats.

As the market expanded so did the need for protection. It is a plant subject to a wide variety of fates, after all. The tulip options market was born.

Hedging:

· Wholesalers bought calls

· Growers bought puts (I'll explain both "calls"

and "puts" later in this chapter.) Soon everyone wanted a piece of the action and not only in Holland. Investors and speculators from all over Europe got in on the act.

There were up to fifteen different kinds of tulips but none more desirable than the Switzer. Considered the most beautiful of them all, the Switzer was radiant and commanded the attention of artists as well as speculators.

Source: The "broken" Semper Augustus tulip as shown in the Brandemandus Tulip Book in the 1600s. PUBLIC DOMAIN

Researchers discovered that prices for these bulbs erupted from December 1636 to February 1637 more than twelve times.

Researchers will downplay the extent investors outside of high society participated in the mania. But the bottom line is the tulip market went bust as an investment vehicle because of out-of-control speculation. Today, Holland is the world leader in tulip production.

I also have to give a shout out to the Japanese for establishing the first option exchange. In the 17th century Japan's elites known as "The Samurai" were paid in rice (just as Roman soldiers were paid in salt and hence the word "salary.") In an effort to make sure their work didn't lose value, they created the Dojima Rice Exchange in 1697.

These days, options trading in the United States is reaching levels normally associated with manias. When I began it was more of an orderly market, sort of like a boxing match governed by Marquis De Queensberry rules. Today options trading is more like MMA fighting with very few rules.

Options Volume Has Gone Off the Rails

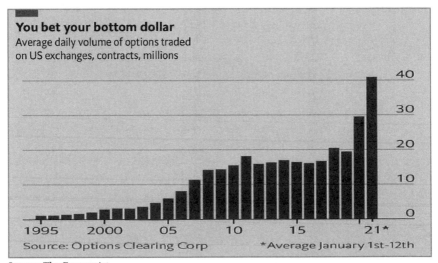

You bet your bottom dollar
Average daily volume of options traded on US exchanges, contracts, millions

Source: Options Clearing Corp   *Average January 1st-12th

Source: The Economist
https://www.economist.com/finance-and-economics/2021/01/16/why-everyone-is-now-an-options-trader

Driving all of this are options that expire daily and the emergence in popularity of zero-day-to-expiration options. Think about this for a moment — these options have a life span that's shorter than a housefly and they have become all the rage.

There are advanced strategies for playing these kinds of options, including hedging. The fact of the matter is the volume is too great to "blame" it on novice retail investors. The returns can be awesomely mindboggling, like buying tulips in the Netherlands in late November 1637.

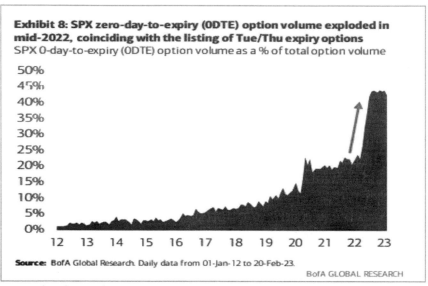

Exhibit 8: SPX zero-day-to-expiry (0DTE) option volume exploded in mid-2022, coinciding with the listing of Tue/Thu expiry options
SPX 0-day-to-expiry (0DTE) option volume as a % of total option volume

Source: BofA Global Research. Daily data from 01-Jan-12 to 20-Feb-23.

BofA GLOBAL RESEARCH

Source: Bloomberg, BofA Global Research

The main reasons for trading options, however, haven't changed.

So, Why Do People Trade Options?

Who wouldn't want to increase their options for trading in the market (pun intended) and be able to make money regardless of whether the market is going up, down, or sideways? Some love seeing a potential stock move coming and being able to make a higher percentage return than if they were only trading the stock. Because option strategies are so flexible, they may also be used to take advantage of a market that's going sideways or down.

In addition to taking advantage of markets that are going up, down, or sideways, some may see risk with their stock positions or their portfolio and will use options as insurance. They want to have peace of mind when there's a turbulent stock market or individual stock. And yet, others are looking for ways to bring in extra capital on a regular basis; they're looking for income. Each of these are compelling reasons why people trade options.

Let me give you a quick example of how an option trade performed, as reported in the track record of my Model Portfolio Alert service. I'll compare it to how the stock performed over that same time frame. Keep in mind, this is not a recommendation and no guarantee of what you'll be able to do consistently. You don't even need to understand the details of it yet. That's why we have this section on options. I'm giving it as an example to demonstrate the power of leverage you can have with trading options. I've had trades that didn't work out, too. Leverage is a knife that cuts both ways.

The following option was purchased on Friday, held for just over a week, and sold the following Monday, netting a profit of 37.85%.

Report: Buy AAL230915C00013000 (AAL)				
Action	Date/Time	Price	P/L $	P/L %
Buy	4/28/2023 1:55:25 PM	$1.77	$0.00	
Sell	5/8/2023 9:34:51 AM	$2.44	$0.67	
Trade Summary			$0.67	37.85%

Over that same time frame, the stock went from $13.49 to $14.38. This would have been a $0.89 profit on the stock, but because the stock costs more, it would have been a lower return on the investment. It would have been a 6.60% profit. That's still not a bad trade for just over a week, but the option made over five times the return than the stock would have made.

What Are Options?

To learn how options are used for speculation, hedging, and income, it's important to understand what options are and to learn more about option terminology. For many, this may be a lot to take in at one time, but it'll be worth it. It might take more than one time to read through this section for it to start to sink in. Please be patient with yourself. Just about everyone has a hard time with these concepts the first time they're exposed to them. It's very much like drinking from a firehose.

Contracts Between a Buyer and a Seller

Let's start by describing what options are. Options are simply contracts between two parties where one party has a right and the other party has an obligation. The two parties are known as either the buyer or the seller of the option contract. The option buyer is also known as the holder of the option contract, whereas the option seller is also known as the writer. Buyers have rights and sellers have obligations. It may seem obvious but I'm going to say it anyway: buyers pay money and sellers receive money.

There are two main types of options, also known as option classes: calls and puts.

- If a call is purchased, it gives the buyer the **right** to buy or "*call* the stock away from" the other party, the seller.

- If a put is purchased, it gives the buyer the **right** to sell or "*put* the stock to" the other party, the seller.

Let me repeat that in a different way.

- The *buyer* of a <u>call</u> has the **right to buy** the stock and the *seller* of the call has the **obligation to sell** the stock.

- The *buyer* of a <u>put</u> has the **right to sell** the stock, and the *seller* of the put has the **obligation to buy** the stock.

This can be represented in the following table and images:

OPTIONS	BUYER Has the <u>RIGHT</u> but not the obligation to:	SELLER Has the <u>OBLIGATION</u> but not the right to:
CALL	Buy the stock	Sell the stock
PUT	Sell the stock	Buy the stock

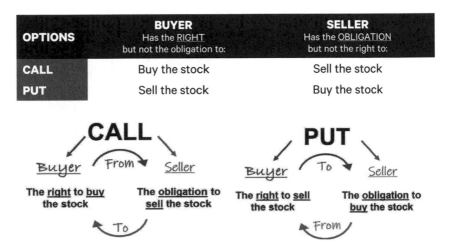

If you are the buyer of a call or the seller of a put, you want the stock price to go up. If you are the buyer of the put or the seller of the call, you want the price of the stock to go down.

There's more to an option contract than just the right (or obligation) to buy (or sell) the stock. If you have a brokerage account, then you can already trade stocks. You don't need an option to trade stocks in the stock market. So, what makes options so special? Once the other terms of the option contract are discussed and we cover more about option terminology, it will start to make more sense and you'll start to see the possibilities of trading options.

Option Terms

Underlying and Derivative

Options in the stock market can be based on stocks, Exchange Traded Funds (ETFs), or Indices. Collectively, the stock, ETF, or Index that the option is based on, is known as the underlying instrument, or simply known as the underlying. An option is known as a derivative because it derives part of its value based on the price of the underlying.

Expiration Dates

Option contracts, just like a coupon or insurance, have an expiration date. They don't last forever. The more time an option has before it expires, the more expensive it will be. It used to be that the only options available on an underlying would be those listed with an expiration date for the third Friday of the month. Limiting the number of options available through having fewer expiration dates will maintain a higher level of liquidity for those options that are listed, which, in turn, helps with the effectiveness of trading options.

As options gained popularity, many underlyings were traded enough that they could have options expiring every Friday, not just the third Friday of the month. The additional options expiring on Friday are known as weekly options, whereas those expiring on the third Friday are known as regular options. The difference between the expiration dates is that sometimes the regular options have more liquidity, meaning it's easier to get in and out of the option trade with better pricing. The main point to remember is that all options have an expiration date.

Strike Price

The buyer of an option has the right to trade the underlying at a specific price. This is known as the strike price. The standard option contract represents the right to trade 100 shares of the underlying. If a company has gone through a stock split or other corporate action affecting the shares of the stock, the option contracts could potentially be adjusted.

Each underlying that offers options will have both calls and puts available. They will have multiple expiration dates and multiple strike prices to choose from. Each option is unique. If someone were to buy a specific option, they cannot choose an option with different terms to sell to close out of it. They need to sell the exact same option to close it out.

Unique Symbol

An example might be a call option on Apple that expires January 17, 2025, with a strike price of $175. Many brokers now hide the nomenclature of the option symbol to simplify it for the option trader but will list the details of the option instead. An example of the option symbol for this option might look like the following:

.AAPL250117C175 or AAPL250117C00175000, or even .AAPL170125C175

Within this option symbols is listed the ticker symbol of the stock, the two-digit code for the year, the two-digit code for the month, the two-digit code for the day, the one letter code for a call or a put, and the strike price of the option. The date might be listed in a different order. These details identify the option from other options.

Premium

An option will list a bid price and an ask price (also known as an offer price). The bid price is referenced for someone wanting to sell the option, the ask price is referenced for someone wanting to buy the option, just like they do for selling or buying the stock. The difference between these two prices is known as the bid/ask spread. It's preferable that these two prices are close to each other. The price that someone buys or sells the option for is known as the <u>premium</u>.

Option Pricing

Since the goal is to make money, it's important for us to be aware of some of the key influences on an option's price. Again, an option is known as a derivative because it derives part of its value from the underlying. Here are a few factors of the underlying that influence the option's price:

1. **Trading volume** — If the volume of the underlying is high, then, usually, the options also have high trading volume. When this happens there's more competition to get a good price, whether that's buying or selling. This, in turn, creates a smaller bid/ask spread. If there's a lot of option trading, we say that the options are liquid.

2. **Price** — The price of the option tends to be greater when the price of the underlying is higher. For example, an option on a $500 stock will be more expensive than an option on a $50 stock.

3. **Volatility** — Some stocks have a lot of volatility; they tend to move up and down a lot more than other stocks. When this is the case, there's more demand for the options. More demand means higher prices.

Other factors influencing the price of the option would include:

1. **Speculation on the underlying** — If there's a lot of buying of the options, it's probably because option traders are collectively expecting there to be high volatility in the stock. This is basic supply and demand at work on the options themselves. The more traders want to buy the options, the higher the price will be in order to have a balance between

buyers and sellers. In fact, the amount at which the options are priced implies what the stock's future volatility will be. You can probably guess what this is called. It's called implied volatility.

2. **Time** — If there were no time at all before the option expired, then there would be no way to speculate on how much the price of the underlying would change. If there's a lot of time between now and when the option expires, there's more time for the underlying to go up or down in value.

Option Greeks

Option Greeks describe the impact that different factors have on the price of an option. Some of them have less impact on the change in the option price while others have more. Option Greeks can be viewed when looking at an option table. Let's focus on the two most followed option Greeks:

1. **Delta** — Delta reflects the change of the options value based on a $1 move of the underlying.

2. **Theta** — Theta reflects the change in the value of the option contract for one day that passes, all the way up to the option contract's expiration. This is also known as "*time decay.*"

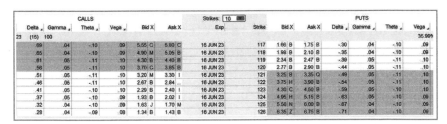

The image above shows an <u>option chain</u>. The expiration date and the strike price are listed in the middle. Calls are listed on the left and puts are listed on the right.

Let's focus on the top row for the call. It shows a Delta of .69. When talking about the value of the Delta, it's usually stated without the decimal. We'd say the June 16th, 117 strike has a Delta of 69. If the stock were to go up $1.00 the option would increase by 69 cents.

That same call option has a Theta of -.10. Like the Delta, it's usually stated as having a Theta of 10. Both the negative sign and the decimal are dropped in speech. It's negative because time decay is always reducing the value of options.

The same convention applies to the Greeks for the puts. The decimal is dropped in speech and so is the negative sign, unless we're drawing specific attention to the fact that it is negative.

So, what can we learn about calls and puts when looking at the Delta and Theta for them? Calls make money when the stock goes up, puts make money with the stock goes down. Time decay erodes the value of both calls and puts. If the stock moves more in your favor than what is lost with time decay, the trade is likely to make money.

Most option chains, that's the name of all the options listed for an underlying, will list other option Greeks. Just so you know but not to focus on them here, Gamma reflects the change in the option's Delta for a $1 move of the underlying. Vega reflects the rate of change in the value of the option contract for a one-point change in volatility.

Buy-to-Open and Sell-to-Close

When an option trader starts out with a new position by **buying** the option, it's known as a buy-to-open order. This is also known as a long option. You might hear the term, "long call,' or 'long put." These terms just mean that the option was purchased. After an option is purchased, the buyer has three actions he or she can take.

1. **Sell-to-close the position**. The difference between what it was bought for and sold for will create a profit or a loss. This is the most common action when trading options.

2. **Exercise the option**. Remember that the buyer of a call has the right to buy the stock and the buyer of a put has the right to sell the stock. When they decide to follow through with this right, it's known as exercising the option.

3. **Let it expire**. I'll explain what the following terms mean, afterwards. You may want to reread this next paragraph after the terms are defined. If the option is one penny or more in-the-money (ITM) at the time of expiration, by default the broker assumes you want to exercise the option and will exercise it for you, unless you give them specific instructions to "do not exercise (DNE)." If it's out-of-the money (OTM) then it will expire worthless. Again, I'll explain these two terms soon, so you understand this better.

Sell-to-Open and Buy-to-Close

When an option trader starts out a new position by **selling** the option, it's known as a sell-to-open order. This is also known as a short option. You might hear the term, "short call," or "short put." These terms just mean the option was sold. After an option is sold as a new position, the seller has three possible outcomes.

1. **Buy-to-close the position**. The difference between what it was sold for and bought for will create a profit or a loss. We always want to buy low and sell high for

a profit. It just happens to be that we're selling first in this situation. Buying-to-close can only be done if the option has not already been assigned.

2. **The option may be assigned**. Remember that the seller of a call has the obligation to sell the stock and the seller of a put has the obligation to buy the stock. Since the seller has the obligation, they don't have a choice about whether this happens or not. They're not the one in control; the buyer of the option is the one with the right to exercise the option or not.

3. **Let it expire**. If the option is one penny or more ITM at the time of expiration, the option is most likely to be assigned. If it is OTM, then the option is most likely to expire worthless. I say the option is most "likely to happen," to be assigned, when it expires ITM because the buyer of an option may give instructions to their broker to "do not exercise." If you happen to randomly be paired up with the person who gives these instructions, you won't be assigned. This scenario seldom happens, but it can. Most of the time it does exactly what you'd expect. When it reaches expiration, if the option is ITM, the option is assigned. If the option is OTM, the option expires worthless.

In-the-Money (ITM), At-the-Money (ATM), and Out-of-the-Money (OTM)

The third possibility listed earlier for both the buyer and the seller of an option has to do with an option that is held until the expiration date. It's now time to define the following terms: in-the-money (ITM), out-of-the-money (OTM), and at-the-money (ATM).

In-the-Money (ITM)

An ITM call option is where the stock price is above the strike price. For example, if the stock price is at $50 while the strike price is at $45, then the call is ITM.

In-the-Money (ITM) Call:

When the Stock Price > Strike Price, then it's ITM.
The strike price is at a better price for buying the stock; therefore, the option is ITM.

Stock Price	$50
Strike Price	- $45
Amount the option is ITM:	$5

Think of it this way: a call option gives the buyer of that call the right to buy stock at the strike price. Which would you rather spend for the stock, the strike price of $45 or the stock price of $50? I would rather pay less. Since this happens to be the strike price, it's considered ITM. In fact, it's ITM by $5 ($50 stock - $45 strike).

The formula is a little different for a put option because we're no longer talking about buying the stock, but rather selling the stock. An ITM put option is where the stock price is below the strike price. For example, if the stock price is at $50 while the strike price is at $55, then the put is ITM.

In-the-Money (ITM) Put:

When the Stock Price < Strike Price, then it's ITM.
The strike price is at a better price for selling the stock; therefore, the option is ITM.

Strike Price	$55
Stock Price	- $50
Amount the option is ITM:	$5

Think about it, a put option gives the buyer of that put the right to sell stock at the strike price. Which would you rather sell it for, the strike price of $55 or the stock price of $50? I would rather sell it for as much as I can. Since the strike price is a better price for selling the stock, this option is considered ITM. In fact, it's ITM by $5 ($55 strike - $50 stock).

The reason that an ITM option is exercised automatically at expiration is because it can be traded at a better price than just letting it expire. If it's not exercised and were to just expire, the value of the option would be gone too.

Out-of-the-Money (OTM)

An OTM call option is where the stock price is below the strike price. For example, if the stock price is at $50 while the strike price is at $55, then the call is out-of-the-money.

Out-of-the-Money (OTM) Call:

When the Stock Price < Strike Price, then it's OTM.
The stock price is at a better price for buying the stock; therefore, the option is OTM.

Stock Price	$50
Strike Price	- $55
Amount the option is OTM:	- $5

You could ask the same question as mentioned with ITM options: which would you rather spend for the stock, the strike price, or the stock price? In this case, the current stock price is a better price to pay when compared to the strike price. When it's better to trade based on the stock price, then the option is considered OTM. It saves money to buy it in the open market rather than using the option to buy the stock.

An OTM put option is where the stock price is above the

strike price. For example, if the stock price is $50 while the strike price is $45, then the put is OTM.

Out-of-the-Money (OTM) Put:	
When the Stock Price > Strike Price, then it's OTM. The stock price is at a better price for selling the stock; therefore, the option is OTM.	
Strike Price	$45
Stock Price	- $50
Amount the option is OTM:	- $5

Again, think about it, a put option gives the buyer of that put the right to sell the stock. Which would you rather sell the stock for, the strike price of $45 or the stock price of $50? Since the stock price would bring in more money when selling the stock, the option is considered OTM.

At-the-Money (ATM)

The option with the strike price closest to the current price of the stock is considered ATM. There are times when this specific option needs to be referenced. The ATM option is usually also either ITM, or OTM. The only time it's not also considered ITM or OTM is when the stock price and the strike price are the same price.

Intrinsic Value and Extrinsic Value

The amount by which an option is in-the-money is the same thing as the intrinsic value, and it's not the only value that it has. Any additional value is called extrinsic value, or time value. It's called time value because it goes away once the option is at the expiration.

For example, when the stock is at $50 and a call option is at $45, it has $5 of intrinsic value. If that option has a few months before expiration, it might have a premium of $8. Both the amount of the intrinsic value and the premium are needed to calculate the amount of extrinsic value. In this example, the difference between the premium and intrinsic value is the extrinsic value of $3. ($8 - $5).

A Couple of Analogies

So, is your head exploding yet? Take a deep breath. You're probably doing better than you think you are. I wouldn't be surprised if you decide to read through this information again. It's a lot to take in. I'm going to give a couple of analogies to help explain calls and puts. These analogies will also help introduce you to a few other key option terminologies.

A Call Is Like a Real Estate Option

I'm using this example of a real estate option because many of us have purchased a home or have, at least, thought about it. Let's say that you found a house that you really like but you're not ready to buy it just yet, nor is the owner of the house ready to sell it yet, unless he can get a really good price for it. In this analogy, the house is currently worth $450,000.

You'd like to have the opportunity to buy it any time between now and two years from now. You know the owner isn't willing to sell it for the current market value, but he is willing to write a contract allowing you to buy it for $500,000, if you are also willing to give him $20,000 to lock in that price for the next two years. The house owner would then net a total of $520,000 ($500k from selling the house and $20k from the contract) if you decide to buy the house.

If the house is never purchased, he's still getting $20,000 out of the deal. He likes the terms and so do you.

You have a right to buy the house, and he has an obligation to sell it. You paid him for this right, and if you do not buy the house, he keeps the $20,000.

Are You Starting To See Some Similarities To Calls?

In this analogy, the house is the "underlying," the contract is a "derivative," because it derives part of its value based on the house. The two years determines a specific "expiration date," $500,000 is the "strike price," and the $20,000 is the "premium." You are "buying-to-open" the contract and the homeowner is "writing" the contract so they are "selling-to-open." You have a 'right,' they have an 'obligation,' and the contract is written up. It's "out-of-the-money" because the "strike price" is greater than the house price.

You have three choices at this point:

1. Trade your contract with someone else to either make money or to not lose the full $20,000 you paid for it,

2. "Exercise" the contract and buy the home, or

3. Let it expire, worthless.

This strategy is known as <u>buying a long call</u> for speculation.

What about the homeowner? What can they do?

1. Buy back the contract from you to get out of the terms (this might be at a gain or a loss),

2. Fulfill on their obligation (sell the home for $500,000), or

3. After two years, the contract might expire worthless, thus keeping the $20,000 (and still own the home) for having agreed to the contract.

This strategy is known as selling a covered call.

A Put Is Like An Insurance Policy (Contract)

Let's keep using a house example. Let's say you own a home worth $450,000 and you buy insurance for one year. Your insurance company (at least in this example) allows you to purchase insurance for different amounts and you decide to buy insurance that is worth $400,000. You'll pay $5,000 for this one year's worth of protection. If your house burns down, the insurance company will buy your home from you for $400,000 so you can go build a new home.

We now have enough to draw a comparison like we did with the call option. In this analogy, the house is the "underlying," the contract is a "derivative," the one year of insurance determines a specific "expiration date," and $400,000 is the "strike price." You are "buying-to-open" the contract, and the insurance company is "writing" the contract, so they are "selling-to-open." You have a "right," they have an "obligation," and the contract is written up. It's "out-of-the-money" because the strike price of $400,000 is less than the current house price of $450,000.

You probably hope that the house doesn't burn down and that the purpose of the insurance was just for peace of mind. You'd rather lose the full premium and see the value of the house continue to go up. If something does happen to the house and it drops in value a lot, the insurance will have been worth it.

This analogy is like someone buying a put to protect their stock. This is known as a protective put. Sometimes investors will buy a put on an index or an ETF that most closely mirrors their portfolio to hedge risk on their portfolio.

If you were the insurance company instead and had cash to buy the home, then this analogy would be like someone selling a put with enough cash to buy the stock. This strategy is known as selling a cash covered put or cash secured put.

If, on the other hand, you didn't own the home and you bought the insurance for speculation, the value of the policy would still most likely increase when the value of the home drops. You could then sell the policy, hopefully for a profit. You could also end up letting it expire worthless. This strategy is known as buying a long put for speculation.

Five Single-Leg Option Strategies

Here's a summary of five strategies that were mentioned while giving the analogies, three buying strategies and two selling strategies. Using one option, regardless of the number of contracts bought or sold, is known as a single-leg option strategy.

1. Buy a call for speculation.

2. Buy a put for speculation.

3. Buy a put for protection (also known as hedging).

4. Sell a cash secured put for income. This is done when the put is sold and there's enough cash reserved to buy the stock if required to do so.

5. Sell a covered call for income. This is done when the call is sold and there's enough stock in the account to sell if required to do so.

More complex option strategies can be traded by combining more than one option at the same time. These are known as multi-leg option strategies. For example, a trader might buy a call and sell a call at the same time. The two options might have the same or different expiration dates. They might also have the same or different strike prices. I don't want to get too complex here in this chapter but want to acknowledge them because you might hear different names for other option strategies.

Some example names you might hear are: vertical spread, calendar spread, butterfly, iron condor, etc. They're basically built using some of the earlier strategies mentioned as building blocks.

I believe that understanding and gaining experience with single-leg option strategies, before making them more complex with multi-leg option strategies, will build a solid foundation of understanding. A trader does not need to master all option strategies to be effective.

Education

As I mentioned, learning options is like drinking from a firehose at first. I know I gave you a lot of information to digest. I covered how options are used for speculation, hedging, and income. I explained a lot of other relevant concepts from rights and obligations, and intrinsic and extrinsic value, to the option Greeks, and more. Now that you have this high-level overview of options, if you'd like to learn more, **I want you to know that my team and I offer option education that covers more practical applications of these concepts. I have instructors with decades of practical experience in trading options, who specialize in simplifying concepts, and give practical examples, giving you the confidence needed to trade options.**

Dividends

When Do Companies Pay Dividends?

Companies love to create value for their shareholders. Typically, when a company is relatively young, they need all the money they can get. They take the money they have from profits and invest it back into the business. For example, they may use their profits to invest in research and development to keep a competitive edge. They may use money to market their products or services to create more awareness and, thereby, create future revenue and earnings growth. Business activity tends to increase the value of the stock.

If investors believe the company is stable and will continue to grow, they tend to be more willing to invest in the company. Eventually, a company may not feel like it needs to hold on to all the funds they're bringing in and they want to reward shareholders. Typically, a company will do this when the returns from investing back into the business start to diminish. This is why, historically, older and larger companies with a strong cash flow pay out dividends. While these companies often have slower revenue growth, the amounts taken in are substantial and usually shared generously with shareholders.

Companies reward shareholders in two ways. The first is through buying back outstanding shares. Buying back shares makes the ownership pool smaller, hence each remaining share becomes more valuable. The other way they reward shareholders is through paying out a dividend.

A <u>dividend</u> is a distribution, usually in the form of cash, from the company to the shareholders. The most common schedule for paying out a dividend is on a quarterly basis, and they're paid out of profits or reserves.

Why Might Someone Look for Stocks with Dividends?

Market participation includes all types of investors, including those who aren't as concerned with growing their principal investment. These types of investors care more about the steady cash flow created by dividends and underplay the significance of what their principal investment is doing. The daily, weekly, monthly, and even the yearly changes in the share price don't matter as much to them. I believe this is right for a small pool of investors, although millions have been misled into believing they belong in this category.

That said, there's room for a steady dividend yield in every portfolio. The kind of exposure you take on is not only determined by your personal investment goals and risk tolerance, but also by market conditions and macro risk factors.

The <u>dividend yield</u> for your portfolio is calculated by dividing the annual dividend payment by your cost basis for the stock. The current dividend yield listed on market sites uses the current price of the stock, and so the yield will change as the price of the stock changes. Increasing dividend payments increases the dividend yield for both those who already own the stock and those who are looking to purchase the stock. Lower stock market prices only help improve the dividend yield for those who haven't already bought into the stock, or for those looking to add more to their stock position. Once you own the stock, it's better if the stock increases in value.

We want to have a high <u>total return</u>, which includes changes in the value of the investment distributions, such as dividends or coupons, and includes the changes in the stock itself. Who wouldn't want to double dip or triple dip and have both a good dividend payment, stock appreciation, and, possibly, income from options?

The financial industry has sold investing households too many dividend and yield products, under the guise of diversification. These products add more risk to portfolios than imagined. I know because I've gone over thousands of investment portfolios chock-full of dividend and yield funds.

These funds are often redundant, and many get confusing when they veer off into certain foreign assets or other investments. There is no reason for investors to settle for owning stocks with high yields when the company's share prices are moving lower. It negates the goal of investing.

Dividend Payout Ratio

When evaluating a company to consider it for the dividend, you might want to review its dividend payout ratio. The dividend payout ratio is the percentage of a company's net income that is paid out to shareholders as dividends. The percentage that isn't paid out to shareholders is called the retention ratio. An investor who is interested in knowing if the company is likely to be able to keep paying out the current dividend needs to look at the dividend payout ratio.

Just because a company is paying out more than its earnings doesn't mean it can't keep paying out the dividend at its current rate. There may be macro issues that are believed to be temporary. It's ok for a company to pay dividends from its reserves. However, if a company is taking out loans to meet the dividend payments, you might want to investigate further into how the company is doing, to make sure it's a temporary issue. A dividend payout ratio of 30-60% is considered healthy.

Dividend Reinvestment Plan (DRIP)

If you're looking to own the stock for the dividend but don't want or need the payments yet, you might want to make sure it has a dividend reinvestment plan (DRIP), which takes any dividend payments received and automatically reinvests them back into purchasing additional shares of that stock. You would simply ask your broker to activate that feature for you. Your broker might allow you to make this change online without you calling them. Some stocks do not offer a DRIP, but your broker might still offer it in-house for you as a benefit.

Four Dividend Dates

There are four dates commonly associated with a dividend payment. The first is the declaration date, which is when the company declares they will pay a dividend. The board of directors for the company decides on a date when you must be on the company's records as a shareholder. This is known as the record date.

Currently, stock trades settle in two trading days, so a person needs to own the stock two trading days prior to be listed as an owner on the record date. Luckily, we don't have to remember this since the Securities and Exchange Commission sets the ex-dividend date, which is the date where it's too late to receive the declared dividend. The ex-dividend date is the date most people pay attention to because it's the date that determines if you'll get the dividend or not. You need to own it the day before and not sell out until the ex-dividend date to be paid the dividend.

The final date is the pay date, which is the date you get paid the dividend. You don't need to still own the stock by the pay date. If you're listed as an owner-of-record, then you'll receive the payment.

Where to Look for Dividend Paying Stocks

There are many places to look for stocks to invest in that pay dividends. The first source we'll consider is the dividend aristocrat list. These are companies found on the S&P 500 that have consistently paid dividends every year and increased the size of the payout for at least the last twenty-five years.

Being on this list implies that they're a large company that consistently pays dividends and can weather bad financial markets, at least the ones that existed over the past twenty-five years. Past performance is not a guarantee of future results or returns but it's a good place to start looking. To find this list, simply do an internet search for "dividend aristocrats."

The Dogs of the Dow is our next list to consider. The Dow Jones Industrial Average, or just "Dow" for short, includes thirty widely watched stocks. A committee selects which stocks to include, and they exclude companies in the industrial and utility sectors. The Dogs of the Dow are the ten highest dividend yielding stocks at the end of the last trading day in December. The high dividend yields may be due to dropping stock prices.

Just because a stock is on this list is no guarantee that it will perform well next year. There might be a legitimate reason why the stock is priced low, and, therefore, the dividend yield is currently high. On the other hand, the company might still be financially sound and offering higher than average dividend yields. To find this list, simply do an internet search for "Dogs of the Dow."

The concept can also be applied any time of the year by pulling up the list of Dow 30 stocks and sorting by the current dividend yield, even if it's not officially on the lists created from the end of the year. Additionally, any list of stocks on an index could be used to find high-paying dividend stocks.

Precious Metals

A History of Gold and of the U.S. Currency

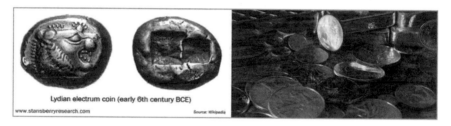

Lydian electrum coin (early 6th century BCE)
www.stansberryresearch.com   Source: Wikipedia

It's helpful to know a little history before I get into talking about investing in precious metals and even the next section on digital assets.

Precious metals are both rare and economically valuable and have been around for a long time. Gold and silver have served as currency for thousands of years. The first notable time the world minted them as an official coin was back around 600 BCE with King Alyattes of Lydia, which is part of present-day Turkey. These coins were made from electrum, an alloy of gold and silver, and had an image of a roaring lion's head on one side, which was a symbol of Lydian kings. The other side was left with the imprint from the pounding of the hammer to create them.

I want to share a short history of gold as it pertains to the U.S. dollar, showing how it was backed by gold and later decoupled from it. This is important to understand because it shows how money was tied to the value of gold and vice versa. It also shows how it's currently a viable asset in which to invest.

Britain was the first nation state to adopt the gold standard and to print promissory notes giving the holders of the notes the right to the gold held in reserve. This was done as early as 1717. This is another way of saying that the paper bill was backed by a physical asset, in this case, gold. The notes were easier to carry around than the actual gold coins, which facilitated the ease with which commerce could transact business. In 1792, the coinage act established the U.S. dollar as legal tender and was introduced on par with the Spanish-American silver dollar.

The U.S. dollar was set on a bimetallic standard of gold and silver beginning in 1879, other than for a period when there was an embargo on gold exports during World War I. In 1900, Congress passed the Gold Standard Act, making the gold dollar the official unit of currency.

U.S. CONSUMER PRICES WERE MOST STABLE ON THE GOLD STANDARD

ANNUAL CPI FOR DIFFERENT PERIODS

	AVERAGE	STANDARD DEVIATION	MINIMUM	MAXIMUM
1789-1996	1.38	5.70	-17.06	22.45
1789-1859	-0.10	5.88	-17.06	18.23
1879-1913	-0.02	1.98	-4.74	4.53
1914-1996	3.33	5.13	-11.47	16.29
1914-1941	1.40	7.16	-11.47	16.29
1946-1996	4.25	3.26	-1.25	13.62

Note: Figures are taken from a Federal Reserve Bank of St. Louis report published in 1998.
Sources: Bureau of Labor Statistics, Federal Reserve Bank of St. Louis, U.S. Global Investors

This listed table shows that the period where paper money was not separate from gold but was fully convertible, was the most stable, compared to the other periods.

During the Great Depression of the 1930s, the public began hoarding gold. In 1931, Britain had dropped their gold standard, which is to say that the currency couldn't be converted back into gold.

In March of 1933, President Roosevelt ordered all banks to stop payment in the form of gold and to not export it. On April 5, 1933, he ordered all gold coins and gold certificates in denominations greater than $100 to be turned in for other money by May 1, 1933, using the set price of gold at $20.67 per ounce. Two months later, Congress did away with the gold clauses in many public and private obligations that required debtors to repay in gold dollars of the same weight and fineness as those borrowed.

In 1934, the price of gold was increased to $35 per ounce, effectively increasing the value of gold on the Federal Reserve's balance sheets, after they had taken a greater position on gold. This was done to increase the money supply and, thereby, create inflation to fight the current economic recession.

In 1971, President Nixon announced that the U.S. would no longer convert dollars to gold at a fixed value, which was intended to be a temporary injunction. In 1974, President Ford signed legislation that permitted Americans to hold gold bullion once again.

In 1976, the "temporary" injunction to no longer convert the dollar into gold became permanent. This is the official beginning of the U.S. currency becoming a fiat currency, meaning that there is no physical asset backing up the value of the dollar, but rather it's maintained by the public's faith in the country's central bank and government.

What I hope you get from this history lesson is a sense of how gold has intricately been tied to the value of currencies initially, and to get a sense of why it still holds value, in part because of its use, historically, as money.

Pros and Cons to Investing in Precious Metals.

Let's now turn our attention specifically to investing in precious metals. It has several pros and cons. Understanding the pros and cons will help you know when investing in them might make sense for you. I believe there can be a place for precious metals in an investment portfolio, but typically recommend only investing 5% or less of your portfolio in precious metals.

You've probably heard ads on TV or the radio encouraging you to invest in gold. Those same ads were probably trying to cause fear or concern about our nation's economy or the world's economy, about wars, or just fear about the future in general. They often focus on how gold is used to protect financial portfolios from extreme catastrophes. That's because investing in precious metals has traditionally been viewed as a "flight to safety," and there are reasons for this.

Pros of Precious Metals

Precious metals are tangible assets, which hold value beyond just being an investment. For example, they're used in dentistry, aerospace, arthritis and other medical treatment, computers, jewelry, etc. They're used regardless of whether the economy is doing well or not.

Another top reason for investing in precious metals is because of their tendency to serve as a hedge against inflation. Precious metals are a scarce resource, a limited asset. The dollar can be printed as much as the government sees fit to do so. The dollar may buy less than it used to, while precious metals appear to be increasing in price. In other words, they're a hedge against inflation. Because of this, it's viewed as an alternative to holding currencies such as the U.S. dollar. Additionally, a distrust in how national governments run may lead to more demand for precious metals.

Precious metals are relatively liquid, meaning it's easy to trade them for cash. This is probably the case, in part, because currencies used to be backed by gold. They also provide diversity to a portfolio, since they don't always move in tandem with how the stock market is moving.

Cons of Precious Metals

There's typically a cost to buying, selling, shipping, storing, and insuring precious metals. For example, typical fees for buying gold could range from 1-3% and, when it's time to sell, there might be another fee around 1-2% for doing so, not to mention there might be a bid and ask price difference. If it's shipped to you, there will be a cost for shipping and for insurance while it's being shipped. Once it's within your possession there is also a risk of theft. If you don't have it shipped to you, there will likely be a storage fee of around 0.5% annually.

Keep in mind that if you were to buy precious metals and were to sell them far into the future, for example in ten years, the fees would play only a very small role in the decision. But investing directly into precious metals seems to only make sense if you're an investor, not a trader.

Other cons could include the fact that they don't pay dividends like stocks might, nor do they pay interest payments like fixed assets might. When they're held for more than a year and sold at a profit, they're taxed as a collectible, which is typically more than capital gains. If held for less than a year, they're taxed as ordinary income.

A new threat to owning precious metals is now on the horizon. Cryptocurrency is viewed as a competing asset. As cryptocurrencies rise in popularity, it's possible that the competition could reduce the demand for precious metals, which may bring down their prices. You'll learn more about cryptocurrencies in the next section of this chapter.

Ways to Invest in Precious Metals

Physical Assets

As I've talked about investing in precious metals, I've been describing it in terms of owning the physical metals directly, either at your home or being stored on your behalf. The current price of precious metals is known as the spot price, because it's the price at which it's traded on the spot, right now.

Futures

Futures are contracts to trade an asset at a set, agreed-upon price on a future date. These two prices, the spot price and the future price, are not the same price. The closer the future contract is to its expiration date, the closer it tends to be to the spot price. As such, it's often used to chart the underlying asset.

I'm not going to attempt to teach you how to trade future contracts because it would be too complicated to try to do so in a short section of a chapter, but I wanted to make sure you are aware they exist. There are futures for many precious metals, for example:

1. Gold (Futures Product code: GC)

2. Silver (Futures Product code: SI)

3. Palladium (Futures Product code: PA)

4. Platinum (Futures Product code: PL)

Stocks

Another way to invest in precious metals is through investing in companies in the stock market that are involved with them. Below are just a few stocks given as examples. If you decide to invest in any of these, please make sure to do your own analysis on them to make sure it makes sense, based on your risk tolerance and portfolio needs.

1. Newmont Mining (NEM) is the world's largest gold mining company and the fourth largest silver mining company.

2. Barrick Gold (GOLD) operates in thirteen countries around the world and engages in the exploration, mine development, production, and sale of gold and copper properties.

3. Franco-Nevada Corporation (FNV) operates as a gold-focused royalty and streaming company.

Exchange Traded Funds (ETFs)

Anytime you use ETFs for investing, it's good to read the prospectus and understand what type of companies they invest in. If an ETF is based on companies who take physical possession of the commodities, then the taxation will be as if you were investing directly in the physical asset, as a collectible. Two examples of this are SPDR Gold Trust (GLD) and iShares Gold Trust (IAU). They buy, sell, and store precious metals. As an ETF, they trade like stocks so you're not paying the high fee for buying or selling since it's built into the ETF.

Other ETFs representing the commodity and holding the physical product in bank vaults include:

1. iShares Silver Trust (SLV)

2. Aberdeen Standard Physical Platinum Shares ETF (PPLT)

3. Aberdeen Standard Physical Palladium Shares ETF (PALL)

4. Aberdeen Standard Physical Precious Metals Basket Shares ETF (GLTR)

If the ETF primarily has exposure to equity-based commodity exposure, then it's treated like stocks for tax purposes. A couple examples are:

1. VanEck Gold Miners ETF (GDX)

2. VanEck Junior Gold Miners ETF (GDXJ)

GDX normally invests at least 80% of its total assets in large-, mid-, and small-cap common stocks and depository receipts of companies involved in the gold mining industry. GDXJ tracks small- and mid-cap companies involved in gold or silver mining for at least 50% of their revenues or at least the potential to generate a minimum of 50% from their mining/royalties/streaming projects.

Cryptocurrency

 It's interesting to note the similarities between Bitcoin and the U.S. dollar, as well as the similarities between Bitcoin and gold or any other precious metal.

Bitcoin is just one type of cryptocurrency. The "crypto" part of the title cryptocurrency refers to how it's managed electronically, through encrypting the data. It's very secure, with a built-in validation process. The "currency" part refers to the similarities it has with real currency. To qualify as a currency, it needs to function in three main ways.

1. As a medium of exchange. It's still far from universal, but more and more mainstream businesses are accepting it as a form of payment. This is one area, some argue, that Bitcoin and other cryptocurrencies shouldn't be considered a currency yet. They need wider acceptance.

2. <u>As a unit of account</u>. It's fungible, meaning one Bitcoin is equivalent to any other Bitcoin. A Bitcoin can also be divided into 100 million subunits known as a "Satoshi."

3. <u>As a store of value</u>. It's designed to become more valuable over time because there's a limited supply of it.

A <u>cryptocurrency</u> is a digital currency that is not backed by any government, person, or entity. For many, this has been one of the appeals. In the rawest sense, Bitcoin can be traded between two parties outside of any bank, exchange, or government; however, it's rapidly being traded more and more through crypto exchanges or through brokers. This is because they provide liquidity and ease of exchanging Bitcoin for "real" money.

Cryptocurrency is also a type of <u>digital asset</u>. The IRS currently treats digital assets as personal property, and it is taxed accordingly. According to the IRS, "Digital assets are broadly defined as any digital representation of value which is recorded on a cryptographically secured distributed ledger."

Every Bitcoin is unique from any other Bitcoin and a history, or a ledger, of the transferring of ownership can be traced backwards to its original creation. This history is only from the perspective of the Bitcoin itself. It does not keep a record of what it is traded for, whether that's for money, products, services, or even other types of cryptocurrencies.

Comparison Between Bitcoin and the U.S. Dollar

Now let's get to comparing Bitcoin to the U.S. dollar (or any other real money, also known as "fiat" money). The U.S. dollar is made legal tender by the decree of the U.S. government. The U.S. dollar became a fiat currency when it dropped the gold standard, meaning it couldn't be redeemed for physical gold anymore. Any currency that's issued purely by the decree of a country's government, without it being backed by any tangible asset, is known as a fiat currency.

Think about that for a moment; there is no intrinsic value to the U.S. dollar. It only has value because we accept in good faith that it has value. Neither the U.S. dollar nor Bitcoin is backed by any other tangible asset.

There are risks associated with cryptocurrencies in that the value can fluctuate dramatically, since it's not typically tied to any physical asset. It's also currently viewed more as a speculative investment than as a currency. Most cryptocurrency disclosures will include the fact that they are highly volatile, and you could lose all of your money.

US SEC sues crypto exchange Coinbase, one day after suing Binance

BY JONATHAN STEMPEL, REUTERS - 6:19 PM ET 6/6/2023

TOP NEWS

NEW YORK (Reuters) - The U.S. Securities and Exchange Commission on Tuesday sued Coinbase, accusing the largest U.S. cryptocurrency platform of operating illegally because it failed to register as an exchange, in another blow to the crypto industry.

The lawsuit is the SEC's second in two days against a major crypto exchange, following its case against Binance, the world's largest cryptocurrency exchange, and founder Changpeng Zhao.

Both civil cases are part of SEC Chair Gary Gensler's push to assert jurisdiction over the crypto industry, which he on Tuesday again labeled a "Wild West" that has undermined investor trust in the U.S. capital markets.

Other risks include governmental regulations that could either add stability with greater oversight, or they could cause more fear in using it, since one of the reasons to invest in cryptocurrencies is to avoid being tied to any government. How other countries view cryptocurrencies varies widely. China, for example, has a complete ban on Bitcoin.

One risk to consider would be how well people adapt to it being used as a form of payment. Another risk is once all Bitcoin is mined, validation will only be compensated by transaction fees. We won't really know how much relying only on the fee structure will impact transactional validations once Bitcoin has been completely mined. I'll explain mining later.

Comparison Between Bitcoin and Gold

Let's compare Bitcoin with gold. They are both viewed as coming from a limited resource. For example, the amount of gold in the world is considered finite. We might get better at mining for gold, but there's still a limit to how much exists. It's the same with Bitcoin. It's capped at 21 million, whereas there are currently over 19 million in existence now.

Having a limited supply of gold can increase its value. The fact that gold can't easily be mined, while more fiat money can easily be printed, is a major cause of the price of gold increasing. This is one cause of inflation. There are other factors influencing the price of gold, of course. The same can be said of Bitcoin. The fact that there is a limited quantity of Bitcoin helps to influence its value. But once again, it's not the only factor influencing its value.

Neither gold nor Bitcoin are tied to a central bank. They're often a flight to safety when you're not at ease with current government policies. To hedge against a country's inflation or overreaching policies, investors may turn to gold or cryptocurrencies. Gold tends to be the traditional way of doing so, whereas younger generations might become more comfortable using cryptocurrencies as a hedge.

Mining

It's interesting that the term "mining" is used with both gold and Bitcoin. There are mining companies for gold and there are mining companies for Bitcoin. At the current rate, it's estimated that all Bitcoin will have been mined by the year 2040. The maximum number of Bitcoins that can exist is 21 million and as of March 2023, over 19 million Bitcoins have already been mined. Bitcoin mining is the process by which new Bitcoins are entered into circulation.

A Bitcoin miner is rewarded with Bitcoin when they verify 1 megabyte worth of transactions, also known as a block. Information can be run through an algorithm generating a sixty-four-digit hexadecimal code called a hash, which increases its level of encryption. This code is used and modified in the header of the next block, linking them together. Since one block is chained to the next block, it's called a blockchain. The linking of the blockchains together makes them immutable, no one can alter it. Changing any part of the transaction data within a block would change that block's header, thereby no longer syncing with the next header.

Creating a hash code is very easy but decoding it could take centuries. A target hash is also associated with the block and is the number miners are trying to solve when they mine to validate the transactions in the block; however, they don't have to get an exact solution. Because of its encryption, it can take billions of attempts from one mining pool to come up with a solution that satisfies solving the algorithm to the point it's viewed as having been verified. The first one to solve it is both the one who verifies the block and receives newly issued Bitcoin. They also receive the transaction fees.

This rate of rewarding Bitcoin is cut in half every 210,000 blocks, which happens approximately every four years and can happen sooner the more Bitcoin transactions occur.

The Process of Investing in Cryptocurrencies Using Blockchain

There are over 18,000 different cryptocurrencies in existence with, perhaps, Bitcoin and Ethereum as the most well-known. What they have most in common is cryptography to keep them secure. The length of time to validate a block varies from one cryptocurrency to the next.

How to Buy Cryptocurrencies

The most common way to buy cryptocurrencies is via a centralized crypto exchange (CEX). They can also be purchased through a decentralized crypto exchange (DEX) or brokers who are set up to offer cryptocurrencies. If you're already investing in the stock market, you could check with your broker to see if they offer, or are associated with, any cryptocurrency services.

Popular centralized crypto exchanges include Coinbase, Crypto.com, Kraken, Gemini, and Binance. Much like stock trading websites, cryptocurrency can be traded at the current market rate, also known as the spot rate. Orders can be entered to buy or sell at the listed market price or as a limit order, which is to trade it at the price you specify, or better. Some exchanges may even allow you to trade on margin, which is borrowing money from the exchange for trading purposes. They will have you associate a bank with your account to move real currency back and forth. This is like a stockbroker, but more specifically for cryptocurrencies. A quick word of warning seems appropriate here. If you're using a broker or a centralized exchange, you need to have some confidence in their ability to keep your digital assets safe from theft or corporate fraud.

GLOBAL 500: THE WORLD'S LARGEST CORPORATIONS

FORTUNE

THE NEXT WARREN BUFFETT?

Owning digital assets requires a digital wallet. However, most centralized crypto exchanges will act as a custodian and hold your digital assets in their own digital wallet. Again, as a warning, keep in mind that you carry the risk of them failing, having fraud, or being hacked. In November 2022, in one of my Payne's Perspective reports, I talked about the collapse of FTX, which was a centralized crypto exchange. CEO Sam Bankman-Fried, who was touted as a wunderkind who wowed Silicon Valley and bought up Washington, DC, was arrested on charges of lying to investors and committing fraud. It's an example of this kind of risk.

Despite these risks, using a centralized crypto exchange is the most common way of investing in cryptocurrencies. They have varying degrees of regulatory oversight, but most follow common compliance rules such as "Know Your Customer," fair pricing rules, and other customer protection protocols to build confidence and trust in using their services. CEXs are probably the simplest way to get your feet wet with trading cryptocurrencies.

Decentralized exchanges are non-custodial, meaning that you'll need your own digital wallet to link to the DEX. They're better for investors looking to switch from one digital currency to another, and not for someone trying to buy and sell using fiat currencies. A digital wallet does not actually contain cryptocurrency. They remain on the blockchain. What it stores is your private key. This private key is what is used to access your cryptocurrency. They may also provide additional features to help you safeguard your information.

Digital Wallets

Digital wallets come in two forms, <u>hot wallets</u> and <u>cold wallets</u>. Hot wallets are those that readily connect to the internet. Examples of hot wallets include: 1) a mobile wallet, found on your mobile phone; 2) a web wallet, which stores your private keys on a server; and 3) a desktop wallet, you guessed it, it's stored on your computer. How easily the information is accessed affects the level of potential risk. They all need to be connected to the internet at the time of spending digital currency.

Cold wallets are simply storage solutions that do not store information online. Cold wallets include, 1) hardware wallets, which may look like a USB device and could have a biometric lock to increase security or 2) physical media, such as printing a QR code that can be kept in a safety deposit box, or other secure place, and scanned when needed.

Here's a few different cryptocurrency wallets for consideration:

1. Ledger Nano X, which is widely viewed as the best hardware wallet. It's paired with the Ledger Live app to provide feature-rich mobile and desktop apps.

2. Coinbase wallet, which was created by the same individuals who created the Coinbase Bitcoin exchange.

3. Trezor wallet, which is an open-source cryptocurrency wallet that links to a desktop computer via USB. It can be used as a cold wallet.

4. Metamask, which has over 30 million users and is one of the most popular cryptocurrency mobile wallets, especially for Ethereum.

Ways to Invest in Cryptocurrencies

If you're not ready to start trading directly in cryptocurrencies but still want to be involved, you can invest or trade through futures, ETFs, or stocks that are involved with the cryptocurrency industry. This is similar to our discussion on precious metals. And like precious metals, I recommend investing 5% or less of your portfolio in cryptocurrencies.

Direct Investment

During this section on investing in cryptocurrencies, I've explained how you can invest through your current broker, a centralized crypto exchange, or a decentralized crypto exchange. There are other ways to begin investing in cryptocurrencies.

Futures

As mentioned earlier in this chapter, futures are contracts to trade an asset at a set, agreed-upon price on a future date. There are future contracts for two of the dominant cryptocurrencies: Bitcoin (Product code: BTC), and Ether (Product code: ETH).

Stocks

Another way to invest in cryptocurrencies is through investing in companies in the stock market that are involved within the crypto economy. Below are just a few stocks given as examples. If you decide to invest in any of these, please make sure to do your own analysis on them to make sure it makes sense based on your risk tolerance and portfolio needs.

1. **Block Inc (SQ)** — They hold about $230 million worth of Bitcoin on their balance sheet. They plan to manufacture the chips and related hardware for Bitcoin mining.

2. **Coinbase Global, Inc. (COIN)** — They provide financial infrastructure and technology for the crypto economy in the United States and internationally.

3. **Riot Platforms (RIOT)** — They operate as a Bitcoin mining company in North America.

4. **Nvidia (NVDA)** — They make semiconductors called Cryptocurrency Mining Processors (CMPs), specifically designed for mining Ether.

5. **Paypal (PYPL)** — They offer trading on 4 different cryptocurrencies: Bitcoin, Ethereum, Litecoin, and Bitcoin Cash

Exchange Traded Funds (ETFs)

Exchange Traded Funds are a common way to provide exposure to sectors, industries, commodities, and even cryptocurrency.

1. Grayscales Bitcoin Trust (GBTC) is a closed-end fund that holds Bitcoin, meaning they cannot create new shares of the trust, nor redeem them, as the demand expands or contracts. If it were an open-ended fund, then it would track the value of Bitcoin much closer. As of March 31, 2023, they held 628,932 Bitcoins. Grayscale applied to turn this fund into an open-ended spot ETF but was denied. There currently are no open-ended spot ETFs in the U.S. Market.

2. ProShares Bitcoin Strategy ETF (BITO) offers exposure to Bitcoin via futures contracts.

3. ProShares Short Bitcoin Strategy ETF (BITI) offers exposure to Bitcoin via futures contracts through short positions.

4. VanEck Bitcoin Strategy ETF (XBTF) is an actively managed alternative to BITO. It holds mostly U.S.

Treasury bills, which are used as collateral for monthly CME Bitcoin futures.

5. Global X Blockchain ETF (BKCH) seeks to invest in companies positioned to benefit from the increased adoption of blockchain technology, whether that's through companies involved in digital asset mining, digital asset transaction, blockchain applications, etc.

6. Bitwise Crypto Industry Innovators ETF (BITQ) tracks crypto industry stocks instead of Bitcoin futures.

7. Global X Blockchain & Bitcoin Strategy ETF (BITS) — offers about 55% exposure to BKCH and about 45% exposure to Bitcoin futures as used in BITO and XBTF.

Collectibles

Some call collectables the ultimate inflation assets since their value often increases as the value of other assets decline.

I am no expert on collectables but I have a seven-figure portfolio of such assets. I try to guess what's going to be cool down the road but I'm the least hip person I know. So, my top rule for this kind of investing is to own things that give you day-to-day enjoyment.

I'm a very esthetic person. I love clean lines (2000 Rolls-Royce Cornice) but I also appreciate the abstract (Aboriginal art).

This was a lesson I learned not on Wall Street but in high school. I had the privilege of attending the High School of Art & Design in New York City. It is the best art high school in America — probably in the world. I wanted to be an architect but we could not afford the educational fees needed, so I majored in commercial art.

In my junior year a teacher, who gave the aura of a college professor, told us to never buy art for an investment but to buy it because you love it. That principle has applied to all my collectable investments since.

History is also a great guide to collectables investing. Kelly bags from Hermes have an amazing track record of price appreciation. Patek Philipe watches are the cream of the crop, although newcomers are climbing the charts fast.

I realize these are expensive but do not get discouraged and focus on great brands with limited editions. You can also use and wear these items, although sparingly and never throw away any of the packaging, even the bag you used to carry it home.

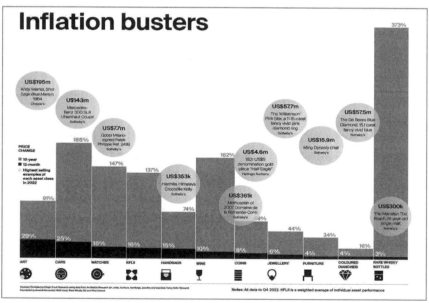

Source: Knight Frank Wealth Report 2023

Summary

Now that you have read through this entire chapter, you're probably feeling like you just drank from a firehose. I promise, my intention was not to overwhelm you, but rather to give you outstanding information to make it possible for you to get involved beyond the model portfolio. Consider this your starting point to greater knowledge and experience.

The topics covered: options, dividends, precious metals, cryptocurrencies, and collectibles go beyond stock investing and can provide greater flexibility and diversity. I spent most of the chapter on options because, as I've reported on FOX Business: "Options trading is projected to surpass stock trading for the first time ever!" Investors are loving the power of options because they can allow you to:

- Turn small stock moves into substantial gains
- Create income on stocks you own
- Hedge against market losses
- Secure returns even when stocks fall

Over the last several years, my team and I have developed an in-depth, interactive option education program. In addition to video and text lessons, we offer live classes, Q&A sessions, and workshops with our team of instructors who have decades of experience trading and teaching others how to trade. Our goal is to help you gain confidence through education and implementation of trading strategies.

After completing this chapter, I'd like you to narrow in on an area that you feel is right for you and act on it to improve your investing and trading. Treat this chapter like a workbook. Don't let this opportunity fall through your fingers without doing something about it.

I don't often quote others, but this is worth repeating. Stephen R. Covey, the author of *The 7 Habits of Highly Effective People* said, "To learn and not to do is really not to learn. To know and not to do is really not to know."

Check for Understanding

There is a great deal of challenging information in this chapter. Rather than quizzing you on all that new information I am going to give you a task.

I want you to pick one of the five areas discussed and make it your goal to explore that investment opportunity more completely.

- Go back over the information I've provided you here, but go beyond that.
- Seek out more information.
- Listen to experts in that specific field.
- Learn more so that you become a bit of an expert yourself.

I don't want you investing in anything until you have done your own research and are comfortable that the investment fits your goals and your level of risk tolerance. I want you to have options for when you might see an opportunity to expand your investment portfolio. If you are like me, there is a joy in learning new things and exploring new possibilities. Have some fun exploring one (or more, if you want) of these opportunities.

7

The Original Diamond Hands — Warren Buffett

Diamond Hands & Buying the Dip

> *Diamonds are forever*
> *They are all I need to please me*
> *They can stimulate and tease me*
> *They won't leave in the night*
> *I've no fear that they might desert me*

~ Shirley Bassey

Part of the psyche in the new, individual investor revolution is becoming wedded to a stock or other investment no matter how high or low it might go. This approach is called "diamond hands." The idea is that by holding the stock they are protecting their investment and pushing back against the establishment that promotes excessive buying and selling.

While Wall Street pitches the notion of long-term investing, the action and real rhetoric has a different focus. It is all about turning the wheels of the machine. Buying and selling generates activity and fees while also creating environments that lead assets to be overbought or oversold in the short term. This "churn" of stocks has resulted in some investors viewing trading like one might a game.

But the gamification wasn't started by investors new to the market. While trading apps like Robinhood are designed to entice more activity, these apps did not invent gamification. The approach was born and is propagated daily by Wall Street. Each day "experts" evaluate stocks that then receive upgrades or downgrades all based on hunches about where a stock will go over the next few months. While some of these "hunches" are more educated than others, they are all still guesses trying to predict the short-term future.

Think about this very carefully. If a company is not hitting its all-time peak share price, why would an investor sell?

Over time I'm sure there have been hundreds of "sell" ratings on stocks like Apple and Amazon and thousands of downgrades to "hold" from "buy." Have these stocks already gone as high as they ever will? I think the answer is probably not...like 99.9% sure it's probably not.

I am not suggesting here that there is never a time to close out a position. I held two different stocks into bankruptcy, in large part because I knew management and let those personal relationships supersede my typical research. I bought into the story and thought the company could make it happen. Even though I lost money on these companies they are not my greatest regrets.

I regret much more the stocks I've owned and took a quick profit on even when my own research said the company was still a strong bet to go higher, even if there was a slight, short-term dip in price. So why aren't we all diamond hands? We know great companies with businesses that should still be around and making money for, at least, the next one hundred years.

On the other hand, why are we diamond hands to a bunch of funds in our retirement accounts that mostly produce lackluster returns?

It all gets back to the one variable that is most difficult to understand and harder to control — being human.

Baptism by Fire

So, you want to be a diamond. Just remember that journey to the polished stone you ogle through the jewelry store window each morning on the way to the office took a lot of time, shaping, and polishing to grab your attention and admiration. It takes millions of years, and incredible pressure, to create a diamond. In the market, the term refers to patience and the ability to withstand pressure.

Why do investors often choose to close out a position? Remember earlier in the book how I said that Unbreakable Investors needed to be able to understand both their own emotions and those of others? Here's another example of what I was talking about. Let me explain.

Often, we sell stocks because of emotions and the need to avoid emotional pain. You may close out a position because it has had a good run and now seems to be plateauing. If it then makes another run, you might assuage an inner feeling that closing when you did was a mistake with one of the old Wall Street axioms like "you never go broke taking a profit" or "bulls make money, bears make money, but pigs get slaughtered." And, of course, if the stock pulls back after you have closed it you really feel brilliant.

If the stock were to move higher you might beat yourself up for the choice you made, I certainly have in the past. However, you don't need to play head games with yourself. You closed out a position for a gain and that's good. You can now sleep better and not have to fret over what some talking head said about the stock on television that day. You are human, and humans love the feeling of relief. But the problem is what do you do with the cash and how close are you to reaching your goal of financial independence. If you invested the cash you made when you closed out the stock, and the new investment is making you more money, great! You're moving in the right direction toward financial independence. The one thing you can't do is just put the money aside and let it be "dead money." Then closing out that position early is truly a mistake. So, you might wonder what "professional" investors do.

Let's look at the original diamond hands: Warren Buffett.

The Oracle of Omaha

Warren Buffett began investing when he was eleven years old and eventually took control of a textile company in serious disarray called Berkshire Hathaway.

He used this company as his investment vehicle, moving into insurance companies that provided him with the cash to buy or take large stakes in other businesses. Most of his investments were companies bought on dips in the market caused when all investments were taking a hit.

This has given Warren Buffett the cache of being seen as a "value investor," but, those stocks or companies that made him extremely wealthy were, at times, huge growth stocks and he continued to hold them. In fact, it's rare he closes out his core holding names — those that made him a legend.

Everyone Else's Fear Is Good

One of Buffett's most famous investment phrases is: "Buy when there is blood in the streets."

In the movie "Wall Street", Gordon Gecko gives a speech at a company's shareholder meeting that has been affixed to the street ever since. I will paraphrase it to explain Buffett's real skill:

Fear, for lack of a better word, or should I say other people's fear, is good.

What is meant by that statement? What Gordon Gecko is saying, and what Warren Buffett acts on, is the idea that when others are fearful, they are the exact opposite of diamond hands — they are paper hands. They will tend to close out positions, sending stock prices down, even when there isn't a real reason to do so. Sometimes, that fear is justified, and the actions are good ones. There are times when a stock can be so fractured that holding it for the length of time it takes to rebound is not as profitable as selling and moving to a more stable investment. However, these fear-driven actions can also provide the savvy investor a great opportunity. Both the real Warren Buffett and the fictional Gordon Gecko recognized these opportunities. This is why you need to understand fundamentals. It is the number one way to not only avoid the emotional losses from following the herd but also gives you a chance to take advantage – to buy the dip.

A Coke and a Smile

That's what Warren Buffett did with Coca-Cola, which he began to accumulate in 1988 as the shares were still sagging from the 1987 crash. His big investment was the epitome of buying the dip, which is what you do when you really believe in a stock. It is a hallmark of a true "diamond hands investor." Of course, Buffett had done his research. He believed in the value of the company where others didn't. He bought and held this company based on that research. This is different than buying and holding a company that is completely shattered.

Researching events of the past is always clouded with the knowledge of what happened. It's easy to lose perspective and think you would have made all the right decisions. But it's important to see what worked and what didn't to inform our own current and future decisions. Let's take a minute and look back at what Buffett had available to him.

I took a look at Coca-Cola's 1987 annual report. Below is some of the information from that report.

The heart of The Coca-Cola Company is selling soft drinks to a thirsty world, one drink at a time, more than 524 million times a day...and counting.

Excerpts

"These actions produced a 6 percent increase in soft drink unit volume, outstanding market share gains and a cash flow of approximately $1.2 billion. Your Company also enjoyed record operating income of $1.3 billion and earnings per share of $2.43- Excluding 35 cents per share of unusual items in 1986, operating income climbed 23 percent, while net income gained 14.5 percent to $916 million and net income per share increased 17.4 percent."

Let's break down a few of these key points.

A 6 percent increase in soft drink unit volume...

Outstanding market share gains!

My investing philosophy begins with wanting to own companies in a growing macro environment that are experiencing fast growth through strong, top line volume gains and pricing power. It was clear Coca-Cola was doing just that. As a result, income grew, and margins expanded. This is a buy signal

Enjoyed record operating income of $1.3 billion and earnings per share of $2.43.

The question was then, could the company keep its volume growing this well and consistently for an extended period of time. Again, we have the benefit of looking backwards and knowing what happened. But put yourself in the place of a shareholder that might have sold, and a potential shareholder like Warren Buffett, just kicking the tires but ready to make a decision.

The report also highlighted Global Volume

> +1% United States
> -4% Germany
> +10% Italy
> +12% Japan
> +19% Brazil
> +26% Thailand
> +31% Great Britain
> +34% Taiwan
> +38% Indonesia
> +162% China

What's really amazing about the growth in China is overall volume was just a drop in the bucket for the company, but it was clear there was more upside potential there than in many other places. This wasn't a value company; this was a growth company with a stock that was treated like a stodgy old value name. Not only was operating income at a new record but operating margins expanded to 17.3% from 12.9% a year earlier. **This is a buy signal.**

Buying Back Stock

Here's another excerpt from the report...

"Often the best use of excess cash generated by our businesses has been to invest in our own stock. After repurchasing 10 million shares in 1986 and early 1987, we announced plans in July 1987 to repurchase over a three-year period up to 40 million shares, more than 10 percent of the company's total number of outstanding shares. By year-end, we had purchased 6.6 million shares, lowering the total number of outstanding shares to approximately 372 million."

I have always had mixed feelings about stock buybacks, which can be great for growing businesses but horrible for those that are failing and trying to manipulate their underlying share price to mask failure. But in 1987, Coca-Cola was growing nicely and investing in their business, which spanned 155 countries.

The cash flow was such there was enough left over to buy back shares.

Not only did management buy back 10 million shares in 1986 and early 1987, they announced a new plan to buy another 40 million shares or 10% of the company's shares over the next three years and, in the process, lower the total number of shares outstanding.

Set Adrift

Going through the 1987 annual report it seemed like the stock was a screaming buy, but the stock wasn't moving. Warren Buffett bought $1.0 billion in Coca-Cola (KO) stock in 1988 which represented 6% of the company. Using my approach, although the story was more powerful than share price action, I would have waited and maybe bought in March 1989, when the stock was in a wonderful cup and handle formation and breaking out to new highs.

Yep, that means I would have been chasing the stock. But I would have been chasing the value proposition, which would be confirmed with this kind of breakout.

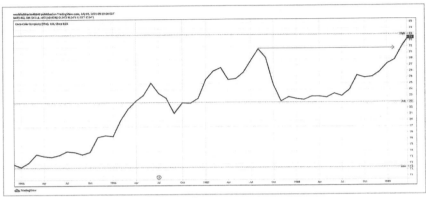

Source: TradingView.com / Coca-Cola Stock

Time to put on the diamond hands. It's always easier said than done and looked especially easy between 1987 and June 1998.

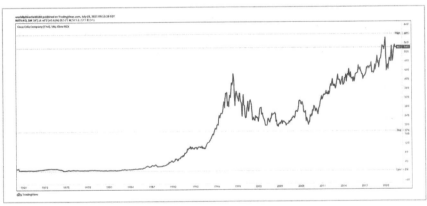

Source: TradingView.com / Coca-Cola Stock

Buy & Hold

The ride in Coca-Cola shares was fantastic once it got off the ground, and even if you waited for the breakout in

March 1989, you would have a straight shot higher until the shares peaked in May 1992. From here the stock traded sideways until breaking out again in August 1994.

That is a long time to hold a stock that's going nowhere. Some would call it dead money.

The dilemma for most investors is having limited funds and whether they have built a sufficient cushion in a winner to endure pullbacks and corrections. I must say, being positioned in the latter is wonderful. I own several stocks and forget what I paid for them because I'm up so much (more than 100%) so it's no problem keeping them on the shelf even as they move sideways.

Everyone's goals and circumstances are different, but I do not think anyone with less than $3,000,000 in the market should put stocks on the shelf when the shares and underlying fundamentals hit a rough patch. This is not the same as selling in a huff or panic.

This is an important distinction.

When you are closing a position on your own terms rather than following the crowd, which will always overreact, you move much closer to your own financial freedom because you have empowered yourself with control.

Remember, this all grows out of knowledge. Knowledge of markets and knowledge of what you own.

Moving On

If bought in March 1989 on that breakout and still held in May 1992, I would have closed the position before 1994. My financial circumstances at the time were not like they are now, and I would have kept my money moving.

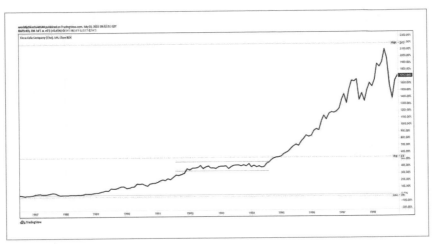

Source: TradingView.com / Coca-Cola Stock

Obviously selling a stock simply because it's moving sideways or drifting lower is anathema to using knowledge and strategy to beat the market.

But it's your signal to look deeper under the hood.

In 1992 Coca-Cola revenue growth slowed to 13.0% from 1991 compared to 18.7% for 1991 from 1990. In addition, operating margin only edged to 21.3 from 20.0 the year before, some of which came from a reduction in costs in stock-related employee benefits.

In September of 1992 the stock stumbled hard and pierced the 50-day moving average.

- By now there were signs of near-term slowing
- Stock moving sideways
- Shares were breaking key support points.

This is where I might have sold — again, with the benefit of hindsight.

Below is a graph of what I would have been seeing at that time.

Source: Yahoo Finance

I would have probably moved out of my position with Coca-Cola in 1992, based on my personal situation and what I was seeing at the time. But I wouldn't have forgotten about the company just because I had made a good profit and then closed out. When you have a huge winner, you never take it off your watch list. All the stars realigned to buy Coca-Cola back at the breakout in 1994.

Warren Buffett Is Different

"You know, the rich are different from you and me."

F. Scott Fitzgerald is supposed to have once said this to Ernest Hemingway. It was a very intriguing comment coming from someone who was born into wealth. It gave him a special insight for sure, but the sentence suggests Mr. Fitzgerald thought of himself as a man of the people. And there is no arguing for all his success that Hemingway was always connected to the people.

But let me get back to Warren Buffett and his "diamond hands" approach to Coca-Cola. Buying Coca-Cola in 1988 was brilliant, and it was easy for him to hold the stock, which had a few mild pullbacks but was, for the most part, a straight shot higher. It was a growth stock in terms of market action and underlying fundamentals. But it wouldn't stay that way forever.

The shares peaked in June 1998 at $43.50 then proceeded to not just slump but stumbled hard. The stock got slammed and slipped into an abyss.

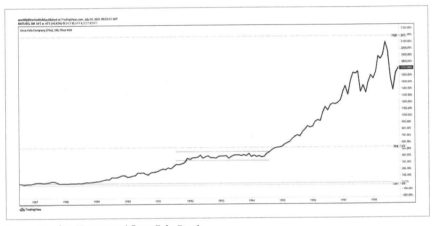

Source: TradingView.com / Coca-Cola Stock

The collapse underscores three important things about business and investing.

- Being the biggest doesn't mean invincibility.
- Once companies lose their way it's rare they get back on track quickly.
- Management is everything.

Robert C Goizueta is a good example of that last point. He was one of the greatest CEOs in business history. His leadership at Coca-Cola is remarkable. He led the company from 1980 to his death in October 1997. The company ran on his momentum. But with his passing everything changed for the company and the entire industry.

Carbonated sodas started to become a major health concern and this concern saw market share shrink in western nations — especially in the United States. Diet sodas were popular for a while, but the same health police that went after the sugar industry came for diet sodas as well.

Coca-Cola shares went into free fall, and, for a while, the company was in a state of disrepair. The free fall lasted almost eleven years before bottoming at $19.60 in 2009.

Warren Buffett, the definition of diamond hands, held and bought even more shares. We have to recognize that Warren is different than you and me. He can afford to be, and it has served him well. Most investors would have cut their position (hopefully at a profit) and moved on.

But it hasn't always been this way, and therein lies the lesson. Earning the right to take shots means building enough wealth through a disciplined approach where you are committed to A) following a plan, B) putting in the work, and C) always learning and making adjustments.

Warren Buffett can afford to have diamond hands whenever he wants. He has built up sufficient reserves to ride out the variations of any particular stock. That isn't the case for most of us, and doesn't always work for Mr. Buffett either, as we'll see shortly. But the Coca-Cola lesson is a good one for all of us. He found a stock that was a quality investment that happened to be out of favor with Wall Street.

The investing lesson for the general investor is that it's worth finding a quality name that's out of favor with Wall Street. But unless you have significant resources, when the underlying fundamentals begin to collapse, it's time to sell the stock.

If a stock is out of favor and has been moving sideways for a while, what might cause that stock to pop again? When a company needs to get back on track, I look at the management. I prefer to see new management that has a track record of innovation for these situations. I also assume it will take about a year or so for companies to get their act together with the new management.

Innovation and fresh thinking are important for getting companies back on track. Remember, they have gone full circle, which means they have to return to their roots and have a startup mentality. I have seen many stocks instantly pop back on new management. How much does management really matter in a huge corporation? Take a look at the chart below and you'll see.

CEOs Matter

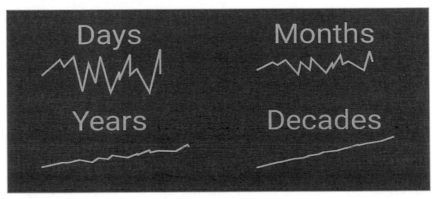

Source: Refinitiv Datastreaml; company reports; press reports

Losing Patience

Although we all know that the further you stand back and look at it, the overall stock market has essentially gone up. But living through periods of anxiety resulting from market corrections makes days and weeks feel like years and decades.

But the longer you hold or stay in the market, the smoother the ride becomes. The chart above is a nice representation of what the market might look like over time.

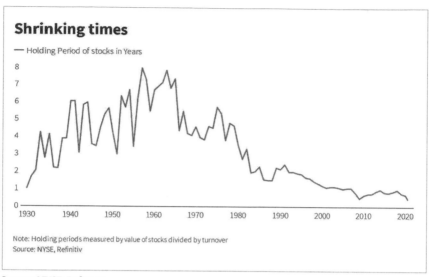

Shrinking times

— Holding Period of stocks in Years

Note: Holding periods measured by value of stocks divided by turnover
Source: NYSE, Refinitiv

Source: NYSE, Refinitiv

Even armed with this knowledge, stock holding periods have become shorter and shorter — it feels like everyone is day trading these days. Look at the chart above. The reduction in holding periods may be a result of the increased availability of information. Remember my story about the people who lived farther away from the brokerage house? The same thing may be happening here. We have to wonder how much of the actions are based on emotions from "partial information" that anyone can now get.

> **Falling in Love**
> Falling in love, it was easy at the start
> I thought I had it in my hands
> Something went wrong, somewhere we lost a part
> It was more than we could stand, yeah
> It was too late when I realized
> That I couldn't see the forest for the trees
> What was wrong with me
>
> ~ Peabo Bryson

If you think you are falling in love with a stock, then get to know that stock and treat it like a personal relationship. One of the most important things is seeing and understanding growth. By that I mean going beyond great and consistent execution. One of the areas of growth and change in this relationship that you need to understand is acquisitions. Takeovers can cause stocks and investors problems if they are not paying attention.

Over the years I have come to view takeovers differently. Usually when a company announces an acquisition its shares decline. This knee-jerk reaction is based on the notion that the pie is getting larger (if stock is used) or there will be extra debt (if cash is borrowed) or there will be culture clash that mitigates any positive impacts from these deals.

That is wrongheaded.

Imagine if your favorite aging athlete or dancer or thinker could get a booster shot that serves as a fountain of youth. Their original skill gets a lift, or they might gain more skills — there would be no need for nostalgia since you could still actively watch and root for them.

The market initially treats acquisitions in the exact opposite way. These companies gain something (to be quantified by research and execution) that, more often than not, supersedes the notion that there are more shares outstanding.

The old rationale for selling these stocks may seem dumb these days, including the so-called "culture clash." Below are some of the most acquisitive companies in the market and how well they've performed. It can take more time to study and understand these deals, but below are a few signs that the deal could be great.

Accretive Deals — this is when the new company immediately adds to the bottom line.

Cash Offers — this means management sees its own shares as more valuable than cash

Stock Rallies — the knee jerk reaction to deal announcements is that the acquiring company shares move lower – don't take the bait. However, when the street sees immediate upside, it's probably a grand slam.

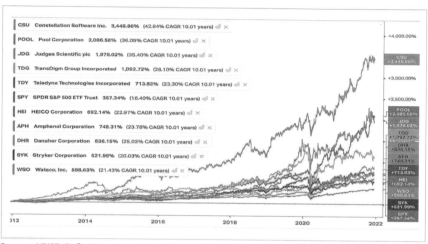

Source: NYSE, Refinitiv

Mistakes Will Be Made

I mentioned earlier that even Warren Buffett misses once in a while. Let's look at one of those examples.

Below is an excerpt from a *Reuters* article about one of those times that Mr. Diamond Hands missed on an investment.

> **"Warren Buffett's $10 billion mistake: Precision Castparts"**
>
> *"The 90-year-old billionaire on Saturday admitted he "paid too much" when his Berkshire Hathaway Inc spent $32.1 billion in 2016 to buy aircraft and industrial parts maker Precision Castparts Corp, its largest acquisition.*

Berkshire wrote off $9.8 billion of Precision's value last August, as the coronavirus pandemic sapped demand for air travel and the Portland, Oregon-based unit's products.

In his annual letter to investors, Buffett said he bought "a fine company - the best in its business," and Berkshire was "lucky" to have Precision Chief Executive Mark Donegan still in charge.

But Buffett said he was "simply too optimistic about PCC's normalized profit potential."

Precision shed more than 13,400 jobs, or 40% of its workforce, in 2020, and only recently has begun to improve margins, Berkshire said.

"I was wrong ... in judging the average amount of future earnings and, consequently, wrong in my calculation of the proper price to pay for the business," Buffett wrote. "PCC is far from my first error of that sort. But it's a big one."

Two years ago, Buffett admitted he "overpaid" for Kraft Foods when Berkshire and private equity firm 3G Capital merged it in 2015 with their H.J. Heinz Co to form Kraft Heinz Co.

And in his 2008 annual letter, Buffett called his 1993 purchase of Dexter Shoe his "worst deal" ever, saying he had bought a "worthless business" and compounded his error by using Berkshire stock rather than cash to fund the acquisition.

"I'll make more mistakes in the future - you can bet on that," he wrote.

> *Tom Russo, a longtime Berkshire investor, welcomed Buffett's candor.*
>
> *"I admire Warren for taking personal responsibility for Precision Castparts," he said. "Few managers are willing to admit their responsibility rather than pass on blame."*
>
> Source: https://www.reuters.com/article/
> us-berkshire-buffett-precisioncastparts/
> warren-buffetts-10-billion-mistake-precision-castparts-idUSKCN2AR0MZ

Mistakes happen to all investors at one time or another. But it is only really tragic if we don't learn from those mistakes and improve our strategy for the next investment.

Warren Buffett & Apple: Additional Lessons for Investors & Procreators

Warren Buffett is notorious for shunning technology stocks. In the 1990s his image took a mighty blow for missing the big tech rally. But by 2002 his legend grew even larger, as all those who sneered and jeered him were licking their wounds and applying for jobs at hardware stores.

In the first quarter of 2016 Buffett took the plunge and bought 9.8 million shares of Apple. This is what you can learn from that purchase and subsequent purchases.

Never Too Old

Buffett began buying shares of Apple when he was 85 years old.

Focus on Management

Management report card from quarterly earnings is a great tool but try to learn even more about their vision and ability to execute.

Own Some Positions for Cash Flow.

In 2022 Berkshire Hathaway received $823 million in dividend payments from Apple. Every time you bought an Apple product or service you handed Buffett money. Start paying yourself.

Make Adjustments

Buffett vowed to avoid tech but changed his mind with Apple. The experts blow it all the time because of the inability to make adjustments.

Never Stop Investing

Americans have been trained to put it in neutral as they approach age 65 and shut it down completely at 65 and that includes investing in the stock market. Why would you ever walk away from the greatest money-making machine in history?

Quiz: Chapter 7

1. **Define "Diamond Hands".**

2. **In order to be a Warren Buffett level Diamond Hand, how much value do I believe you should have in your portfolio?**

3. **What do we mean when we say that other people's fear is good?**

4. **What has happened to the average holding time for an investment over the last few years?**

Answers

1. The term refers to the willingness to hold on to a position even as the stock moves sideways or shows a dip.

2. I suggest that you have at least $3,000,000. This provides you with enough cushion to ride out any dips that might occur. Of course, you don't want to stay in a stock if your research indicates that the fundamentals have changed or there is some macro event that would indicate you should close a position.

3. This is a paraphrase of Warren Buffett's statement and indicates that when others are fearful there may be an opportunity to get into a stock at a depressed price. His Coca-Cola purchase is a good example.

4. The average hold time has been decreasing. Investors are moving in and out of positions much more quickly. This can sometimes present opportunities to those who are doing their homework!

8

Federal Reserve

Federal Reserve: Unparalleled Power

> *Money*
> *Get away.*
> *You get a good job with more pay and you're okay.*
> *Money*
> *It's a gas.*
> *Grab that cash with both hands and make a stash.*
> *New car, caviar, four-star, daydream*
> *Think I'll buy me a football team.*

> ~ Pink Floyd

The rapid growth of the United States made it a beacon for investment, particularly for rich European money seeking new fortunes in the new world. But the tides turned quickly resulting in economic "panics" which almost always also meant recession. It was a feast or famine, which is no way to run a nation. Finally, the Panic of 1907 set into motion the eventual creation of the Federal Reserve.

Panics

1786 (National)
1789 (Northern States)
1792 (National)
1796 (National)
1857 (National)
1863 (New York)
1873 (New York & National)
1884 (New York)
1890 (New York)
1893 (MidAtlantic)
1896 (Midwest)
1899 (New York)
1901 (New York)
1903 (MidAtlantic)
1907 (National)
1910 (National)
1913 (New York)

Cartoon for the Panic of 1873 which sparked the 'Long Depression

Bipartisan Support

In 1913 the U.S. Senate passed the Federal Reserve Act and set into motion the creation of an entity that has become the most powerful in the world.

The Fed can't wage physical war but its ability to move the U.S. economy and even, indirectly, the global economy is without equal. The power of the Fed was recognized very quickly, which is why it took years of horse trading and wrangling in Congress before it was officially passed into law.

In the end, fingerprints from a top Republican lawmaker and the progressive U.S. president can be found on what many call "the Creature from Jekyll Island" (the first meeting place of wealthier bankers and lawmakers that set the creation in motion). Below is an article reflecting the history of the passage of the bill creating the Federal

Reserve. I think it is helpful to have a bit of historical understanding about how this incredibly powerful and influential entity came into being. I think it is important to know something about the past to better understand the present and have an insight into the future.

The Senate Passes the Federal Reserve Act   🖨

December 23, 1913

It took many months and nearly straight party-line voting, but on December 23, 1913, the Senate passed and President Woodrow Wilson signed the Federal Reserve Act. The need for a central bank became painfully evident during the financial panic of 1907, when the stock market collapsed, banks failed, and credit evaporated. Because the federal government lacked the tools to respond, it had to depend on private bankers, such as J. P. Morgan, to provide an infusion of capital to sustain the banking system. To correct the problem of an "inelastic currency," Congress created a National Monetary Commission, chaired by Rhode Island Republican senator Nelson Aldrich. Aldrich proposed a system that would be run by private bankers who would act as federal agents. Progressives adamantly opposed what they called a surrender to the "Money Trust" and blocked its passage.

In 1912 Democrats won the White House and majorities in both houses of Congress. Even before his inauguration, President-elect Woodrow Wilson began encouraging congressional leaders to enact banking and currency reform. In March 1913 the Democratic Senate created its first Banking and Currency Committee, chaired by Oklahoma senator Robert D. Owen. The House Banking Committee was chaired by Virginia representative (and future senator) Carter Glass. In June President Wilson formally proposed creation of a government-run Federal Reserve system. The House took up the issue first and passed a bill in September, after which the Senate Banking Committee began holding hearings.

By December the Senate was debating and voting on its version of the bill. When all of the Senate Republicans voted for a substitute measure, Senate Democrats opted to make the banking and currency bill a "party question." At that time, the Democratic Conference had a "binding caucus" rule, by which whenever two-thirds of the conference voted in favor of a bill, all of its members agreed to support it and not to offer amendments on the floor. The Senate therefore passed the Federal Reserve Act by an almost party-line vote. The bill then went to a conference committee, which forged the necessary compromises and reported it back on December 22, when it was accepted by the House.

On December 23, 1913, the Senate adopted the conference report by a vote of 43 to 25, with every Democrat present voting for the measure and all but four Republicans voting against it. (Twenty-seven senators were "paired" or chose not to vote.) Most senators immediately rushed to Union Station to catch trains home for the holidays, while the chief sponsors went to the White House. President Wilson signed the Glass-Owens Act at 6:00 p.m. He used four pens, then gave one to each of the leading sponsors. Wilson commented that he was not accustomed to using a series of pens. The Democratic whip, Senator J. Hamilton Lewis of Illinois, responded, "The bill itself was made in installments, Mr. President." "Yes," said Wilson, "and very slowly." The Oval Office filled with cheers for what became the most lasting legislative accomplishment of the Wilson administration.

Source: senate.gov
https://www.senate.gov/artandhistory/history/minute/
Senate_Passes_the_Federal_Reserve_Act.htm#:~:text=It%20took%20
many%20months%20and,signed%20the%20Federal%20Reserve%20Act.

A Question of Accountability

Despite pronouncements from Woodrow Wilson about small groups of dominant men controlling the nation's system of credit, the Federal Reserve was never going to be a democratic entity.

Ironically, a series of gaffs at the start of the Great Depression saw changes to the Federal Reserve via the Banking Acts of 1933 and 1935 including moving power of the Fed to the Federal Reserve Board and away from the twelve Reserve Banks as was the case initially.

The Board now set discount rates and held most seats on the Federal Open Markets Committee (FOMC). In addition, the Fed itself saw its power reduced as the U.S. president and Treasury gained more sway over monetary policy. The president had the authority to revalue the dollar in terms of gold and regulate the gold standard. The Treasury, via the Exchange Stabilization Fund, could manage the dollar.

The tide would later turn back in favor of the Fed. Currently, after economic or financial upheavals the Federal Reserve is taking, or being given additional powers and oversight. Although the Chairman of the Federal Reserve makes a bi-annual visit to be grilled by Congress, there is no real oversight.

"A great industrial nation is controlled by its system of credit. Our system of credit is concentrated. The growth of the Nation, therefore, and all our activities are in the hands of a few men ♦ ♦ *, We have come to be one of the worst ruled, one of the most completely controlled and dominated Governments in the civilised world — no longer a Government by free opinion, no longer a Government by conviction and the vote of the majority, but a Government by the opinion and duress of small groups of dominant men."
— Woodrow Wilson, The New Freedom

tags: banking-system, banks, corruption, economy, federal-reserve, oligarchy, plutocracy, politics, usa 0 likes

"The Federal Reserve is an independent agency. And that means basically that there is no other agency of government which can overrule actions that we take. So long as that is in place, and there is no evidence that the administration, or congress, or anybody else is requesting that we do things other than what we think is the appropriate thing, then what the relationships are don't frankly matter. And I've had very good relationship with presidents."
— Alan Greenspan

tags: federal-reserve   0 likes

Source: goodreads.com

While the Federal Reserve may lack significant oversight, the Fed can still be impacted by the actions of Congress. The Fed has several mandates to shape its actions and decisions. Congress can make those decisions more interesting. Below is an example of two acts passed by Congress thirty-two years apart that had a direct impact on the Fed's mandates.

Congress Steps Up

Employment Act of 1946

February 20, 1946

President Harry S. Truman signed this law on February 20, 1946, as hundreds of thousands of American soldiers returned home from World War II and the economy transitioned from wartime production.

Source: federalreservehistory.org
https://www.federalreservehistory.org/essays/employment-act-of-1946

With soldiers coming home from the war and looking for work, Congress took it upon itself to step up and get vets back to work. It was laid out in the heart of the Employment Act of 1946:

The Congress hereby declares that it is the continuing policy and responsibility of the federal government to use all practicable means consistent with its needs and obligations and other essential considerations of national policy with the assistance and cooperation of industry, agriculture, labor, and state and local governments, to coordinate and utilize all its plans, functions, and resources for the purpose of creating and maintaining, in a manner calculated to foster and promote free and competitive enterprise and the general welfare, conditions under which there will be afforded useful employment for those able, willing, and seeking work, and to promote maximum employment, production, and purchasing power.[1]

After several drafts, the final bill removed a claim that citizens have a "right" to a job. In addition, the final bill also removed acknowledgment of the importance of maintaining purchasing power. That would have required Congress to find ways to keep inflation in check, which some saw as a bridge too far in a nation that embraced free markets and not the visible hand of government.

The act created the Council of Economic Advisers (CEA) to aid and advise the president. In turn, the president would be required to submit a report to Congress within ten days of submitting the federal budget, forecasts on the future state of the U.S. economy.

The act also saw the creation of the Joint Economic Committee (with members of both parties) tasked with reviewing the president's report and making recommendations to Congress on economic policy.

Congress Passes the Baton

Full Employment and Balanced Growth Act of 1978 (Humphrey-Hawkins)

October 1978

This amendment to the Employment Act of 1946 was signed in October 27, 1978, by President Jimmy Carter, establishing new goals for the nation's economic policymakers.

Source: federalreservehistory.org
https://www.federalreservehistory.org/essays/humphrey-hawkins-act

The Humphrey Hawkins Act amended the Employment Act of 1946 and established several objectives.

Public Law 95–523
95th Congress

An Act

To translate into practical reality the right of all Americans who are able, willing, and seeking to work to full opportunity for useful paid employment at fair rates of compensation; to assert the responsibility of the Federal Government to use all practicable programs and policies to promote full employment, production, and real income, balanced growth, adequate productivity growth, proper attention to national priorities, and reasonable price stability; to require the President each year to set forth explicit short-term and medium-term economic goals; to achieve a better integration of general and structural economic policies; and to improve the coordination of economic policymaking within the Federal Government.	Oct. 27, 1978 [H.R. 50]

Source: govinfo.org
https://www.govinfo.gov/content/pkg/STATUTE-92/pdf/STATUTE-92-Pg1887.pdf

Unemployment was not to exceed 3.0% for people twenty years or older.

Inflation to be reduced to 3.0% or less (provided reducing inflation didn't interfere with employment goals). Initially, the goal was for the inflation rate to be zero by 1988.

The Federal Reserve had three general mandates. They were to:

· Stabilize Prices

· Maximize Employment

· Moderate Long-Term Interest Rates

The Fed would very quickly flex its authority in ways that made Congress very nervous. The country was suffering from crippling inflation and the Fed decided to take decisive action. Fed Chairman Paul Volker vowed to crush inflation, but while doing so unemployment spiked to more than 10% and lawmakers were in a panic. Summoned to DC, Volker insisted he had to whip inflation and then unemployment would come down. He was adamant that the task of bringing down runaway inflation had no other solution.

His firm stance is the stuff of legends. Eventually, inflation would fall, GDP would climb and hold steady, and unemployment fell back as well. It ushered in a period known as The Great Moderation.

Great Moderation

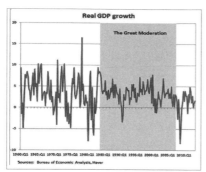 

Source: Bureau of Economic Analysis, Haver https://www.federalreservehistory.org/essays/great-moderation

Source: Bureau of Economic Analysis, Haver https://www.federalreservehistory.org/essays/great-moderation

When Paul Volcker became chairman of the Federal Reserve on August 6, 1979, the S&P 500 was changing hands at 104. At the end of The Great Moderation, the S&P 500 was trading at 1,478.

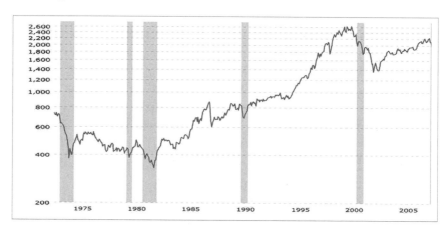

Paul Volcker had a showdown with Congress and won. But his real victory was propelling the office of the Federal Reserve into superstar status.

1982

Source: time.com
https://content.time.com/time/
covers/0,16641,19820308,00.html

2005

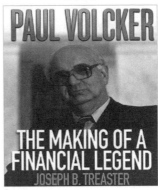

Source: amazon.com
https://www.amazon.com/
Age-Turbulence-Adventures-World
-traditional-Chinese/dp/9862130016

From Tough Love to Sweet Love: Enter the Maestro

Who can take the rainbow?
(Who can take the rainbow?)
Wrap it in a sigh
(Wrap it in a sigh)
Soak it in the sun and make a groovy lemon pie?

The Candy Man (the candy man)
The Candy Man can (the candy man can)
The Candy Man can cause
He mixes it with love
And makes the world taste good
(Makes the world taste good)

~ Sammy Davis

While Paul Volcker used tough love to carve out a place in history, Alan Greenspan used aggressive accommodation to become a legend. Appointed the chairman on June 2, 1987, and confirmed on August 11, 1987, Greenspan was greeted with the biggest single-day market crash ever on October 19th otherwise known as "Black Monday" when the Dow Jones Industrial Average was slammed 22.6%.

Greenspan Springs Into Action

Greenspan had been on his way to Dallas for a speaking engagement when the news about the crash reached him.

After huddling with his team, it was decided that going on with the speech would seem out of touch. Now the focus was on the action — a mixture of calm and strength.

Within the Fed there were concerns about any weak links in the system but mostly their goal was to get bankers to step up to the plate. Specifically, what Greenspan and his team wanted was for the banks to agree to make loans and take on some risks that might have seemed counterintuitive at the time. At the same time, Greenspan honed in on a message for the markets and decided to make it short and to the point. On October 20 at 8:41 (before the market opened) Greenspan issued this statement:

"The Federal Reserve, consistent with its responsibilities as the nation's central bank, affirmed today its readiness to serve as a source of liquidity to support the economic and financial system."

Behind the scenes, the Fed encouraged/pushed banks to make loans. Ben Bernanke noted, "Making these loans must have been a money-losing strategy from the point of view of the banks (and the Fed); otherwise, Fed persuasion would not have been needed. But lending was a good strategy for the preservation of the system as a whole"

The "Put" is born.

Greenspan Put

By coming to the rescue after Black Monday and subsequent crises in a swift and decisive manner the market came to believe Alan Greenspan would always save the day, and this led to the notion of the Greenspan Put, the name given to his monetary policy to financial crises.

Human nature being what it is, saw investors push the envelope more and more believing that if "you-know-what" hit the fan, Greenspan would save the day.

Prior to the appointment of Alan Greenspan to the Chairmanship, the Federal Reserve and its counterparts in other countries achieved easy money goals by keeping interest rates low.

The low cost to borrow would fuel economic growth and super-size the growth of value in assets while at the same time discouraging savings (which rarely kept the pace of even low inflation). Over time the Federal Reserve used its tools based on the status of the economy.

That all changed dramatically with the arrival of Alan Greenspan...also known on Wall Street as "The Maestro."

Greenspan lowered rates and restored calm, which was unthinkable as the Dow Jones Industrial Average was free-falling 23% on that fateful day.

Greenspan provided the template for the more visible role of the Federal Reserve and its relationship with the stock market and wealthy benefactors. Black Monday also coincided with the collapse of Long-Term Capital Management: a hedge fund founded by Ivy League professors who had won Nobel Prizes in economics on their theories.

Plenty of money was thrown at these guys but the real world is also different from the academic world where emotions can have a tremendous impact. The smartest guys in the room blew it.

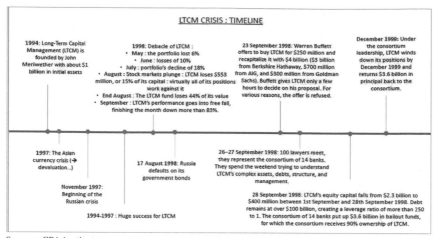

Source: CFA institute
https://extreme-events-finance.net/resources/ltcm-crisis/

For the "greater good," LTCM was bailed out, which was a de facto bail out of the stock market. If there was any doubt before, it was clear that Main Street's needs were subordinate to Wall Street's.

WALL STREET BAILOUT

By **Robert D. Novak**
September 28, 1998

As the Federal Reserve's policy-making body meets tomorrow amid expectations of an interest-rate cut, Chairman Alan Greenspan faces reproof for bailing out a highly speculative hedge fund and then helping it more by altering the central bank's grand strategy.

Long-Term Capital Management, which makes risky bets worldwide, was saved from bankruptcy by an emergency meeting at the New York Federal Reserve Bank that raised $3.5 billion from Wall Street giants to pay the company's creditors. The next day, Greenspan hinted that monetary easing by the Fed will take place this week.

This looks like the Fed caricature painted by populists for much of the past century: impervious to woes of businessmen and farmers in the real economy but ready for quick action when high-flying investors are imperiled. A former Fed vice chairman sitting as a principal of Long-Term Capital adds to the perception of the buddy system at work.

Source: washingtonpost.com
https://www.washingtonpost.com/archive/opinions/1998/09/28/wall-street-bailout/
de0b66c4-360c-4d86-9c9e-d1abe990fc7e/

Eventually, the mistakes were so egregious they led to the Global Financial Crisis of 2007-2008. Later Greenspan would admit to mistakes that played a role in the GFC although he never took responsibility.

Bernanke Put

Ben Bernanke introduced quantitative easing or QE when Greenspan's tools stopped working during the GFC. The program was straightforward — flood the economy with money. A monetary *printing press on steroids, Bernanke's plan was based on the following concepts:

1. Central Bank creates money to buy bonds and, in this case, mortgage-backed securities.

2. The extra demand for bonds lowers their yield.

3. This lowers interest rates across the economy.

4. Businesses and consumers are incentivized to spend and invest.

5. That extra spending lifts the economy.

This plan increased the Fed's balance sheet at a remarkable rate, something that was not greeted with enthusiasm by all economists.

The Balance Sheet Swells

For years economists argued against the Fed's balance sheet crossing $1 trillion, feeling it would be a dark day for the economy — a sure sign of instability and far too much money at the central bank. After three rounds of quantitative easing, the Fed's balance sheet swelled to $4.4 trillion from $870 billion.

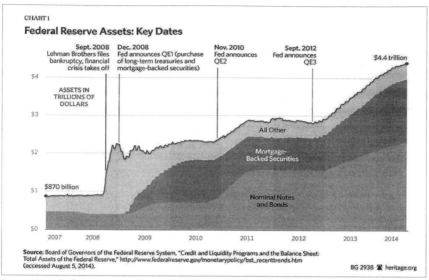

Source: Board of Governors of the Federal Reserve System
http://www.federalreserve.gov/monetarypolicy/bst_recenttrends.htm

Yellen Put

Janet Yellen followed Bernanke into the chairmanship in 2014. As Fed Chair, Yellen was expected to keep rates low. In fact, she hiked Fed Fund rates 25 bps, and the stock market had a temper tantrum. This headline is an example of the general concern at the time.

> DEC. 16, 2015
>
> Janet Yellen Is Trying to Slow Down the Economy. But Why?

Source: nymag.com
https://nymag.com/intelligencer/2015/12/janet-yellen-is-trying-to-slow-the-economy-why.html

The stock market stumbled for the rest of 2015 and the first ten sessions in 2016 were among the worst in history for that same time frame.

The thing about the market is that when it feels like it can intimidate the Federal Reserve, when the Chairman blinks stocks rally. Once it was made clear that Janet Yellen got her mind right, the stock market took off.

Fed officials rarely comment on the market in part because any negative observations without actions will be seen as a weakness. An example would be when Alan Greenspan called the 1996 market rally "irrational" but only took action to cool the market years later. Chairman Yellen understood this dynamic. Here is a graph of what she was looking at during the early years of her first term as chairman.

S&P 500

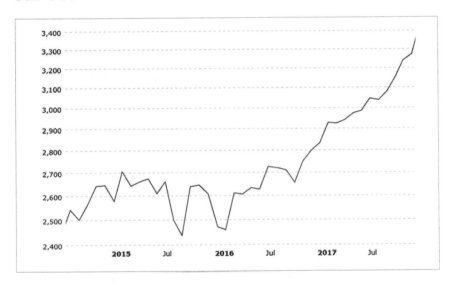

Janet Yellen learned her lesson and the Fed waited until after the 2016 presidential election results were in before hiking rates again. Another reason stocks recoiled from the rate hike is global conditions were already deteriorating and the rate hike was seen as unnecessary. This is the worst kind of move a central banker can make, adding interest rate pressure to an economy already lurching into freefall.

Trichet Folly

Jean Claude Trichet, the head of the European Central Bank, had the aura and personality that came straight out of central casting: the arrogant aristocrat banker with little time to listen to his underlings. Trichet was determined to hammer inflation even after it was clear inflation had peaked. At the same time that the U.S. was heading into the biggest financial crisis in generations, Trichet was misreading the situation in Europe.

Source: newyorker.com
https://www.newyorker.com/magazine/2011/09/05/europes-big-mistake

Not only was inflation coming down, but it was in free fall and soon the ECB would need to cut rates and commence QE (money printing), which meant a higher balance sheet.

This episode in central banking history doesn't get nearly as much attention as Arthur Burns' pause on rate hikes before inflation had run its course in the 1970s but it's a cautionary tale for bankers and citizens.

More elegant solutions need to be created by central banks to combat inflation rather than the irresponsible notion of breaking everything (and everybody).

Fed officials are loath to let inflation run amok but society is loath to see the value of their assets crushed and job losses mount and jobs become less plentiful.

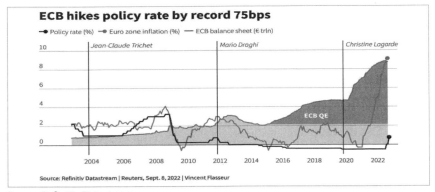

Source: Refinitiv Datastream
https://www.reuters.com/markets/europe/australia-new-zealand-keeps-global-rate-hikes-up-ward-swing-2022-10-05/

Powell & COVID-19 Whiplash

We cannot critically discuss financial actions taken during the COVID-19 pandemic, particularly in the initial months of the lockdown, and national fear of this unknown disease, and rising death rates.

The world hadn't seen anything like this for one-hundred years.

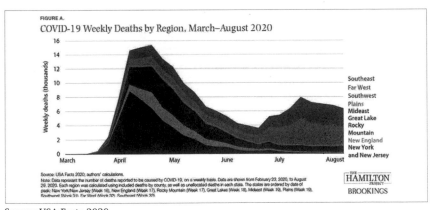

Source: USA Facts 2020
https://www.hamiltonproject.org/publication/economic-fact/
ten-facts-about-covid-19-and-the-u-s-economy/

The economy quickly lurched into recession. In fact, no recession had ever been as swift, it was like a swarm of locusts descended upon society and the economy overnight.

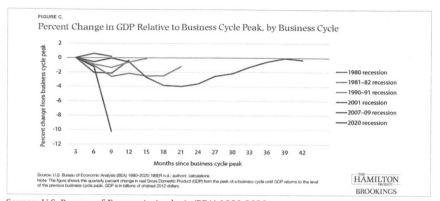

Source: U.S. Bureau of Economic Analysis (BEA) 1980-2020
https://www.hamiltonproject.org/publication/economic-fact/ten-facts-about-covid-19-and-the-u-s-economy/

Hardships Lingered

I remember coming home from the supermarket and wiping down everything with disinfectant even fruit to the point where most of it became inedible.

People were told not to go to work, and many businesses closed. Paying rent was difficult for more than 20% of households late in 2020.

There was no doubt lots of money would have to be deployed into the economy, but nobody knew just how much. Below is a chart that exemplifies the difficulties many families faced through 2020 and 2021. This is what governments, both state and Federal, as well as the Federal Reserve were seeing and reacting to at the time.

But the reason for these hardships was no longer steeped in a shutdown economy but in runaway inflation that rose out of all the money poured into the economy in a very short period of time.

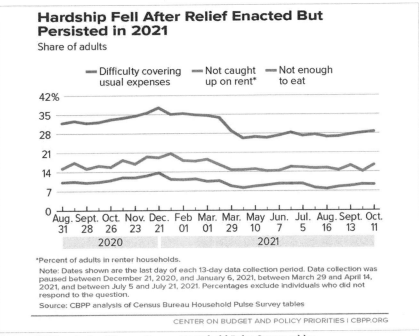

Hardship Fell After Relief Enacted But Persisted in 2021

Share of adults

Legend: — Difficulty covering usual expenses — Not caught up on rent* — Not enough to eat

*Percent of adults in renter households.

Note: Dates shown are the last day of each 13-day data collection period. Data collection was paused between December 21, 2020, and January 6, 2021, between March 29 and April 14, 2021, and between July 5 and July 21, 2021. Percentages exclude individuals who did not respond to the question.

Source: CBPP analysis of Census Bureau Household Pulse Survey tables

CENTER ON BUDGET AND POLICY PRIORITIES I CBPP.ORG

Source: CBPP analysis of Census Bureau Household Pulse Survey tables
https://www.cbpp.org/hardship-fell-after-relief-enacted-but-persisted-in-2021

Financial Rescue

The Federal Reserve and Federal Government (Trump and Biden administrations) reacted with the most cash ever distributed in the history of mankind. Stimulus funding was 27% of the U.S. GDP.

No country sent out more checks than the United States, and only Singapore distributed more as a percentage of GDP.

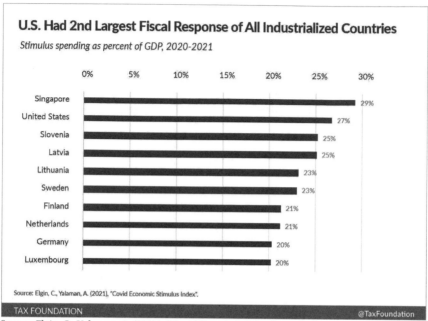

Source: Elgin, C., Yalaman, A. (2021), "Covid Economic Stimulus Index".
https://taxfoundation.org/us-covid19-fiscal-response/

And Now for My Next Trick...

The Fed sprang into action in the weeks after COVID-19 made its way into our lives.

The Federal Reserve issued $4.7 trillion out of the $7.1 trillion it was prepared to offer. Here is a brief breakdown of how the Fed attacked the crisis.

The Federal Reserve resurrected and created a number of facilities to get money into banks and then Main Street. That is something that has to be applauded by all.

Most of the cash had an immediate positive impact, and by the end of 2020 miraculous things were happening with the economy.

TABLE 1
Pandemic-era Federal Reserve facilities
The Fed established various emergency lending programs under Section 13(3) of the Federal Reserve Act to support households, businesses, governments, and financial markets.

Facility	Sector targeted	Funding	Date announced	Date opened	Date closed	Maximum capacity ($ bil.)	Peak assets ($ bil.)	Assets as of 12/8/21 ($ bil.)	Treasury backstop ($ bil.)
Commercial Paper Funding Facility (CPFF)	Commercial paper market	Fed, Treasury (ESF)	3/17/20	4/14/20	3/31/21	Unlimited	4.2	0.0	10.0
Main Street Lending Program (MSLP)*	Small and mid-sized businesses, non-profits	Fed, Treasury (CARES Act)	4/9/20	7/6/20†	1/8/21	600.0	16.6	13.4	75.0
Money Market Mutual Fund Liquidity Facility (MMLF)	Money market mutual funds	Fed, Treasury (ESF)	3/18/20	3/23/20	3/31/21	Unlimited	53.2	0.0	10.0
Municipal Liquidity Facility (MLF)*	State and local governments	Fed, Treasury (CARES Act)	4/9/20	5/26/20	12/31/20	500.0	6.4	4.2	35.0
Paycheck Protection Program Liquidity Facility (PPPLF)*	Small businesses	Fed	4/9/20	4/16/20	7/30/21	953.0‡	90.6	39.9	-
Primary Dealer Credit Facility (PDCF)	Broker-dealers	Fed	3/17/20	3/20/20	3/31/21	Unlimited	33.4	0.0	-
Primary Market Corporate Credit Facility (PMCCF)*	Large businesses	Fed, Treasury (CARES Act)	3/23/20	6/29/20	12/31/20	750.0	0.0	0.0	50.0
Secondary Market Corporate Credit Facility (SMCCF)*	Large businesses, exchange-traded funds	Fed, Treasury (CARES Act)	3/23/20	5/12/20†	12/31/20	Combined with PMCCF	14.3	0.0	25.0
Term Asset-Backed Securities Loan Facility (TALF)	Securities markets (e.g. student, auto, & credit card loans)	Fed, Treasury (CARES Act)	3/23/20	6/17/20	12/31/20	100.0	4.1	1.4	10.0

Source: Federal Reserve. ESF refers to the Treasury's Exchange Stabilization Fund.
* Programs new for 2020.
† The MSLP began purchasing loan participations on 7/6/20 for for-profit businesses and 9/4/20 for nonprofits. The SMCCF began purchasing ETFs on 5/12/20 and corporate bonds on 6/16/20.
‡ The PPPLF maximum capacity listed is the amount allocated to the PPP by Congress.

Hutchins Center
on Fiscal & Monetary Policy
at BROOKINGS

Source: Federal Reserve
https://www.brookings.edu/articles/fed-response-to-covid19/

Balance Sheet Goes to New Heights

If you polled every single economist in the world and proposed to them the Fed's balance sheet would rocket to $7.0 trillion and asked what the corresponding condition of the world would be, I'm sure most would say it as A) preposterous or B) the planet was being invaded with space aliens.

The Federal Reserve was putting out the fire of recession but also creating kindling for the next financial crisis: runaway inflation.

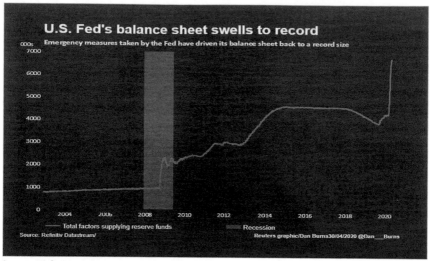

Source: Refinitiv Datastream
https://www.reuters.com/article/us-health-coronavirus-fed-borrowing-idUSKBN216418

Interestingly, inflation wasn't an issue despite all the cash that came into the economy. I should rephrase this and say inflation wasn't an issue for the Federal Reserve as Jay Powell told everyone it was temporary.

One issue that was out of Powell's control, however, was the record-breaking gusher of money from the federal government.

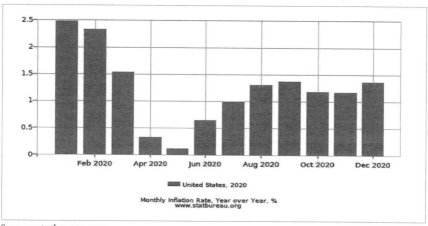

Source: statbureau.com
https://www.statbureau.org/en/united-states/inflation

Inflation Takes Flight

Although there were far too many deaths from COVID-19 and many jurisdictions leveled restrictive policies on their population that slammed local commerce, the nation was already back on its economic footing.

There is a legitimate argument that households and businesses in America had never been so rich going into 2021 as the household debt was a record low against income and GDP and corporations were sitting on record cash with record-low debt.

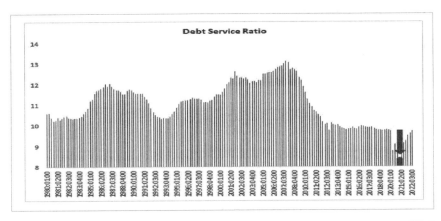

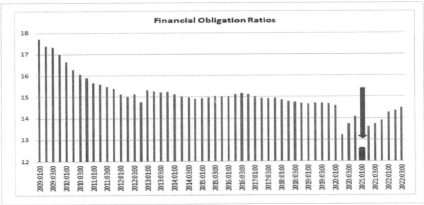

America didn't need an additional $1.9 trillion in economic relief, but it got it.

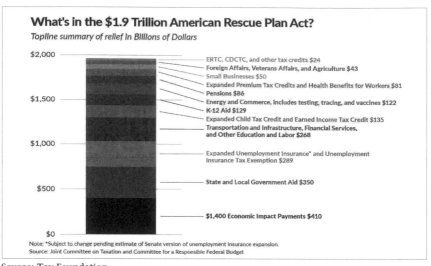

Source: Tax Foundation
https://taxfoundation.org/american-rescue-plan-covid-relief/

The Great Depression notion of "a chicken in every pot" was taken to new levels and billions were sent to states for dubious programs like a guaranteed income. Very little was used or needed for COVID-19 related issues.

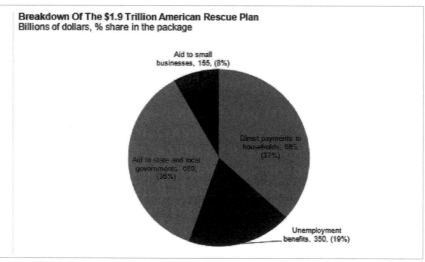

Source: SPGlobal
https://www.spglobal.com/ratings/en/research/articles/200120-enel-esg-and-credit-rat-ings-11311565

Inflation Erupts

There was no need for $1.9 trillion back in 2021, but once it was signed into law the motions began, not unlike that of a volcanic eruption. The lava (money) was going to flow and there was no stopping it. The devasting impact could last for years.

And that's exactly what happened in the United States where inflation climbed to the highest level in forty years.

Powell Blows It

Source: KITCO News

There were signs inflation was moving too high, too fast, and soon could be out of control. The nation looked to Jay Powell, the current Chairman of the Federal Reserve, for assurance, and he was firm in his convictions. Inflation was transitory. Chairman Powell's beliefs proved overly optimistic. Here is what he thought was going to happen. The reality proved to be something entirely different.

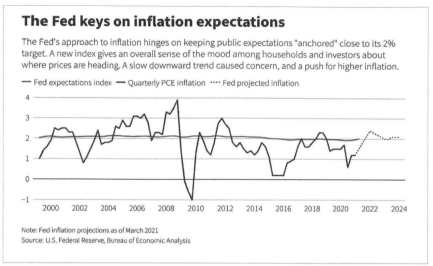

The Fed keys on inflation expectations

The Fed's approach to inflation hinges on keeping public expectations "anchored" close to its 2% target. A new index gives an overall sense of the mood among households and investors about where prices are heading. A slow downward trend caused concern, and a push for higher inflation.

— Fed expectations index — Quarterly PCE inflation ···· Fed projected inflation

Note: Fed inflation projections as of March 2021
Source: U.S. Federal Reserve, Bureau of Economic Analysis

Source: U.S. Federal Reserve

Yikes!!

Consumer prices climbed to the highest level in forty years. Half the nation had never dealt with that kind of inflation and the other half thought it was a relic of the past. The Federal Reserve's main mandate, after all, is keeping inflation in check. The following Consumer Price Index graph is a good representation of how effective the Fed had been in maintaining a consistent rate of inflation, which stabilized consumer costs. But that was not the case beginning in 2021. Families began to see a serious, negative impact on their daily lives.

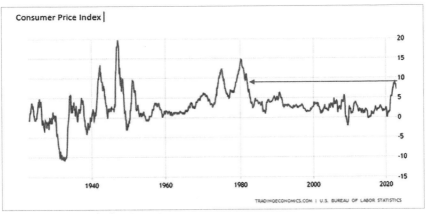

Source: U.S. Bureau of Labor Statistics

Wages adjusted for inflation immediately were negative the month the $1.9 trillion package became law and lasted for more than two years. Something needed to change.

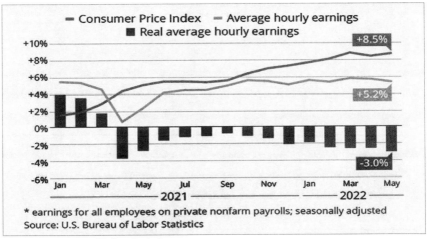

Source: U.S. Bureau of Labor Statistics

Powell Pivots

In a series of humiliating admissions, Jay Powell retired the word "transitory" and acknowledged inflation was stubborn and had to be uprooted by the Federal Reserve.

The reaction was the most aggressive rate hiking cycle in history. Even then, service inflation was so deeply rooted it remained elevated.

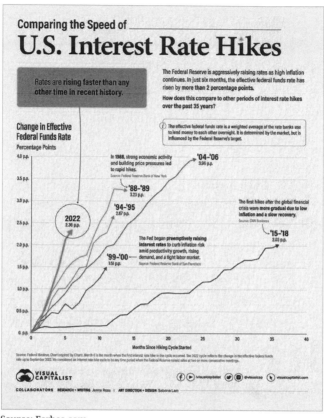

Source: Forbes.com
https://www.forbes.com/sites/investor-hub/2023/05/02/
investing-in-a-high-interest-rate-environment/?sh=10331a8423c2

Record Cash

The big problem for Jay Powell is the record amount of cash folks were sitting on and spending. The combination of the restrictions during the pandemic and the large stimulus grants created a cash flow situation that was really remarkable.

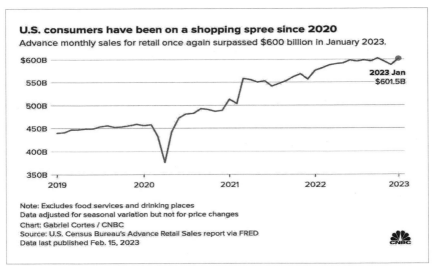

Source: CNBC / U.S. Census Bureau

Inflation was becoming embedded in the economy and the Fed risked pushing the nation into a deep recession to bring it under control. Ironically, time was a weapon that wasn't considered.

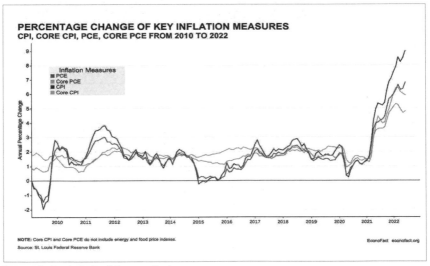

Source: St. Louis Federal Reserve Bank

Excess Savings

Economists talked a lot about "excess savings" as a reason not to fear a recession in 2022 and 2023. Moreover, many said it was a reason the Federal Reserve had to remain aggressive in its efforts to take money out of the economy. This really upset me tremendously. There certainly was excess cash, but it was not evenly distributed.

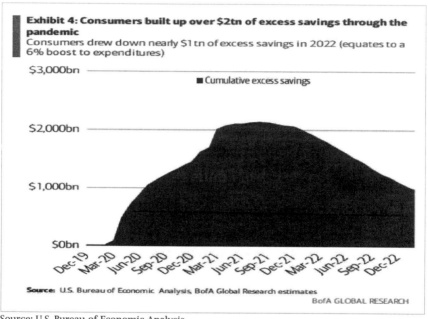

Exhibit 4: Consumers built up over $2tn of excess savings through the pandemic
Consumers drew down nearly $1 tn of excess savings in 2022 (equates to a 6% boost to expenditures)

Source: U.S. Bureau of Economic Analysis, BofA Global Research estimates

BofA GLOBAL RESEARCH

Source: U.S. Bureau of Economic Analysis

The top quartile of the economy had the largest share of excess savings, which they accumulated through reduced spending. Aggressive rate hikes weren't going to move the needle with this crowd. Please, I understood that the folks at this top of this quartile were always going to end up with all the money. And I wasn't the only one to recognize the upward movement of all this cash.

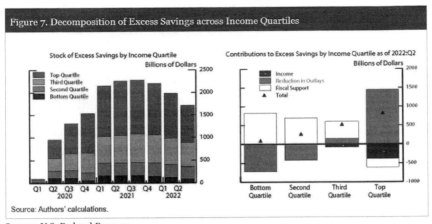

Figure 7. Decomposition of Excess Savings across Income Quartiles

Source: Authors' calculations.

Source: U.S. Federal Reserve
https://www.federalreserve.gov/econres/notes/feds-notes/
excess-savings-during-the-covid-19-pandemic-20221021.html

Trickle Up

In February 2023 Stanford University issued a paper explaining how all the stimulus money would find its way into the pockets of the top 1.0% over a five-year period.

Source: Stanford (SIEPR)

The poorest households with the highest Marginal Propensity to Consume spend down their excess savings the fastest, increasing other households' incomes and their excess savings. This leads to a long-lasting increase in aggregate demand until, ultimately, excess savings have "trickled up" to the richest savers with the lowest MPCs, raising wealth inequality.

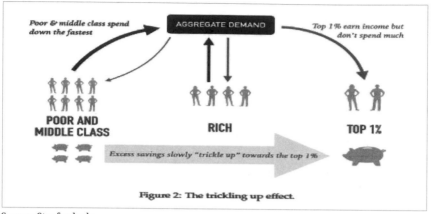

Figure 2: The trickling up effect.

Source: Stanford.edu
http://web.stanford.edu/~aauclert/tricklingup.pdf

Rewarding the Wealthy

The Fed hiked rates so much that interest-earning assets began to benefit. Money market yields surged, bond yields surged, and certificates of deposit made a comeback. By the same token, interest rates zoomed higher, adding even more misery to those households that already spent their excess savings. Increased interest rates don't have the same impact on all people. If you are in the bottom 70% economically, you are losing ground with higher interest rates. This illustration demonstrates the impact, both positively and negatively.

Every One Percent Increase in Interest Rates

TOP 30%	BOTTOM 70%
Own $1.3 trillion interest-earning assets	Holds $4.8 trillion in consumer debt
Earns $60 billion	Cost $40 billion

The Fed decided to destroy the economy from the bottom up, and while that's a way to kill inflation, it rubs me the wrong way. It really stinks.

There was room for personal accountability just like the housing boom in the mid-2000s when people knew they couldn't afford the home they were buying but planned to flip it before their starter loan interest rate doubled. When the housing market crashed, they were in deep trouble.

With record-high credit card debt and auto loans that climbed to an average monthly payment of $730 (16% were $1,000 a month) the American public paid a huge price for Powell missing the threat of inflation and President Biden adding too much money into the economy.

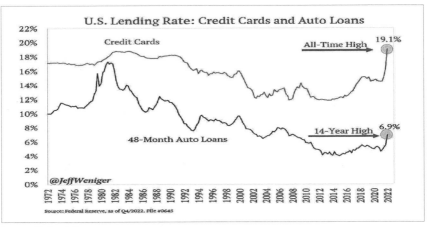

Source: Federal Reserve

Federal Reserve & Stock Market

So, the Fed has a tremendous impact on the economy generally. The Unbreakable Investor needs to understand the Federal Reserve, its history, and its current actions to better understand where the economy may be heading and how to best make use of that information.

Rate hikes generally elicit fear in stock investors, in part because historically at the start of a rate hiking cycle, the stock market moves lower — an average of 6% in the first three months after the first hike.

The game plan says to buy stocks with low valuations ahead of the first rate hike.

Then the script says to buy momentum stocks.

There will be a greater focus on:

> Strong balance sheets
>
> Solid dividend yields
>
> Low volatility
>
> Strong margins

Wall Street has taken to calling these stocks "quality" but remember, these are places to park cash for a few months.

Our focus is always on the best individual names that can significantly outperform over time. But during bear markets and aggressive rate hiking cycles or recessions, it's fine to have more cash and shift the portfolio to overweight safer sectors. But always remember your fortune will be made by going against the grain and against the talking heads.

Exhibit 3: Value stocks tend to outperform around the first rate hike
as of January 13, 2022

	Median returns			
	Months PRECEEDING first rate hike		Months FOLLOWING first rate hike	
	6 months	3 months	3 months	6 months
S&P 500	6 %	5 %	(6)%	5 %
Long/short factors				
Valuation (low vs. high)	5 %	3 %	1 %	5 %
Momentum (high vs. low)	2	(5)	7	2
Growth (high vs. low)	1	(2)	(4)	1
Size (R2K vs. SPX)	0	1	(2)	0
Bal. Sheet (strong vs. weak)	(1)	(3)	4	(1)
Dividend yield (high vs. low)	(1)	2	3	(1)
Volatility (low vs. high)	(3)	(0)	4	(3)
Margins (high vs. low)	(4)	(3)	3	(4)
Returns (high vs. low)	(6)	(3)	4	(6)

Source: Yahoo Finance
https://au.finance.yahoo.com/news/what-happens-to-the-stock-market-when-interest-rates-rise-115245445.html

History of Rate Hikes & Market Reactions

What Happens After the First Fed Rate Hike?
S&P 500 Index Future Returns

Date of First Hike	Next 3 Months	Next 6 Months	Next 12 Months
8/8/83	2.0%	-0.7%	2.1%
4/1/87	19.1	20.9	1.5
5/11/88	3.4	8.6	20.7
2/4/94	-5.9	-2.5	2.4
3/25/97	13.6	20.6	39.6
6/30/99	-7.6	6.6	6.0
6/30/04	-2.3	6.4	5.2
12/16/15	-1.1	0.1	9.1
Average	2.7	7.5	10.8
Median	0.5	6.5	5.6
% Positive	50.0	75.0	100.0

Source: LPL Research, Bloomberg

Bloomberg

Source: Bloomberg
https://www.bloomberg.com/news/articles/2022-03-13/what-happens-to-stocks-when-the-fed-hikes-a-historical-guide

Over the course of rate hikes the stock market normally turns around.

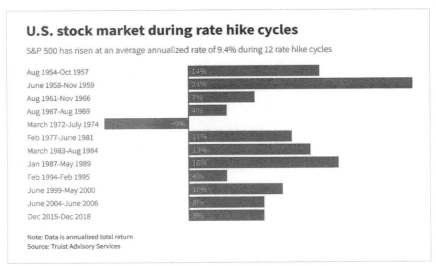

U.S. stock market during rate hike cycles

S&P 500 has risen at an average annualized rate of 9.4% during 12 rate hike cycles

Period	Return
Aug 1954-Oct 1957	14%
June 1958-Nov 1959	24%
Aug 1961-Nov 1966	7%
Aug 1967-Aug 1969	4%
March 1972-July 1974	-9%
Feb 1977-June 1981	11%
March 1983-Aug 1984	13%
Jan 1987-May 1989	16%
Feb 1994-Feb 1995	4%
June 1999-May 2000	10%
June 2004-June 2006	8%
Dec 2015-Dec 2018	8%

Note: Data is annualized total return
Source: Truist Advisory Services

Source: Truist Advisory Services
https://www.reuters.com/business/futures-climb-ukraine-peace-talks-fed-decision-ahead-2022-03-16/

History of Rate Cuts & Market Reactions

I have mentioned before that I'm a student of history. Here is another example of where understanding history can help the Unbreakable Investor increase his or her financial position.

When we look at all rate cuts together, history suggests the initial move in the stock market is lower, and while that could be the case because the economy is in trouble, soon after the market surges. Unfortunately for many investors, the ghosts of the tech bubble bursting prevents them from buying.

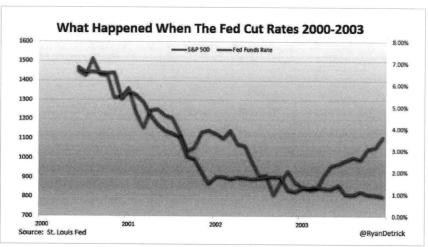

Source: St. Louis Fed

But you want to be ready to leap into the market when the Fed starts cutting rates. In fact, if they cut and there is no recession, fortunes can be made.

Quiz: Chapter 8

1. **What is the primary purpose of the Federal Reserve?**

2. **How did the crash of 1907 influence U.S. fiscal policy?**

3. **Paul Volcker took very aggressive action as the Fed Chair. Why and what were the results of his actions?**

4. **Who is the current Chairman of the Federal Reserve?**

Answers

1. The primary purpose of the Fed is to control inflation.

2. The crash set in motion the acts that would, eventually, result in the creation of the Federal Reserve Banks. These would become the Federal Reserve as we now know it.

3. He was determined to halt the rapid inflation of the time and raised rates in an incredibly aggressive manner. This resulted in the loss of jobs.

4. Jerome Powell is the current Chairman of the Federal Reserve

Chapter

9

Roaring 2020s

The world, led by the United States, has entered the fourth industrial revolution and with this will come a whirlwind of upheaval including the destuction of millioins of jobs as well as the creation of millions of jobs. Comforts currently enjoyed by a few will be ubiquitous. Fortunes will be made in industries that currently only exist in the minds of innovators. This will provide the backdrop to wealth creation never seen before in the history of mankind.

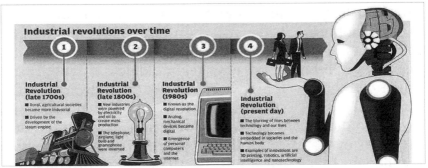

Source: bbntimes.com
https://www.bbntimes.com/technology/artificial-intelligence-in-the-4th-industrial-revolution

While the fourth industrial revolution makes for a sexy backdrop for a big-time party celebrating man's latest leap, it will mostly super charge the innovation cycle that will bridge the sixth and seventh waves.

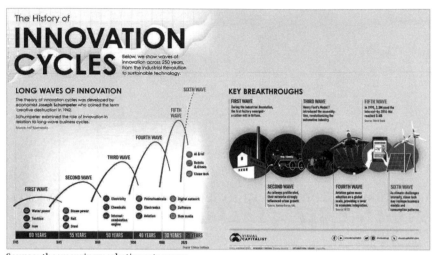

Source: theemergingmarketinvestor.com
https://www.theemergingmarketsinvestor.com/category/technology/

I'm looking for a repeat of the 1920s during the 2020s based on a combination of factors of which many have already occurred.

These factors are a test and surviving them is the equivalent of a caterpillar emerging from a cocoon into a butterfly.

That test has several components. One is that Americans are developing a wider zest for life, just like we did following the First World War. The next component would be the development of new technologies. In the 1920s much of that development came out of the war and the Spanish Flu. Today we have COVID-19 and the War on Terror to drive some developments, but innovation has a life of its own and continues at an amazing pace. The final component that occurred in the 1920s was a pro-business administration in Washington DC That one still remains to be seen, but I'm hoping we get that final piece because if we do, the ride could really be amazing!

Parallel to 1920

I know it sounds kind of corny and even flippant to suggest the 2020s could be a repeat of the 1920s and, in fact, much has been written about the parallels between the 1920s and the 2020s. For example:

- Spanish Flu = COVID-19
- WWI = War on Terror
- Sharp Recession 1920-1921 = Economic Shutdown Shock 2020

Let's take a stroll back in time to the set up that sparked one of the greatest periods of economic growth in American history.

The Spanish Flu took 675,000 American lives and 40 million around the world, and the end of WWI saw a million soldiers enter the workforce.

The Federal Reserve printed up a ton of money to offset economic struggles. This created a new problem: runaway inflation.

A pair of shoes that cost $3.00 in 1918 cost as much as $12.00 in 1920. The Fed pivoted to hiking rates and that made matters worse as the economy had already peaked. Left to its own devices, inflation would have faded without assistance.

- In 1920 the United States was in the grip of economic demise
- Unemployment climbed to 12% from 4%
- Gross National Product (GNP) declined 17%

So, what happened to change this incredibly bleak picture? Historically it is generally accepted that the U.S. government took no action or intervention. Rather, it allowed the economy to organically climb out of that harsh recession.

But there was action — just not the kind of intervention we have become accustomed to. Our most recent economic crisis saw the government pump billions of dollars into the economy. While economists might argue about the timing or the volume of money, it was generally accepted that some positive action was necessary. There was a completely different approach in the 1920s.

The nation was reeling and, just as with the most recent crisis, action had to be taken. To his credit President Wilson chose to cut government spending by 20% and use surplus funds to pay off WWI debt.

President Harding cut government spending an additional 35%, raising the surplus to $736 million despite urging of federal stimulus by Commerce Secretary Hoover. Harding then went even further.

In addition to less spending, Harding began lowering taxes across all income brackets:

Top Rate
   · 1922 58% from 73%
   · 1924 46% from 58%
   · 1925 25% from 46%

The 1920-21 recession lasted eighteen months and many say its severity and short duration are both due to the fact the federal government didn't save unhealthy banks or businesses. While this approach might seem rather draconian to us today, it worked.

The Stage Is Set

President Harding died in office on August 2, 1923. His Vice President, Calvin Coolidge, was administered the oath of office as President of the United States in the early-morning hours of August 3.The economy was beginning to turn around when he took office, but heavy-handed policies could have still derailed it. Coolidge did not get in the way. He believed in the organic growth of the United States.

He was famous, or infamous, for not saying much, which earned him the nickname Silent Cal. It was his reluctance to use government might to intervene in the economy that sparked the ire of his critics. They wanted him to do more, to intervene directly.

He favored lower taxes, less government spending, preferring to move out of the way and let the rapid modernization take its course. Critics of this laissez-faire approach have long used it as a reason to curb prosperity, to promote big and intrusive government that limits the power and scope of business, which in turns limits the power and scope of the individual. Individual wealth and freedom have always been the enemy of big government.

In my opinion criticism of laissez-faire government is completely off base. A hundred years ago President Coolidge used this approach to usher in one of the most remarkable periods of economic and innovative growth in our history, and yet the criticism still exists. It exists because it gives those in opposition power.

There is big money in promoting big government.

Pro-Business

One of Coolidge's most famous quotes, that is often misquoted, presents his understanding of the economy.

After all, the chief business of the American people is business. They are profoundly concerned with producing, buying, selling, investing, and prospering in the world.

It was spoken during an address President Coolidge gave to the American Society of Newspaper Editors in Washington, DC on January 17, 1925. He let business evolve and along the way it created an amazing time to be alive.

Even though there is heavy political opposition toward business and free markets back then even those on the other side of the aisle recognized the impact of Coolidge. Alfred E Smith remarked Coolidge was "distinguished for character more than for heroic achievement." Could he have been referring to Coolidge's strength of character and conviction to trust in the American economy and American creative ingenuity at the time? Perhaps. He went on to say, "his great task was to restore the dignity and prestige of the Presidency when it had reached the lowest ebb in our history... in a time of extravagance and waste...."

That time of scandal refers to President Harding's administration and the infamous Teapot Dome scandal and other shenanigans within his administration. Still, Harding was forward-thinking, including his idea that there should be less government in business and more business in government.

Harding embraced technology, established the federal budget system, and acknowledged the challenges of Black Americans and women.

Coolidge was the son of a village storekeeper born in Vermont. He endeavored to guide a nation that followed old school morality and at the same time enjoyed material prosperity for all Americans

And he succeeded. It was called "Coolidge Prosperity."

The extravagance part was a little trickier.

The ultra rich, nouveau rich, and hangers-on engaged in endless fun. Many called it hedonism and it was made famous by F. Scott Fitzgerald in his novel "The Great Gatsby."

But this extravagance wasn't just about material gain but about freedom. It was a time of creation in the arts, music, and society at large that matches scientific milestones.

There was also a sense of rebellion of youth that has since become a rite of passage although since the 1960s it has been a faux rejection and America success and wealth back in the 1920s it was a celebration.

Hallmarks of the Time

- Jazz Age
- Youth independence
- Flappers
- Speakeasies

It was a wild time but, in retrospect, a lot of the complaints seem quaint. Yes, young women became more independent and the divorce rate zoomed to 16.3 out of every 100 marriages up from 8.8 in 1910. The music and dances seemed scandalous to the older generation. And there certainly was a change (loosening?) of the morals and social expectations of the younger generation. Where have we heard those complaints before?

But the economy was booming. There were wonderful new innovations to explore. There was money to spend. Tomorrow promised to be better than today with new things becoming available at an incredible rate. The 1920s saw the culmination of the first two industrial revolutions shift to the next level.

The first industrial revolution had allowed mankind to leverage their strength and output starting with the mechanical innovations like the loom.

The second industrial revolution saw railroads connect the world and carry people to distant lands.

Together these seismic shifts in advancement were the personification of man's imagination.

The movement of people, commerce, and ideas has always had a profoundly positive impact on civilization, and it all came together in the roaring 1920s. These innovations began to reshape the country. For example:

Automobiles

The adoption of the automobile was instrumental to growing the suburbs. The automobile allowed families to move away from city centers, to live farther from work. In 1920 there were 8 million registered automobiles. By 1930 there were 23 million.

Ancillary businesses included development of vulcanized rubber, newly built roads, motels, diners, and other businesses associated with the boom.

The Spanish Flu also triggered an exodus out of major cities into small specs on the map. Miami saw its population climb 400% to 150,000 by 1926.

Air Travel

The 1926 Air Commerce Act expanded commercial air travel. While still in its infancy, using airplanes to move people and goods was shrinking the country dramatically. Even things as mundane and routine as mail delivery were being impacted.

Electricity

The expansion of the electric grid allowed for factories to power up and churn out new products at a rate that the country had not seen before.

Electricity became the main source of power for factories, climbing to 70% by 1929 from 30% in 1914. This was an even more dramatic shift when we consider that in 1900 80% of that power came from steam. The expanded electric grid also ushered in household appliances, including washing machines and vacuum cleaners along with improved lighting and heating.

By the mid-1920s, half the population had electric lights.

Radio

The spread of radio saw sixty stations by 1927, which ushered in the era of commercials and the advertising industry. The "wireless" changed the communications game forever which means commerce was changed forever.

Telephone

The expansion of the telephone and long-distance communication.

All of these changes and developments, over such a short period of time, had a tremendous impact on the national economy.

Economic Boom

The Gross National Product averaged 4.2% per year from 1920 to 1929.

Real GNP averaged 2.7% The chart below tracks the increases for the decade of the 1920's.

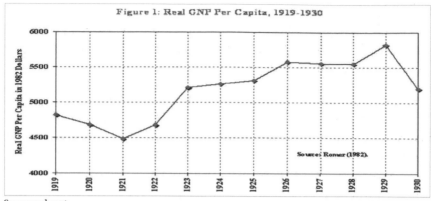

Source: eh.net
https://eh.net/encyclopedia/the-u-s-economy-in-the-1920s/

It is interesting, and informative, to look at the national productivity and capital growth by decade, leading up to and immediately after this incredible growth. One might call it a miracle.

Productivity Miracle

Labor Productivity:	Capital Productivity:
1899 to 1909 1.30%	1899 to 1909 -1.62%
1909 to 1919 1.14%	1909 to 1919 -1.95%
1919 to 1929 5.44%	1919 to 1929 4.21%
1929 to 1937 1.95%	1929 to 1937 2.38%

Table 3: Average Annual Rates of Labor Productivity and Capital Productivity Growth.

Period	Average Annual Labor Productivity Growth	Average Annual Capital Productivity Growth
1899-1909	1.30%	-1.62%
1909-1919	1.14	-1.95
1919-1929	5.44	4.21
1929-1937	1.95	2.38

Source: Devine (1983), Table 2. The average annual percentage rates of growth are calculated as instantaneous rates of change.

Source: Devine (1983)
https://www.eh.net/page/2/?s=taylor+rule

Along with increased productivity came increased wages. As wages went up so did buying power and demand for goods and services. Look at the tremendous increases during this decade. Wages grew for all workers from 1921 to 1929.

- Skilled men +24.5%

- Unskilled men +25.7%

- Women +17.7%

Table 1: Real Average Weekly or Daily Earnings for Selected Occupations, 1920 to 1930.
(1929=100)

Year	(1) Weekly: Skilled and Semi-Skilled Male Production Workers in 25 Manufacturing Industries	(2) Weekly: Unskilled Male Production Workers in 25 Manufacturing Industries	(3) Weekly: Female Production Workers in 25 Manufacturing Industries	(4) Weekly: Bituminous Coal-Lignite Mining	(5) Farmworkers Daily Wage Rate
1920	29.16	22.28	15.14	--	2.82
1921	26.19	19.41	14.96	--	1.96
1922	28.73	20.74	16.19	--	2.04
1923	30.93	22.37	17.31	25.51	2.36
1924	30.61	22.45	16.78	23.47	2.40
1925	30.57	22.41	16.78	25.64	2.30
1926	30.60	22.47	16.72	27.51	2.32
1927	31.09	23.22	17.14	23.85	2.32
1928	31.94	23.89	17.15	24.46	2.30
1929	32.60	24.40	17.61	25.11	2.30
1930	29.93	22.47	16.40	22.61	2.21

Source: U.S. Department of Commerce, Bureau of the Census, *Historical Statistics of the United States: Colonial Times to 1970* (Washington, DC: USGPO, 1976). Col. (1): Series D844. Col. (2): Series D841. Col. (3): Series D838. Col. (4): Series D811. Col. (5): Series K181. All dollar figures were deflated by the Consumer Price Index from series E135 set to 1929=100.

Source: U.S. Department of Commerce, Bureau of the Census
https://www.eh.net/page/2/?s=taylor+rule

Consumer Credit & American Dream

While American factories were churning out cars, vacuum cleaners, and refrigerators, consumer access to credit made it possible to live in ways that only the wealthy could, thus starting the cycle of the democratization of consumption. Some might even call it conspicuous consumption.

Cars were initially for the rich, but by 1925 25% of the nation owned one.

In the 1940s a second bathroom was considered a luxury.

In 1960 color TV was a luxury.

In 1980 personal computers were a luxury.

There was the revolutionary process of shopping via mail and the Sears catalog where you could even purchase a house. The department store also took off with James Cash Penney's going from a few stores in 1920 to 500 by 1924 and 1000 by 1930.

While the American consumer was enjoying this boom of goods and services, certain investors were also getting in on the act. Some investors were offered and accepted 90% margins to buy stock. This fueled an incredible ride, for a while. It was an amazing ride that has turned into a cautionary tale.

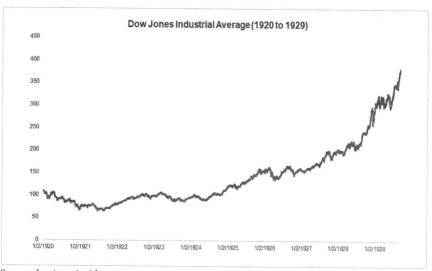

Source: businessinsider.com
https://www.businessinsider.com/
the-stock-market-crash-of-1929-what-you-need-to-know-2018-4

So, are we off to the races again?

The answer is yes, maybe, yes.

Indulge me for a moment here to allow me to explain what I see happening with inflation. Remember, President Coolidge basically took a "hands-off" approach, once the worst of the recession had passed. I think we find ourselves in a similar situation today. We certainly needed decisive actions taken, like those of Presidents Wilson and Harding, at the beginning of the 1920s recession. Now we find ourselves in the "Coolidge" recovery period.

Low taxes and regulations have allowed this economy to flourish before and since the arrival of COVID-19. Wages were on fire before the pandemic, led by a surge in blue collar wages. The rate of innovation and amazing product and services development speak for themselves!

The question is, at what point can that organic, Coolidge-like growth of low taxes and regulations grab the economic rally baton? Will it even have a chance with the spending and taxing schemes currently on the drawing board?

Unlike the 1920 recession, there was swift intervention by the federal government and Federal Reserve. These actions were needed when the government forced the economy to shut down. These days those actions promise to continue to contribute to inflationary pressures.

Not Transitory

Annual inflation right now is running at a thirteen-year high of 5.4% and some of the main drivers, including rent and, to a lesser degree, wages will keep the number elevated.

In addition, the workers' strikes, the supply chain crunch, and government transfer payments will keep the pressure on for some time. It is also possible that crude oil prices might move considerably higher from here.

Wage gains will eventually help power the economy higher, but I hope we slow down on all the transfer payments that are not only adding to the inflation crisis, but disincentivizing work.

Headline Inflation

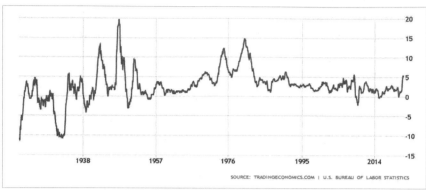

Source: tradingeconomics.com

Core Inflation

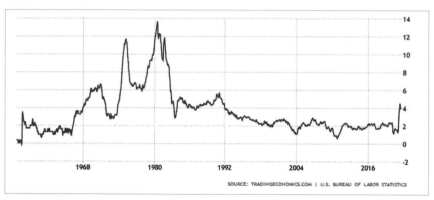

Source: tradingeconomics.com

If these inflationary pressures persist too long the Federal Reserve will have to reverse course and, after tapering current monthly asset purchases, continue hiking rates.

That could be an economic killer.

It's a serious wildcard and right now I think Jay Powell should take a conservative approach for as long as possible. I don't believe there is the political will to do what Paul Volker did to beat inflation back in the 1980s.

Yet this is one of the biggest challenges to a repeat of the roaring 20s. There are other challenges that I will discuss later.

Right now, let's stay focused on the building blocks of the current Roaring Twenties 2.0. The most recent productivity report saw the biggest decline in productivity in forty years, but most analysts, including myself, see this as a one-off, reflecting issues associated with the COVID-19 Delta variant. The Congressional Budget Office (CBO) reported 1.7% average annual non-farm productivity but that number is far too low.

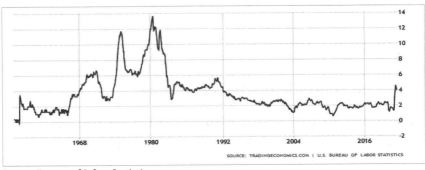

Source: Bureau of Labor Statistics
https://www.washingtonpost.com/business/2021/08/18/us-productivity-boom/

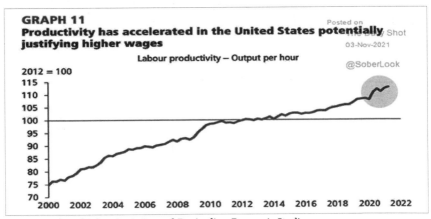

Source: Bureau of Labor Statistics and Desjardins, Economic Studies

This will continue for years with the capex boom that is only just beginning.

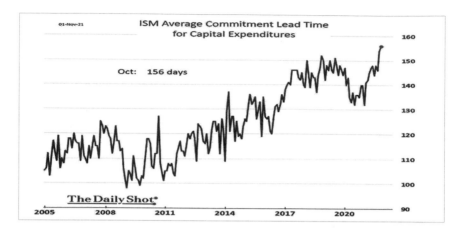

Source: thedailyshot.com

Third and Fourth Industrial Revolution

Right now, artificial intelligence or AI is all the rage even though it has been around since the 1950s and part of everyday lexicon for thirty years.

But the spread of ChatGPT awakened possibilities promised by science and science fiction writers overnight. It took five days for ChatGPT to gain one million users versus 75 days for Instagram.

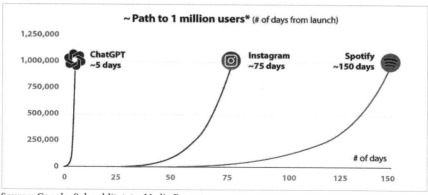

Source: Google, Subredditstats, Media Reports

AI was always going to be the central part of the fourth industrial revolution and is so much more. From an investing point of view the initial market reaction has been to zero in on picks and shovels — those companies that make the computer chips for the public. As time goes on there will be winners based on products and services powered by artificial intelligence.

There are also lots of private companies in the picks and shovels race that are raising billions of dollars. Most of these names will never dominate the industry, but Silicon Valley is only banking on the hype creating a groundswell of demand from individual investors. Be very careful because Main Street will be left holding the bag as the players buy new yachts.

On that note, traditional valuation methods will mean missing grand slams.

Focus on PEG ratios, market share gains and pricing power.

Brave New World

Just as the maturation of the first and second industrial revolutions sparked a new phase in the lives of the average American household in the 1920s, we are entering a wonderous period that will generate mindboggling economic opportunities and gains while changing our lives into an existence that was once only considered science fiction.

The best way to think about where the world is going with America leading the way is to follow the actions of the world's wealthiest folks. They've borrowed from the scripts laid out by the so-called robber barons of yesteryear.

We can take our lessons from the movers and shakers of the past, leveraging the industrial changes to the movement of commerce, ideas, and even people the way

JD Rockefeller, Cornelius Vanderbilt, Henry Ford, Andrew Carnegie and in the world of banking and finance JP Morgan did in earlier generations.

There is a new land grab, of sorts, that is the modern-day gold rush.

- Space
- Tunnels
- Farmland
- The Metaverse

To rule these areas, we will see monster investments and new tools from quantum computers to artificial intelligence to advanced robots to virtual reality headsets that will give way to augmented reality headsets. They all represent amazing opportunities in a wide variety of areas.

Space Taxis and Rockets: COVID-19 helped kickstart the age of cargo drones and air taxis.

Startups promising to usher in the age of air taxis and cargo drones started popping up at the end of the 2000s. For most of their existence, they were underfunded and relegated to niche applications like delivering blood in rural Rwanda or publicity stunts like the Taco Bell-backed "tacocopter." The pandemic changed all that overnight.

This year, startups building autonomous drones to carry passengers and packages have raised $5.1 billion, up from $1.1 billion in 2020. That compares to just $438 million in venture capital funding for the entire decade between 2009 and 2019, according to data from the investment tracking firm PitchBook. Most of the recent wave of funding has gone to a few startup winners, including Joby Aviation ($1.6 billion raised), Lilium ($842 million), and Archer Aviation ($656 million).

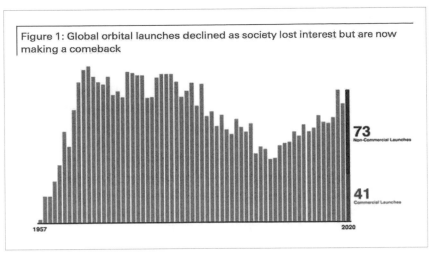

Figure 1: Global orbital launches declined as society lost interest but are now making a comeback

73
Non-Commercial Launches

41
Commercial Launches

1957   2020

Source: BryceTech
http://brycetch.com

The billionaire space race has captured the public's imagination after years of waning interest in traditional space launches, which eventually saw American astronauts hitching rides on the rockets of other nations to get to the international space station.

While the space race is ostensibly being billed as the foray into space tourism, it's a lot bigger than that.

When we talk about the cloud we are talking about outer space and the 4,000 satellites that already orbit the Earth, which are now seeing an additional 990 a year. Last year India launched its most ambitious rocket with a budget that was less than the budget to make the space movie "Gravity."

For business the increased interest in space has led to more exciting ideas beyond the occasional tourist venture. The idea of asteroid mining is huge. And beyond the idea of space tourism, actually moving mankind to outer space is on the drawing board. Imagine if you invested in the stock of one of those companies and could get paid for owning Earth 2.0.

There are some estimates saying space will be a $3.0 trillion industry by 2050. I think those numbers are far too low. In fact, work by Morgan Stanley sees Space X becoming more valuable than Tesla. But space isn't the only element of transportation that is gaining interest. Remember how the automobile allowed the growth of the suburbs? The auto industry remains basically the same today. But maybe things are changing.

Friendly Skies

There is no individual titan or group of billionaires dominating the skies yet, but there is movement to take advantage of all the room in the skies.

Several companies are working on flying cars.

Aero Mobile 2023

Source: AeroMobil
https://futurism.com/now-possible-earn-degree-flying-cars

HT Aero 2024

Source: Xpeng
https://www.cnbc.com/2021/10/24/
xpeng-launches-flying-car-that-can-also-operate-on-roads.html

Ubiquitous Air Travel

And air taxi companies are moving fast and a couple are already publicly traded, including Joby.

Source: Joby Aviation
https://www.cnet.com/science/watch-the-first-video-of-jobys-air-taxi-in-flight/

Electric Vehicles

With governments around the world putting their fingers on the scale, the electric vehicle market will grow exponentially in the next decade. Attractive financial incentives for EVs and financial discouragement for combustion engine vehicles will have an effect that would not have been the case if left to consumers and the marketplace.

Be that as it may, the EV space has become exciting with upstarts, the old guard auto makers, and Tesla.

Estimates vary on growth with one report suggesting the U.S. will go from 1.4 million EVs in 2020 to 6.9 million in 2025. As the federal government and 90% of states offer lucrative incentives to make the switch, this number may be conservative.

Autonomous Vehicles

These are far more exciting than EVs for me because these vehicles will free up people to do things that will make them more productive. These vehicles, that will not have steering wheels or pedals, will be packed with sensors that measure and record everything. Imagine, for a moment, the value of the technology to gather all that information and the information itself. It will be measured in the trillions of dollars.

Tunnels

While his fellow billionaires battle it out with their space race, Elon Musk has been underground trying to do something that could be so revolutionary it would be like the move to paved roads. Musk has promised the ability to deliver tunnels at $10.0 million a mile, which might sound expensive until you stop to think what major subway projects cost.

San Francisco Central Subway cost $1.57 billion for 1.7 miles, which comes out to $920 million a mile. The least expensive public tunnel project is the Atlanta I-20 East Heavy Rail at $170 million a mile.

Line	Type	Cost	Length	Cost/mile
San Francisco Central Subway	Underground	$1.57 billion	1.7 miles	$920 million
Los Angeles Regional Connector	Underground	$1.75 billion	1.9 miles	$920 million
Los Angeles Purple Line Phases 1-2	Underground	$5.2 billion	6.5 miles	$800 million
BART to San Jose (proposed)	83% Underground	$4.7 billion	6 miles	$780 million
Seattle U-Link	Underground	$1.8 billion	3 miles	$600 million
Honolulu Area Rapid Transit	Elevated	$10 billion	20 miles	$500 million
Boston Green Line Extension	Trench	$2.3 billion	4.7 miles	$490 million
Washington Metro Silver Line Phase 2	Freeway median	$2.8 billion	11.5 miles	$240 million
Atlanta I-20 East Heavy Rail	Freeway median	$3.2 billion	19.2 miles	$170 million

Source: Metro.net
https://www.metro.net/projects/westside/

It is unlikely a network would be built in time to transform the 2020s but if there are signs of early economic success, we could see a move that takes a page from Eisenhower's Interstate Highway project in the 1950s. Consider what an impact all those highways had on our way of life.

If you haven't had a chance to read the article below, take a moment to do so. It is a change that is coming to the economy that is worth knowing about.

Making Money on the Digital Revolution

Pandemic Hastens Shift to Asset-Light Economy

Value increasingly attaches to intangibles like brand and R&D rather than to physical assets like machinery and in-person stores

https://www.wsj.com/articles/pandemic-hastens-shift-to-asset-light-economy-11602087201

I understand if you are a bit hesitant to the hype around things like Web3.0 and the metaverse. After all, we've heard it all before with things like nano-technology or 3D printing. Yet so many scientific miracles that have failed to live up to the hype could still become a reality that has a major impact on our lives.

Wall Street learns how to value intangibles and see the benefits of building greatness ahead of building share prices. The following is a statement from Bill Gates about this shift of thinking.

Bill Gates

It took time for the investment world to embrace companies built on intangible assets. When we were preparing to take Microsoft public in 1986, I felt like I was explaining something completely foreign to people. Our pitch involved a different way of looking at assets than our option holders were used to. They couldn't imagine what returns we would generate over the long term.

The idea today that anyone would need to be pitched on why software is a legitimate investment is laughable, but a lot has changed since 1986. It's time the way we think about the economy does, too.

Source: Bill Gates

Jeff Bezos

Jeff Bezos has an interesting take on intangibles and building greatness with time and patience.

Our first shareholder letter, in 1997, was entitled, "It's all about the long term." *If everything you do needs to work on a three-year time horizon, then you're competing against a lot of people. But if you're willing to invest on a seven-year time horizon, you're now competing against a fraction of those people, because very few companies are willing to do that. Just by lengthening the time horizon, you can engage in endeavors that you could never otherwise pursue.* At Amazon, we like things to work in five to seven years. We're willing to plant seeds, let them grow—and we're very stubborn. We say we're stubborn on vision and flexible on details. Showing 49 comments In some cases, things are inevitable. The hard part is that you don't know how long it might take, but you know it will happen if you're patient enough. Ebooks had to happen. Infrastructure web services had to happen. So you can do these things with conviction if you are long-term-oriented and patient

Source: Jeff Bezos

In the 1920s companies measured their tangible assets, and there was amazing growth. In the 2020s the growth is still there but the assets have changed.

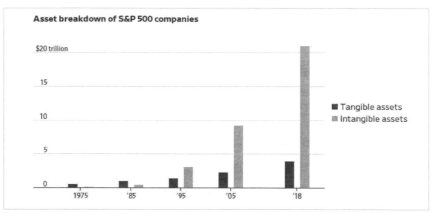

Source: Carlyle Group

Technology & Life Expectancy

The amazing increase in life expectancy in the twentieth century followed the path of knowledge and technology. The greatest gains in life expectancy happened in the 1920s despite all that partying. Medical advances resulting from WWI and the Spanish Flu certainly contributed, as did all the advances in other technologies that made life easier. Note that the only decade that comes close is the 1940s with the advances, again in medicine and technology, that resulted from WWII.

INCREASES IN U.S. LIFE EXPECTANCY	YEARS
1870 to 1900	+1.3
1900 to 1920	+3.2
1920s	+5.6
1930s	+3.2
1940s	+5.3
1950 to 1973	+1.4
1973 to 1990	+2.4
1990s	+1.7
2000s	+1.4

The COVID-19 pandemic revealed amazing advancements being made in medicine and health while also spurring innovations in drug creation and applications. Certainly, the record-breaking vaccine development we just witnessed is only part of the medical miracle scene in the pipeline.

According to the Business Research Company, MedTech is already a $600.0 billion industry with 70% of the large players based in the United States.

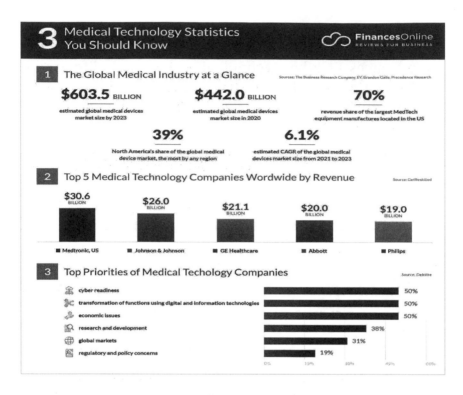

There are other components of Medtech that have seen billions in venture capital investments in the past decade.

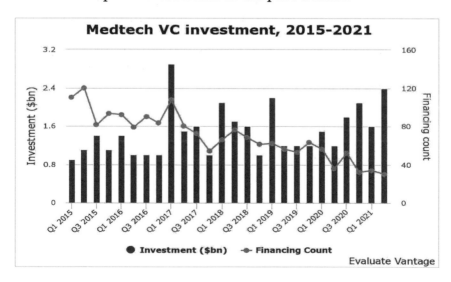

In the years to come implanted computer chips will treat Parkinson's, paralysis, epilepsy, eating disorders and bring hope to hopeless brain and spinal injuries of today.

Biotech is also in a horse race to improve the lives of humankind.

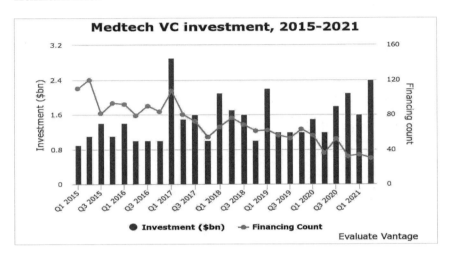

In addition, even industries as basic and fundamental as farming are going through their own revolutions just as millennials and Gen-Z are demanding healthier options. Farmers are becoming more efficient and productive each year.

This is a huge Business and Investing Opportunity

Note: *I got into some names in 2021 and took a beating – make sure there is a clear path to profitability and ability to grow the top line in an industry that is also growing 40% Compounded Annual Rate of Growth (CARG).*

- FarmTech (aka AgTech) Industries
- Component Technologies
- Environmental Controls
- Irrigation & Fertigation

- Lighting Systems
- Crop Monitoring
- Nursery Automation
- Environmental Monitoring
- Pest & Disease Monitoring
- Crop Management
- Farm Management
- Automated Crop Care
- Internal Transport
- Harvest Robotics
- Post-Harvest Automation
- Container Systems
- Greenhouse Production Systems
- Sunless Production System
- Next-Gen Growers
  - Greenhouse Growers
  - Sunless Growers

We are also beginning to see significant social changes, just as occurred in the 1920s.

Societal Changes

Although the term Robber Barons appeared in the late 1800s it was used throughout the Roaring 1920s. And certainly the term has come to carry some negative connotations, but the popularity of folks like Henry Ford was undeniable. Today we have a new group of the mega wealthy. And just as in the previous time, they seem to have an outsized influence on our culture and our lives.

It's true, abuse of power that can be endemic to being

ultra-wealthy, is a major issue but most people in America want to be rich. We want to be able to have the same amazing opportunities that occurred in the 1920s. Why do I feel that way? Personal observations. Let me explain.

America was born and has prospered under the notion that all men and women are born equal and as such individual effort should have its own rewards including that of wealth creation.

Obviously, the nation is not without blemishes because human beings in general are not perfect. The execution of ideas and pledges are going to be uneven at times and even disregarded. Therein lies why I think America is the greatest nation in the world.

We've dealt with our humanism (yes, things like slavery and mistreatment of others are steeped in the nature of humans to exercise unfair power over another) and overcome its darker aspects by relying on the Constitution as a guide.

Another human trait is guilt and remorse. It is so powerful that we are seeing nations around the world self-implode and deliberately crush their own economic well-being. In the United States such guilt and remorse has also resulted in policies designed to make amends but all too often have made overcoming real obstacles in life even more difficult.

With that said, our relationship to the rich is complicated but also simple. Supposed resentment toward the rich is another human trait: jealousy. This isn't as rampant as the media makes it out to be but is exploited by politicians. What's amazing is many elected officials who preach politics of envy go to Washington DC and become millionaires are "public servants." Go figure.

And some of the resentment is hypocritical considering we want the same chances at attaining more wealth. A survey of affluent Americans (household income of $125,000+) sees only 26% of them believe the top 1% is paying their fair share of taxes and yet 67% of these same folks agree it is their right to minimize their own tax burden under existing laws.

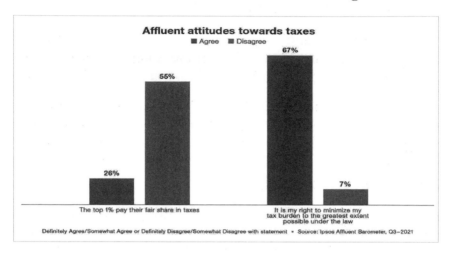

Here's the real deal. We love rich people in America when we watch them earn their wealth. In 2022, the National Institute of Health published a piece on attitudes of the rich. It explains how rich folks who pulled themselves up by the bootstraps can seem insensitive to those stuck in impoverished conditions.

This has been portrayed as rich folks pulling up the ladder once they reached the top when it should be portrayed as rich folks urging everyone to grab the ladder, even if it's the bottom rung, and make the journey. They are not cold or callous. They know if they could do it, so could everyone else.

That was a key part of the Roaring 20s. A sense of economic well-being for everyone that harkens back to the spirit of the founding of America.

The research report also reveals that 88% of Americans admired the rich when we know they've earned it.

We spend a lot of money to watch millionaires and now even billionaires play sports or perform concerts. We read their books and cheer when those books are made into movies and theme park attractions.

If I Could Do It, So Can They: Among the Rich, Those With Humbler Origins are Less Sensitive to the Difficulties of the Poor

Attitudes toward the rich might be influenced by how the rich are deemed to have gained their wealth; a public survey showed that only 27% of respondents agreed with the statement that they admire the rich; however, this trend was reversed when people were asked if they admire the rich who earned their wealth—now, 88% of respondents said they did (Pew Research Center, 2012).

When it comes to business and technology superstars, we not only get to watch them and enjoy their products and services in real time, we get to ride their coattails as well.

If I'm right, we will be cheering the billionaires for the next decade as we watch our own wealth swell from their accomplishments.

Luxury Living for Everyone

I went to a few malls in 2021 the weekend when stimulus checks were sent out. They were all jumping but the thing that was most amazing to me was that the biggest buzz and biggest lines were at stores like Louis Vuitton, Gucci, and the sneaker department at Neiman. It was a madhouse. Just as in the 1920s, coming out of a pandemic and having the stress of global conflict reduced has led to a desire for the finer things in life.

Already, there are signs that this new taste for luxury is impacting the stock market. Here's an example of what I'm talking about.

LONDON--(BUSINESS WIRE)–Capri Holdings Limited (NYSE:

CPRI), a global fashion luxury group, today announced its financial results for the second quarter of Fiscal 2022 ended September 25, 2021.

- Second Quarter Fiscal 2022 Highlights
- Revenue increased 17%, with better than anticipated results across all three luxury houses
- Adjusted gross margin expanded 440 basis points versus prior year
- Adjusted operating margin of 18.5%
- Adjusted earnings per share of $1.53
- Raised full year adjusted earnings per share outlook to $5.30

John D. Idol, the Company's Chairman and Chief Executive Officer, said, "We are pleased with our second quarter results with revenue, gross margin, operating margin and earnings per share all exceeding our expectations. This performance reflects the power of Versace, Jimmy Choo and Michael Kors as well as the execution of our strategic initiatives. Capri Holdings' strong results are a testament to the dedication, resilience and agility of the entire team across the globe."

Mr. Idol continued, "We remain confident in the strength of our luxury houses and are pleased to be raising revenue and earnings guidance for the year. Our new outlook reflects both stronger revenue performance as well as greater than anticipated gross margin expansion driven by the execution of our strategic initiatives. The success of these initiatives is currently offsetting the COVID-19 related industry headwinds including supply chain delays and increased transportation costs. Looking forward as the world continues to recover from the impact of the global pandemic, we remain confident in the growth opportunities for Versace, Jimmy Choo and Michael Kors. As we execute on our strategic initiatives, Capri Holdings is positioned to deliver multiple years of revenue and earnings growth."

https://www.businesswire.com/news/home/20211103005463/en/Capri-Holdings-Limited-Announces-Second-Quarter-Fiscal-2022-Results

Source: Versace

A couple weeks after this big beat from Capri, I was strolling through Bloomindale's flagship store in Manhattan and was struck by an entire bedroom decked out in Versace.

Source: Carlyle Group

There is no doubt the look is unapologetically over the top and screams new money but that's what's happening not just in America but around the world.

Living in a Material World

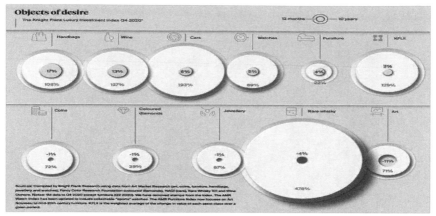

Source: KightFrank
https://www.knightfrank.com/research/article/
2021-03-01-covid19-and-its-impact-on-luxury-investments

If you ever wondered why luxury brands are investing in in-game experience on platforms such as $RBLX: 86% of folks who purchased luxury in-game items also bought the corresponding physical goods. That's a significant ROI.

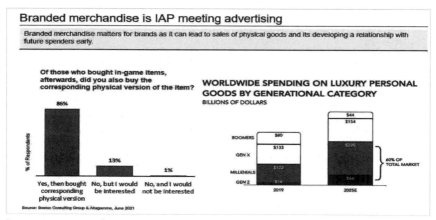

Source: Boston Consulting Group

Hard Asset Investments

Watches

https://qz.com/1946771/sales-of-super-expensive-watches-bounce-back-fast-in-the-pandemic/?utm_source=email&utm_medium=daily-brief&utm_content=10436993&utm_term=members-only

SHATTERS ANOTHER WORLD RECORD WITH SALE OF HERMÈS BLACK CROC BIRKIN WITH DIAMONDS

Other Highlights from Global Luxury
Auction Announced

Los Angeles, California – October 8, 2020 – Kruse GWS Auctions, the world-record-breaking auction house specializing in entertainment memorabilia, fine jewelry, iconic fashion items and royal artifacts shattered yet another world record during their Luxury Jewelry, Timepieces and Handbags auction which was held Saturday, September 26, 2020 in Los Angeles. Founder and lead auctioneer of Kruse GWS Auctions, Dame Brigitte Kruse presided over the auction.

In a stunning round of fast and furious online bids from around the globe, Kruse GWS Auctions sold a **Hermès Shiny Black Porosus Crocodile, 10.70ctw Diamond & White Gold Birkin Bag**, never used, in box for a remarkable **$287,500.** This sale marked yet another world-record garnered by the auction house, proving **Dame Brigitte Kruse**, who was knighted this year, may add "**Queen of Handbags**" soon to her title.

Coveted for their rarity and craftsmanship, Birkin bags have also carved out a rare and lesser-known niche, paving the way for luxury handbags as investments. Over the past 35 years Birkins have out-performed both the value of Gold and the **S&P 500** stocks. Since April of 2020, Dame Brigitte Kruse has sold over **$2,000,000** worth of handbags from the most sought-after luxury brands around the globe, including **Hermès, Chanel, Gucci, Judith Leiber, Fendi, Valentino, MCM, Dolce & Gabbana, Christian Dior, Versace, Louis Vuitton**, and more. Selling at $287,500, the Hermès Birkin bag secured the world-record for the highest sale ever achieved for a **Black Hermès Birkin** handbag.

Other highlights of the auction included the **Ford 2016 Shelby GT-H 50th Anniversary Hertz Rent-a-Racer Edition**.

The highly collectible and sought-after vehicle was #30 of 171 total of these cars made as a collaboration with Hertz and sold for **$93,750**.

In this auction, one of the fine watch highlights was the sale of a **Rolex 1979 Cosmograph Daytona Solid 18K Yellow Gold 37mm Watch** sold for **$37,500**. The handsome timepiece is one of the most highly sought after and collectible models of the brand and is crafted of solid 18k yellow gold.

The world-record-breaking sale by Kruse GWS Auctions further solidifies the renowned Los Angeles based auction house as one of the most influential auction houses dealing in iconic fashion brands and accessories. Having created the exclusive fashion runway auctions and setting many other world-records in the entertainment memorabilia sector, the auction house has become one of the most popular and trusted auction houses in the world amongst sellers, buyers, celebrities, and royal families alike. **Dame Brigitte Kruse** is the founder and lead auctioneer of **Kruse GWS Auctions**.

About Kruse GWS Auctions

Kruse GWS Auctions is the world-renowned auction house specializing in **Hollywood** memorabilia, fine jewelry, luxury timepieces, Royal artifacts, and estates. Founder, and fifth generation auctioneer **Dame Brigitte Kruse** was the first female auctioneer to set a **Guinness World Record**, a member of the **Forbes Business Council Los Angeles**, and the President and Chairman of the board of iSynergy Network, the innovative network for entrepreneurs. The auction house has sold iconic and historical items including **Elvis Presley's** personal jet, **Marilyn Monroe's** black wool dress, **Marlon Brando's** Rolex watch, Elvis & Priscilla Presley's mobile home, Royal family owned one-of-a-kind items, and much more. Kruse also created what are now known as **"Runway Fashion Show Auctions."** Kruse GWS Auctions offers a wide range of global experience in every phase of the auction business, including research, advertising, inventory management, liquidations, personal property appraisal services, exhibition management, cataloging and sales. With a dedicated team of experts worldwide, they offer the highest level of service. The auction house has featured items representing countless celebrities, 16 Royal families, 3 U.S. Presidents, and many more. Kruse GWS Auctions has also featured iconic fashion designers and extensive collections of vintage, haute couture and fine jewelry and royal artifacts. **www.gwsauctions.com**

Pinball Scores

Pinball is scoring with more time spent at home and kids and parents looking for alternatives to video games. Jersey Jack Pinball was already seeing annual sales growth of 30% a year, but sales are surging even higher during the pandemic. Their latest game has a Guns N' Roses theme and interactive experience — when the band's 2020 stadium tour was pushed to 2021, Slash, the famous guitarist (who owns seven pinball machines himself), visited the factory to launch the release of the new game. Jersey Jack sold out its 500 collector's edition games, which cost $12,500, within two hours of going live. They'll sell 5,000 limited edition machines for $9,500, and the standard game for $6,750. Other manufacturers are also seeing a jump in sales as coronavirus puts a new focus on in-home entertainment. We report from the world's pinball manufacturing capital, the Chicago suburbs. Elk Grove Village is home to the largest pinball machine manufacturer, and we dig into the trend from a small business seeing brand new interest.

All of this provides incredible opportunities for the Unbreakable Investor. New innovations and products present exciting chances, but we can't lose sight of the opportunities that are there under the surface. New technologies, whether in tunnel development or flying cars, have components that can also be great investments. The move toward owning the finer things in life offers another road one might choose to travel to gain financial security. Right now opportunities seem to be everywhere. So what might derail this juggernaut?

There are several areas that we need to watch carefully. We need to be aware of world markets, and specifically China. The world is a smaller place today than it was in the 1920s and events globally impact our investments. China is actively working to be a player in markets all over the globe and we need to be aware of how the U.S. is addressing this economic threat.

We need to watch areas of conflict around the world. We have seen how an interruption in the global supply chain has a tremendous impact. Conflicts in areas that produce raw materials necessary for technology and other industries have to be considered.

More locally we need to be aware of changes in tax policies and any major decisions by our local or the federal government that move us away from a free market economy.

I'm hopeful that we see a move towards a business-friendly economy like we saw in the 1920s.

We are poised to see a period of remarkable growth if we are smart enough to take advantage of it.

Quiz: Chapter 9

1. **What approach did President Coolidge take toward the recovering economy when he came to office?**

2. **How did increased access to the automobile change American society in the 1920s?**

3. **How has the continued influx of federal funds to individuals impacted the economy?**

4. **What things should we watch, locally, in regards to the continued growth of this current economic cycle?**

Answers

1. He took a "hands-off" approach, allowing the economy to organically grow out of the recession.

2. It allowed families to live farther away from jobs and shopping. It allowed the creation of the suburbs.

3. The excessive cash has created an inflationary condition with which the Federal Reserve is currently dealing.

4. We need to watch for significant changes in tax policies and laws or regulations that might move us away from an effective free market system.

Chapter

10

Putting What You've Learned into Action

Create the Reality You Desire

For years the stock market was only for an elite class of people with the funds and wherewithall to take advantage of capitalism that truly rewards risk-takers. Wall Street, the institution, didn't really have to build a moat around investing since stories of market crashes and ensuing hard times left indelible images on the minds of folks on Main Street.

Even today when someone invokes the idea of a new Roaring Twenties there is a swift reply that the first one didn't end so well (read the crash in 1929).

When one thinks of the stock market in the 1930s, it's easier to conjure up this famous "Migrant Mother" photo taken by Doretha Lange...

Source: conchamayordomo.com
https://conchamayordomo.com/2020/05/28/dorothea-lange/

Rather than picture the wealth created by those that were buying stocks during the ultimate stock market dip.

Signalling to offices, curb market, New York City
Digital ID: (b&w film copy neg.) cph 3c19557 http://hdl.loc.gov/loc.pnp/cph.3c19557
Reproduction Number: LC-USZ62-119557 (b&w film copy neg.)
Repository: Library of Congress Prints and Photographs Division Washington, D.C. 20540 USA

Both were a reality, but investors with the right knowledge and mindset found life-altering opportunities even in the darkest of times. They were unbreakable.

Inspiration

Whether you're diving headfirst into the market for the first time or have been an investor for years looking for a new approach, it has to begin with your motivation.

We are all inspired by something that motivates us to get into motion and to take risks along the path to satisfying that inspiration. We often call that path the journey, and satisfying or honoring that inspiration is the goal.

Throughout time, much has been written about the human journey, both as individuals and also as families, towns, countries, and all humankind. Our history is rich with stories of overcoming challenges, of growth and success. Each story features the same characteristics: inspiration followed by action.

Genesis

The birth of our inspirations could have come years before we were born or could be part of an extended legacy.

Like this MLK Jr. quote from April 3, 1968

"We've got some difficult days ahead. But it really doesn't matter with me now, because I've been to the mountaintop... I've seen the Promised Land. I may not get there with you. But I want you to know tonight, that we, as a people, will get to the Promised Land"

Sometimes we can have multiple sources of inspiration that can be satisfied by reaching the same goal. My inspiration to give my newborn daughter a great life dovetailed perfectly with the established goal of growing up to help my mother.

Uphill Obstacles

Each journey has uphill obstacles — starting in a position of disadvantage and finding ways around imbedded challenges designed to dissuade or extinguish dreams.

Downhill Obstacles

Each journey has downhill obstacles — self-inflicted wounds that often occur once we have overcome a fair number of uphill obstacles. This happens when we put life on cruise control, become arrogant, forget lessons learned, forget our own values, and ignore the terrain in front of us.

Mistakes

There will be decisions made that will seem disastrous for the moment. These mistakes are unavoidable, but it's better to embrace them as learning lessons than try and tiptoe around them. There is a straight line between the genesis of your declaration to change your life and the ultimate goal. If you dance around too much trying to be perfect or waiting for the perfect time, the clock will run out.

Breaks

We all need breaks, and we all need to recognize breaks. I have been so blessed to have been given key breaks at certain points of my life that made all the difference. Do not think of big breaks as something that can only be bestowed by powerful people and organizations. Remember that these breaks reflect the goodness in the heart of the giver, but also the light inside the receiver.

People want to help people who are trying to help themselves and who then express gratitude.

Doubt

Everyone has doubts. In recent years we are learning more and more that top performers, from recording artists to professional athletes, suffer from debilitating self-doubt. Their skills get them through these pangs of angst. For you, as an investor, it will be your knowledge that sees you through. Never stop learning. It's the best medicine to offset naturally recurring doubt.

Success

There are layers of success and I think you should embrace them but not frolic in them too long, for you will lose sight of the greater picture. There is a saying about stopping to smell the flowers. You should. With every home I have owned, I always took time to look around. I like to do this when nobody else is around. I would find certain vantage points I could enjoy while thinking about the road that brought me to that very moment, in that very place.

Then I would always look ahead, not because I want more, but because I want to continue to enjoy the feeling of new achievements.

Sharing

For me, sharing my good fortune is critically important. Growing up in Harlem I came home one night with a buddy and learned my mother had hit the number and won $600. She was so thrilled and gave me and my buddy $20.00 each. That was a lot of money back then, but I was baffled about why she gave my friend the same amount she gave me. She explained how important sharing was to her.

My mother was deeply religious, and her faith and internal fortitude were tested in the most significant of ways when we left my father in 1975. I came home from school and my mom said, "We're leaving." Me, my mom, and two younger brothers proceeded to the bus station where we took a Greyhound to Harlem, NY.

We left a wonderful two-story house with a big yard, in a neighborhood where we didn't have to lock our doors. Summer was approaching and school was almost over. All I could think about at that time was all the fun we'd have riding bikes all day and rushing home for a quick peanut butter and jelly sandwich, before heading outside again.

We got to Harlem, and it was the most amazing mix of circumstances and spirits. The raw energy and soul were palatable but so too was the desperation of poverty.

We had never wanted for anything in life, and I had never thought about money, not even for a single moment. Now, as the oldest, I was thrust into the position of having to help my mother and brothers.

That's when I sought out the greatest source of money ever invented — the stock market.

Meanwhile, my mother's strength and poise under the stress of poverty, crime, and the never-ending feeling the world was against us, never wavered. She taught us to share our blessings.

I honor her by doing that in so many ways.

So, my friend was in the right place at the right time when my mother cheerfully gave him the same amount she gave me.

Beating the Odds

Hitting the number was like getting struck by lightning. People who played every day lost much more than they could ever win, but the act alone provided hope in a place where there was little hope. Abandoned buildings, huge lots of rubble, drug addiction, alcohol addiction, and rampant crime were just part of the daily landscape.

It always slays me when rich people speak of folks playing the numbers as being stupid because the odds are against them. There is an intangible that cannot be measured but makes up for the odds — hope. That sliver of thinking, even for that day, your ship might come in and you might be able to do stuff you stopped dreaming about, to be able to help a lot of people through their day. That hope was better than addiction.

Hitting the number gave one the feeling of sticking it to society. For a fleeting moment, you won in a game of life where everything was stacked against you.

In many ways that's what's been happening with the Individual Investor Revolution.

People want to hit it big, but they always want to stick it to a system that has churned them up for years. Folks got out of their lane and Wall Street and its tentacles, which includes most of the financial media, have worked overtime to humiliate these folks.

This is one reason I love the Individual Investor Revolution. My goal is to get all investors to arm themselves with the ability to learn and evolve. I do not claim to have all the answers. I am very good, but I am a student of the market, and I have the tools to learn and the skills to adapt to every market condition.

That's how you become *unbreakable.*

The Evolution of the Economy, Trading, & Investing

In 2020 the world went through a traumatic period as a new virus engulfed the planet, catching governments flat footed and unprepared. In the panic the collective decision to do a lockdown, to require people to shelter in place indefinitely, triggered something inside folks in the United States that nobody anticipated.

It was a move back to the roots of the nation, to what propelled this upstart country from a bunch of ragtag states into a republic focused on freedom and individualism. It reminded us of the understanding that individual dreams, talents, desires, and love of self, family, nation, and God were collectively more powerful than government-picked winners and losers.

The result was a nation that climbed to the top. The dollar became the world's reserve currency, and the U.S. military became the police and firefighting force that brought peace and put out fires and conflicts around the world. This, coupled with American contributions including money and knowledge, sparked the growth of one billion folks into the world's middle class.

It's been a wonderful journey but along the way things became skewed. Middle-class wealth stalled, even as wealth in America continued to grow. In more recent years this phenomenon has become even more acute. Here's the kicker — as illustrated in the chart below, after each financial emergency, subsequent wealth growth has happened faster for those at the top than everyone else.

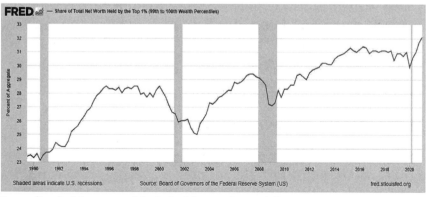

Source: Board of Governors of the Federal Reserve System (US)
https://www.weforum.org/agenda/2022/05/we-cant-create-shared-value-without-data-heres-why/

Some see this as an indictment of capitalism and have politicized the issue. The problem is, more often than not, their issue isn't with middle-class wealth growth stalling, but with capitalism itself. Their prescriptions always focus on punitive actions, like higher taxes and more regulations.

Sadly, these actions have made getting into the middle class more difficult and punish those in the middle class as they are on the cusp of moving up the ladder of success. Let's face it, when you hear a politician rail against Jeff Bezos, the policies being promoted have a far more deleterious impact on the local homebuilder who was ready to hire more workers and invest in more equipment.

The one percent of the one percent are so many steps ahead of Washington they are able to evade any changes. And when there are no loopholes for their businesses they simply hire less, slow pay, and charge more. Mastering the right investing skills and mindset to adapt to changing economic conditions, to recognize opportunity even in the toughest times, and to have the confidence to act quickly on your knowledge, can give you the same type of evasive power.

Your Piece of the Pie

This is a lesson shared by John Bogle, the man credited with popularizing the index fund.

The Prussian General Clausewitz has said, "The greatest enemy of a good plan is the dream of a perfect plan." And I believe that an index strategy is a good strategy. For what Warren Buffet calls the "know-nothing investor" the good plan ironically is better than the theoretically perfect plan.

https://25iq.com/2013/09/28/a-dozen-things-ive-learned-from-john-bogle-about-investing/

After reading this book you are far from a "know-nothing investor" and I already shared earlier how I feel about passive, index investing. I want more for you.

My goal has always been to help people maximize their economic potential. And I mean beyond any kind of scraps promised to folks by those on Wall Street pushing index funds. The fact of the matter is this might be the last window of opportunity for Americans to be able to follow the well-worn path to success.

A) Work hard, pulling themselves up by the bootstraps, before artificial intelligence, virtual reality, augmented reality, robots, and algorithms limit work opportunities and upward mobility for those who are not owners or programmers.

B) The mountain of debt becomes an avalanche. This warning has been in place for more than a decade, and I have no idea when the tides might change, but they will. The smart move is not to hide in a fallout shelter waiting but aggressively building wealth to weather the storm.

C) Naked antagonism for those in other political parties is reaching levels that have preceded civil wars and attacks. Presidents used to say, "my fellow Americans," but these days you might be called a fascist or some other name that opens the door for the next step, personal harm, or loss of freedom.

I don't present these as a foreshadowing of doom, but rather to encourage you to act now. It's too easy to "wait for things to calm down." Each day is an opportunity for you to get closer to your dream of financial security. I want you to take that opportunity, to take advantage of the stock market, the greatest money-making machine ever invented.

But before you can truly become an Unbreakable Investor, you must first break through the things that have been holding you back. You must realize that everything you've been through, and everything you're going through has been preparing you for something bigger in your life.

You must use everything that has tried to break you to motivate you to breakthrough.

You must draw upon all that inspires you to find the courage to put your journey in motion now. Not next week, next month, or next year, but now.

So, for my last Check for Understanding I am going to ask some questions that can only be answered by you.

1. What is your dream of financial security? Be specific. The more detail you have in that dream the more likely you are to make decisions that get you closer to reaching it.

2. If you were to make one change to improve your financial future and move you closer to your goal, what would it be?

3. Referring to question 2, what is preventing you from making that change? How can you overcome that obstacle?

4. When you reflect on all that you have read and learned in this book, what was the biggest "AH HAH!" moment? How will you use that new knowledge to improve your financial life?

Your Next Step

There are always multiple steps we must take in any journey in order to reach our desired destination. My objective is to help you become an Unbreakable Investor in as few steps as possible. To achieve that, and to pick up where this book has left off, I created the following web page.

UnbreakableInvestor.com/NextStep

This page is constantly updated and will give you access to free resources and live training events that my team and I host designed to fast track your journey and eliminate time-consuming trial and error.

We would be honored to help you put what you've learned into action and empower you to transform your actions into results.

Simply visit the web page above to continue your journey!

file